Linux at Work

Linux at Work

Building Strategic
Applications for Business

Marcus Goncalves

Wiley Computer Publishing

John Wiley & Sons, Inc.

NEW YORK • CHICHESTER • WEINHEIM • BRISBANE • SINGAPORE • TORONTO

Publisher: Robert Ipsen
Editor: Marjorie Spencer
Assistant Editor: Margaret Hendrey
Managing Editor: Angela Murphy
Electronic Products, Associate Editor: Mike Sosa
Text Design & Composition: North Market Street Graphics

Designations used by companies to distinguish their products are often claimed as trademarks. In all instances where John Wiley & Sons, Inc., is aware of a claim, the product names appear in initial capital or ALL CAPITAL LETTERS. Readers, however, should contact the appropriate companies for more complete information regarding trademarks and registration.

This book is printed on acid-free paper. ∞

Published by John Wiley & Sons, Inc.

Published simultaneously in Canada.

No part of this publication may be reproduced, stored in a retrieval system or transmitted in any form or by any means, electronic, mechanical, photocopying, recording, scanning or otherwise, except as permitted under Sections 107 or 108 of the 1976 United States Copyright Act, without either the prior written permission of the Publisher, or authorization through payment of the appropriate per-copy fee to the Copyright Clearance Center, 222 Rosewood Drive, Danvers, MA 01923, (978) 750-8400, fax (978) 750-4744. Requests to the Publisher for permission should be addressed to the Permissions Department, John Wiley & Sons, Inc., 605 Third Avenue, New York, NY 10158-0012, (212) 850-6011, fax (212) 850-6008, E-Mail: PERMREQ@ WILEY.COM.

This publication is designed to provide accurate and authoritative information in regard to the subject matter covered. It is sold with the understanding that the publisher is not engaged in professional services. If professional advice or other expert assistance is required, the services of a competent professional person should be sought.

Library of Congress Cataloging-in-Publication Data:

Goncalves, Marcus.
    Linux at work : building strategic applications for business /
  Marcus Gonçalves.
      p. cm.
    Includes index.
    ISBN 0-471-33349-2 (pbk.)
    1. Linux. 2. Business—Computer programs. 3. Operating systems
(Computers) 4. Computer network resources. I. Title.
HF5548.4.L5G66   1999
005.4'469—dc21   99-10789

Printed in the United States of America.

10 9 8 7 6 5 4 3 2

I dedicate this book to an awesome couple, Chris and Diana Hopper, for their love and care for Josh, my son, which I deeply appreciate from my heart.

I also dedicate this book to my wife Carla and children Samir, Andrea, and Joshua, as well as to my mother-in-law, Maria Duenas, for her love and dedication.

Most importantly, I thank God for the talents and gift of life he gave me and for allowing me to contribute to a better world this way. Glory be to Him.

CONTENTS

Foreword   xi
Preface   xv
Acknowledgments   xix

| **Part I:** | **Linux Operating System** | **1** |

| **Chapter 1** | **An Overview of Linux and the Market** | **3** |

Introduction   3

Linux Community   5

Linux Technocracy   5
  Open Source   5
  Linux: A Religious Experience?   7
  Engage Your Primal Urge To Leave a Legacy   8
  Linux Support Exceeds All Other Commercial
     Operating Systems   12

Linux Power   15
  A Stable Solution for Information Technology   15
  A Customizable Solution   15
  Linux's Technical Specifications   21

References   24

| **Chapter 2** | **Under the Hood of Linux** | **25** |

An Overview of the Linux Kernel   26

Processes and Files: Midlevel Management   31
  Processes   34

Linux Applications   37
  Linux Standards Compliance   38
  Managing Strategic Use of Product   40

References   48

| **Chapter 3** | **Managing and Administering a Linux Server** | **49** |

Linux as a Self-Sustaining Server   51

Linux Applications   52

Basic Linux Administration 52
    Managing User and Group Accounts 54
    Monitoring System Resources 55
    Writing Scripts for Recurring Tasks 58
    Adding Hardware 61
    Performing Backups 62
    Network Printers 63
    Handling E-mail, Net News, and Chat 64
    Netscape, the Internet Workstation 66
    Man Pages 66
    GUI/X-Windows 67
    More on System Configuration 69

Advanced Linux Administration and GNU Tools 69
    Configuring Servers for Mission-Critical Applications 70
    Building File Security Models To Meet Specific Needs 71
    Building Systems for a Bullet-Proof Network 71
    Building Custom Applications in Every Major Language 74
    Security Resources 75

Part II: Linux for Business Applications 77

Chapter 4 Linux for Internet Applications 79

Using Linux for Internet Applications 79
    Internet Protocol 81
    sendmail 82
    Web Browsing with HTTPD 83
    A Patchy Server, err . . . , Apache Server 84
    Perl 85

Bandwidth Issues, Ethernet, Fast Ethernet,
Asynchronous Transfer Mode, and Frame Relay 86
    Serial Line Protocols: Point-to-Point Protocol and
        Serial Line Interface Protocol 86
    Ethernet, Fast Ethernet, and Gigabit Ethernet 86
    Integrated Services Digital Network 87
    Frame Relay 87
    Asynchronous Transfer Mode 88
    Miscellaneous Protocols 88

Intranet and Extranet Business Models 88

Linux as a Secure Server 91
    Setting Up a Firewall 93
    Linux as a Bastion Host 96
    Other Security Servers 99

References 100

Chapter 5   Linux for Business Advantage   **101**

Selling Linux to Corporations   102

Integration with Heterogeneous Platforms   108
   In-House Solutions: A Case Study Approach   108

Cisco Systems: Linux Print System at Cisco   116
   Introduction   116
   Printing Strategies   118
   Initial Cisco Configuration   122
   Linux Takes Over   136
   The Future   136
   Conclusion   137

Fluke Corporation   137

Triton ETD   139

U.S. Navy   140

U.S. Army   141

References   142

Chapter 6   Integrating Linux Solutions with Business   **143**

Linux as an Alternative   145

Integrating Linux and Windows 98   147

Integrating Linux with Existing Platforms   148
   The System   149

Reducing Training Time   159
   Setting Up a Linux Training Environment on a Network   159

Chapter 7   Subverting the Push for New Technology   **163**

Linux Is Quietly Replacing Servers   164
   Linux Everywhere?   164
   Linux in Business   170
   Running Windows Programs under Linux   176
   Why Linux Is Not Ready for Prime Time   177

Chapter 8   Linux versus Windows NT   **179**

Linux and NT: Aside from the Halloween Document   179
   A Little Bit of History on Windows NT   180
   The Need for Porting Windows-Based Applications to Linux   185
   NT versus Linux: A Matter of Security   187

Part III: References and Resources for Linux   **193**

Chapter 9   Why Does Microsoft Need Linux?   **195**

Chapter 10   Using Linux Business Products and Tools   **201**

    Business Applications Overview   201

        Knox Software's Arkeia Network Backup Product   204

        Using Arkeia for Mission-Critical Application Backup:

          A Case Study   206

        Adobe Acrobat Reader   212

        Applixware Office Suite   213

        BB Stock Pro   215

        Credit Card Verification System   215

        Ishmail   218

        Maxwell Word Processor   220

        StarOffice   221

    Linux for Manufacturing: Considering Real-Time

        Linux Applications   222

Appendix A   The Care and Feeding of a Linux Systems Administrator   **227**

Appendix B   List of Internet/Web-Based Linux Resources   **231**

Appendix C   What's on the CD-ROM   **233**

Appendix D   Partial List of Linux Consultants   **239**

Index   **353**

Working day-to-day at Red Hat Software, it's easy to forget that the whole world doesn't already know about the Linux operating system. However, even though industry giants such as IBM and Netscape have embraced the open source philosophy on which Linux was founded, the vast majority of the business world doesn't even know that Linux exists. In the entertainment world, the phrase "overnight success" is seldom accurate, as most successful entertainers work long and hard before the general public discovers them. Now that Forbes magazine and CNN have started to mention Linux, it's a sure bet that Linux will be branded an overnight success. Unfortunately, it's also easy to predict the result of all this hoopla—a dire lack of Linux information geared to people trying to make sense of it all.

Fortunately, *Linux at Work* is geared towards the people that need Linux information the most—business people interested in turning Linux's technological strengths into real business advantages. In these pages you won't find compubabble geared toward a system administrator, but you will find concise, easy-to-understand descriptions of the technology behind Linux, and what that technology means to your business.

As with most things technical, it's important to look at the end result of using Linux in your business, and not to be dazzled by the Linux mystique. With all the praise being lavished on the open source movement in general (and Linux in particular), it's easy to fixate on the new and radical concept of making an entire operating system freely available. But if you do this, you'd be making not one, but two mistakes.

The first mistake is that this open source business is new. It's not; it's been a time-honored technique used by many of the world's most skilled programmers for the past twenty years. Most of the Internet was built using open source methodologies, for example. The second mistake is to overlook the reason *why* Linux (combined with the open source way of doing things) has become an "overnight success." It really boils down to one thing: Quality. Higher quality software, and higher quality support: two sides of the same coin. I was fortunate to personally experience the benefits of the open source approach more than a decade before the word "Linux" was coined, in what was then one of the most traditionally "closed source" of places—a large computer company.

My first job out of college was as a technical support specialist. It was a great job—we took phone calls from our company's field reps, got to play with all sorts of computer equipment, delve into source code, and generally have a ball. Most of the time, the resources we had at our disposal were sufficient, and we were able to resolve the field reps' problems in short order.

However, there were times when we needed additional help. In these cases, after a review by a senior support specialist, we could speak with "the engineers"; the people who actually wrote the software we supported. Invariably, these sessions were interesting; even though we worked with the source code daily, the engineers often had a deeper, more complete understanding of how things operated. That didn't mean that they were smarter than those of us in Support—there were times when our fixes were gratefully accepted by the engineers—but it did mean that the creators of the software brought a certain "something" to resolving problems with the software they had written.

A few years later, I found myself on the other end of that support hotline, and more often than not, I wished I had the ability to go down the hall and speak directly with the person who wrote the code. But now, I could only speak to a support specialist, and hope that my problem was interesting enough to warrant a discussion with the engineers. After a job change, where I was now "just" a customer, the only contact I had from an engineer was a two-sentence "I can't help you" response to a year-old support request for a problem I had long since learned to live with. Obviously, things weren't moving in the right direction; the further I got from the original engineer, the poorer the support. And as a customer, I was paying dearly for this poor support, both in terms of dollars as well as missed business opportunities. At about this time, a coworker told me about an "operating system you can download for free." As you might have guessed, that operating system was Linux. After giving it a try, I came to a few conclusions:

- This operating system seemed to be more full-featured than other operating systems I'd worked with. If I found some interesting software on the Internet, most of the time it was easy to get it running under Linux. Suddenly, tools developed by thousands of people around the world became readily available.

- It never crashed, even when I stressed it mercilessly. It ran flawlessly, easily running several web browsers "tag-team" style (looking at one browser while the other one loaded), checking mail on a remote system, and building software, all while downloading something from the Internet. Whether as a server or a desktop system, Linux's reliability made it a pleasure to work with.

- It was efficient. If run on the same hardware as other operating systems, it was faster. But perhaps more importantly, it could do more with less. This made it easy to get a Linux system running (and running well) on hardware that might be considered obsolescent for other, less efficient operating systems. What might have been a long-in-the-tooth desktop system could continue to serve admirably as a departmental file/print server.

Okay, for a technical person, all this was good stuff. But I'd seen well-constructed software before. The clincher didn't come until a year or so later, when I was working on a book project that used many Linux-based tools. We were trying to turn the files containing the book's text into typeset images of each page. The project's deadline was looming near, and the conversion software, a standard part of most Linux distributions, just didn't seem up to the task. I could feel the first twinges of panic starting.

However, my coworker didn't. With a few quick commands, he found the name and email address of the program's author. He then fired off a quick message stating the nature of our problem, what we had tried, how it had failed, that we were in a bit of a time-crunch, and any-help-you-could-provide-would-be-greatly-appreciated-thank-you-very-much. About an hour later, a response came (paraphrased somewhat): "I never thought anyone would try using my program on such a large file! Try the following command; if that doesn't work, let me know—I have some thoughts as to how you can customize my program to work in this situation." As it turned out, the author's first hunch was correct. A simple command change, and we were off and running again. That was when it hit me—I had just had one of those same "engineer" moments that I had had years before. More importantly, this short, timely response quickly put a derailed project back on track, defusing a situation that could have lost money by making our product late to market. That this high quality, timely support came free of charge was icing on the cake.

Having spent the past four years working with Linux on a daily basis, I've seen this open-source operating system beat commercial offerings so many times it's become second nature to me, as I'm sure it has for many other computer professionals. However, as Linux becomes more widely-used in the corporate world, it's important to make sure that the advantages those of us using Linux day-to-day take for granted are communicated to the rest of the business world. I think *Linux at Work* is a good first step in spreading the word.

Edward C. Bailey
Documentation Manager
Red Hat Software, Inc.

L *inux at Work* thoroughly discusses Linux as a rapidly increasing operating system being adopted all over the world by hundreds of thousands of professionals as an alternative to expensive Unix systems (and to Windows NT) for the development of software applications, networking (intraoffice and Internet), and as an end-user platform.

Not many professionals know that Linux is a freely distributed, independent Unix-like operating system for x86, Motorola 68k, Digital Alpha, Sparc, Mips, and Motorola PowerPC machines. Many are unaware that Linux is an implementation of the POSIX (Portable Operating System Interface for Unix) specification with which all true versions of Unix comply.

Many people don't know that Linux is growing very fast, especially in Europe. A recent survey conducted by *iX*, a Unix and networking magazine based in Germany, showed some startling results. Linux is used at work by 45 percent of the readers. Solaris 1 and 2, taken together, come in second with 36 percent, followed by HP-UX with 27 percent. Of companies with fewer than 50 employees, 56 percent use Linux; 38 percent of firms with more than 1000 employees use Linux. In addition, 60 percent of the readers use Linux on their computers at home.

Other places Linux has significant market penetration are in Web servers and as the operating system of choice at universities. In addition, many individuals who realize they need to learn about Unix for career advancement have decided to use Linux on their home computers as a training tool.

Linux is also becoming popular in embedded and turnkey applications, including Internet firewalls, routers, point of sale (POS) systems, and many other business applications. It is on the latter, business applications, that this book focuses.

Linux at Work tries to answer the common questions asked by many chief information officers (CIOs) and information technology (IT) professionals, as well as systems managers as a whole: "How can I be convinced that Linux is an excellent operating system for business use?" and "How do I convince upper management that Linux is an excellent operating system for business uses?"

Linux has many advantages; this book not only discusses them but also one of Linux's major disadvantages: There is no way of knowing how many people might be using it. Not knowing how many users an operating system has causes many problems, especially for companies who work in the Linux market. For instance, companies cannot plan properly without knowing if they are dealing with thousands or millions of potential customers, and the same goes for support. This book addresses this problem.

The book is divided into three parts. Part I, Linux Operating System, provides basic technical grounds for understanding the Linux operating system. It includes three chapters. Chapter 1, "An Overview of Linux and the Market," introduces the Linux community and technocracy as well as the open source concept. It looks into the power and stability Linux can deliver to your enterprise. Chapter 2, "Under the Hood of Linux," adopts a more technical approach, providing an overview of the Linux kernel, processes, and file management. It also discusses Linux networks and administration tools. Chapter 3, "Managing and Administering a Linux Server," deepens the technical approach to present Linux as a self-sustaining server. It looks into applications and administration as well as systems resources monitoring and configuring for mission-critical applications.

Part II, Linux for Business Applications, is a business strategies section, in which Linux business implementations and implementation scenarios with key result areas and rationales are discussed and case studies are presented. It includes four chapters. Chapter 4, "Linux for Internet Applications," covers the use of Linux for Internet applications, including mail server, Web server, and gateway applications. Chapter 5, "Linux for Business Advantage," discusses resolutions of management issues and Linux integration with legacy systems, and it presents a few case studies of companies already adopting Linux for business advantage, including Mercedes-Benz, Sony, Yellow Cab, Rogers Cable, Pacific Digital Interactive, Cisco Systems, and some government agencies. Chapter 6, "Integrating Linux Solutions to Business," discusses tangible advantages for adopting Linux for business applications, from reducing training time and increasing network resources to relying on a stable and robust system. Chapter 7, "Subverting the Push for New Technology," analyzes the expansion of Linux into the operating system market, where it quietly (not so quietly, actually) is replacing servers (and other major operating systems (OSs). Chapter 8, "Linux versus Windows NT," provides a down-to-earth overview of Linux and Windows NT. It goes on to show that Linux and NT don't actually compete against each other.

Part III, References and Resources for Linux, outlines the major players, developers, vendors, and supporters for the Linux market, including their products, their business applicabilities, comparison tables, and specification. It also provides pros and cons of using each one and describes what users should watch for and be aware of. Chapter 9, "Why Does Microsoft Need Linux?," takes the discussion of Chapter 8 deeper, shows how Linux affects Microsoft's OS strategies and eventually its desktop application market, and shows how Linux fits in. Chapter 10, "Using Linux Business Products and Tools," provides a partial overview of some of the most-used Linux business application products. Appendix A, "The Care and Feeding of a Linux Systems Administrator," attempts to provide a profile of a typical Linux systems administrator and his or her everyday work. Appendix B, "List of Internet/Web-Based Linux Resources," provides a great source of references for finding additional information about Linux. Appendix C, "What's on the CD-ROM," provides a map of the files and applications found on the CD-ROM accompanying this book. Appendix D, "Partial List of Linux Consultants," provides a partial list of worldwide Linux consultants. (A more comprehensive list is on the CD-ROM.)

By the end of this book, you should have a full understanding of the state of Linux implementations for business applications, where this market is heading, what the technical issues are, as well as where Linux stands among the heavy gunners—both Windows NT and Unix, as well as Novell. You will also have a reasonable knowledge of the main products and implementation solutions being proposed and where to look for support and additional information.

Who Should Read This Book?

This book is designed for systems managers, network administrators, systems integrators, Internet managers, and even chief information officers implementing or planning to implement Linux-based businesses applications. It's also for those professionals wondering where the OS industry is going, where Linux stands compared to NT, Unix, and Novell, and whether Linux should be considered as an option.

Many were the people that helped to make this book a reality. Starting with the many professionals, I would like to thank Leam Hall for his Linux/Unix expertise, substantial support, and help in the development of the first four chapters of this book. I would also like to thank Red Hat, in particular, Ed Bailey, for its great support, not only for arranging for its Linux distribution and tools to be bundled with this book but also for making its vast Linux resources available to me and writing the foreword.

I thank Vince Ackerman, Charles Kitsuki, and Cliff Seruntine for sharing their knowledgeable work on Linux and allowing me to use it. Many thanks also goes to Damien Ivereigh, from Cisco Australia, for allowing the use of one of his Linux projects at Cisco as a case study in this book. In addition, I thank Ken Creten and Brett Lamb for their keen perceptions of the OS market and how Linux fits in and for allowing me to use their article in the book. Finally, I thank Martin Michlmayr for his extensive support with the list of Linux consultants, and Sam Siegel, president of Knox Software Corporation, for his great support.

As always, I would like to thank my awesome wife Carla for always supporting me, and my three joys, my kids Samir, Andrea, and Joshua, for their willingness to sacrifice some of our family time so that this book could be finished! Most importantly, I am eternally thankful to God, for all of the above, and for allowing me to glorify Him in this way. Surely, I wouldn't be able to accomplish it without Him.

Marcus Goncalves
goncalves@arcweb.com

Marcus Goncalves holds an M.S. in CIS and has several years of inter-networking consulting experience in the IS&T arena. He's a senior IT analyst for Automation Research Corporation, advising manufacturers on IT, industry automation, and Internetworking security. He has taught several workshops and seminars on IS and Internet security in the United States and internationally. He has published several books related to the subject, such as *Firewalls Complete* (McGraw-Hill), *Protecting Your Web Site with Firewalls* (PTR/Prentice Hall), *Internet Privacy Kit* (Que), *Windows NT Server Security* (PTR), and *IPv6 Complete* (McGraw-Hill). He's also a regular contributor to several magazines, such as *BackOffice, Developer's,* and *WEBster.* He's a member of the Internet Society, National Computer Security Association (NCSA), the Association for Information Systems (AIS), and the New York Academy of Sciences.

To contact him, please send e-mail to mgoncalves@arcWeb.com or goncalvesv@aol.com.

PART ONE

Linux Operating System

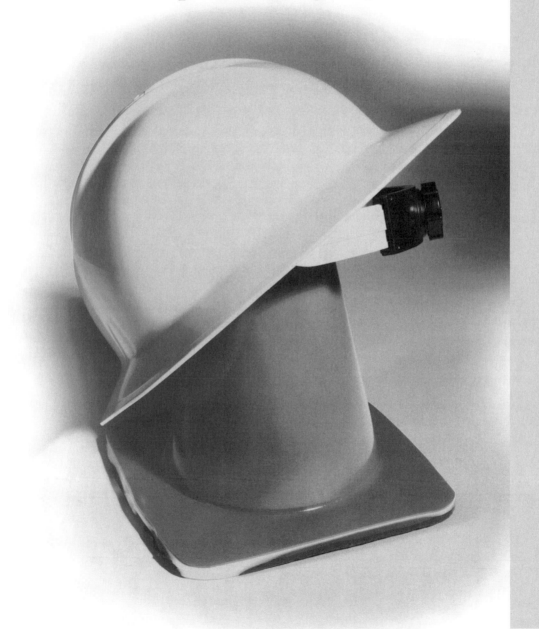

CHAPTER 1

An Overview of Linux and the Market

L inux provides resource control to the person who needs it most—the information technology (IT) professional. Any technical definition is secondary to the need for IT solutions, and Linux provides them, not only in the world of academia and tinkering, but in the real world of data availability, network scalability, and mission-critical applications.

Introduction

Linux* provides power to the manager. This power lets you control how the system functions, how the servers interact, and how the entire network is arranged. The ability to build sections of a growing network, scaling each part as needed, is a strength of Linux. It will provide you the tools you need to perform the job you are tasked to do.

*Pronunciation: There are several opinions on the pronunciation of *Linux*. Linus Torvalds has very clearly stated that he doesn't care how you pronounce it, as long as you like it. Other, less gentle folks have pointed out that since Linus's name pronounces the *i* as an English long *e*, then obviously *Linux* should follow the same standard. Others are habituated to using the long *i*, as in the English pronunciation of *Linus*, like the Peanuts character's name. There is a silent majority that just mentally point out that since we usually communicate through e-mail, who cares?

Linux lets the person responsible for the network actually have authority over it. How many professionals today are actually in control of the networks they supervise? Are they actually able to open the code for their operating systems and see how it functions? Are they given the tools for the job? Are they even allowed to influence how the processes run? Or, more likely, are they at the mercy of another for-profit company who does not keep the same level of importance attached to the IT managers' networks as they do? More importantly, are their very jobs controlled by someone who would not lose near the percentage of income the professionals would when critical resources are down because of some software incompatibility? Again, who is in control?

Linux provides essential network solutions to many of the headaches and problems IT professionals face today. Its support model exceeds most other platforms, its collection of robust tools allow finely crafted problem-solving possibilities, and its customization scheme allows you to modularly migrate your existing network at a pace you feel appropriate.

More importantly, Linux has developed a reputation for stability while keeping current with technological trends. As a direct descendant of Unix, Linux has the legacy of development of the past 30 years. Further, since Linux is written in ANSI C, there is a wealth of personnel resources available for use. Combine these facts with the open source nature of Linux, and you have a tremendous pool of talent able to help you customize any application, focus on any industry-specific task, and resolve any stubborn issue that prevents you from doing excellent work.

One thing you must take responsibility for in Linux is your own attitude. For any endeavor, you can choose to do well or poorly. If you might try Linux but don't really care to investigate it, don't bother. Linux is a difficult subject to conquer for the lazy. Although very user-friendly, Linux is choosy about who its friends are.

However, if you are particularly tired of settling for adequacy and thirst for a chance to excel, Linux is for you. Linux will give you the power to run your network and to resolve issues as you see fit. It will enable you to exceed *good* and go for the best. It will allow you to craft solutions, to really build something of elegance—not just click another series of buttons.

In the best of traditions, Linux will let you build your empire.

Linux Community

The Linux community is unique, technocratic, and, in a way, picky. However, it has healthy reasons to be: performance orientation and skill-set building, both good for profitability.

Linux Technocracy

When you step into a Linux world, you step into a technocracy: a place where performance is expected of systems and skill is expected of the population. Fortunately, these provide you with profits. They also help your organization focus on the important issues of hiring and retention. (You can learn more about these issues in Appendix A.)

Open Source

Software that falls under the open source label must meet several criteria. These standards are used to provide the best growth environment for the software in question. There are several licensing options and the open source definition.

The short form of the Open Source Definition (OSD) states that it provides for the distribution of the software and its source code openly. There are no restrictions on certain groups of people, businesses, or agencies allowed to use the software. The model behind the open source movement can readily be translated to the business world.

TIP

For more information about open source, including some rationales behind the statements and links to several different licensing schemes, check www.opensource.org/osd.html. Also, www.opensource.org itself has a lot of good information and links to different aspects of the model, including case studies from different perspectives.

The open source model creates the ability to take advantage of the talents of people you don't have to put on the payroll or pay benefits. This works for you, entrepreneur and IT professional alike, as it can have significant advantages.

For instance, security may be one of these advantages. A recurring nightmare for most managers and systems administrators alike, system security can be categorized in several ways: internal threats, physical security, and information reliability all are different. The following focuses on two and how the open source model deals with them.

The first is buggy software. Just about every program ever written has some problems, and the number of problems generally increases as the size and power of the program increases. This is a natural phenomenon because the software is written by humans, and humans tend to think in certain patterns and look at solutions in the same manner. As a result, programs are written that have weaknesses, often invisible ones.

Alternatively, there are weaknesses in the tools, such as the language or the interaction between the program and the hardware, that can cause potential problems. It is possible to hire additional developers and software testers to run each section of the program through the mill and find the holes. However, the more work you do to develop this software, the more the final product will cost, not just in terms of developers, but in the infrastructure to support them—machines, managers, physical facilities, and so on.

What open source does, in this case, is allow you to add the developers without having to pay for the infrastructure or the developers' time. Not only do you get more people involved, but you also avoid the common problem of a team of developers working so closely together that they tend to share the same blind spots and thought patterns. If you get only ten open source developers, estimate the cost if you had to bring them into the business. Yet, if you open the software up for review, you can have people who think differently from your development team review the product and provide peer review at no cost.

The second security aspect is the interaction of the software with the operating system. For example, some programs require substantial authority to run their processes. If these programs don't have the authority, they don't run. However, if the program is not completely safe and it has absolute privileges, it can completely destroy any system security you might have had.*

---

*Linux and several other network operating systems use the concept of *privileges.* This means that a program can only be run by a certain person or system account. Often programs request the superuser or root account privileges to run. The problem with this is that the root account has supreme authority over the system and can completely take down the server and destroy its functionality. This is why intruders focus on getting root privileges. Buggy software can allow them to do so.

TIP

> To get an idea about the importance of the open source initiative, check www
> .netaction.org/articles/freesoft.html, which provides an interesting look at a world
> that did not use free software.

Linux: A Religious Experience?

There are some who defend Linux, the open source movement, and
Unix religiously. Many trade show demonstrations have gained atten-
dance by discussing the merits of different operating system platforms
and different network structures. Although there are some benefits to
be gained from both sides of the argument, the Linux and open source
folks seem to view their position as the morally correct one.

To a great degree, this stance is justified. When you exist in the auto-
cratic world of dispensed solutions without benefit of response, the
enlightenment of Linux tends to provide the emotional equivalent
of freedom from enslavement. No longer are you bound to work for
someone else, who you must pay to be allowed to work. No longer
are you treated as if the answer you seek is too complex for your
untrained, ungifted mind. No longer do you have to settle for the
pretty baubles while trying to keep your job because the network continues to fail.

Linux breaks the bonds and sets you free. You are allowed to test yourself in the field of source code, and if your skills are strong enough,
you can enter the hallowed ranks of developers. In addition, if you fail
to comprehend, you are still perceived as valiant for making the effort.
Should you have the perseverance to return for another joust, you will
find wiser, seasoned warriors willing to help you gain victory. They
realize the struggle is not against them, but against your own limitations. If you choose to struggle to make yourself better, you will
improve. That is the victory. Whether you design the ultimate solution
to the most pressing problem is really not the issue. It is whether you
are willing to test yourself repeatedly against the iron of source, and in
that testing, sharpen your skills and contribute a snippet here, a frag-
ment there.

Yet, there are places for those who successfully contest skill versus
problem. These are the people who see needed solutions and focus
their efforts on victory. Repeated attempts, trial solutions: These are

the meat of the developer's life. Moreover, when the challenge is met, they can proudly return from the field and display their trophies—solutions for all, moments of enlightenment for them.

Yes, Linux can be viewed as a religious experience, not only in the personal attention to improvement, but in the societal benefits reaped from the efforts of the faithful.

Deep personal satisfaction comes from contributing to the code. However, lest you think this is the only avenue to greatness, do not be discouraged at your lack of understanding of the mysticism of C and kernel internals. Linux, in particular, and the open source movement, in general, provide a plethora of paths for contributions. If you code, head for the source—but kernel development is not the only path, just the most esoteric. There are other paths to reach your personal Olympus. If you Web, there are many pages that have good content but the hosts do not have the time or skills to master both technical design and visual information transfer. If you write, there are man pages (manual pages) to be updated, documentation on systems integration to be detailed, and skills to be shared.

If you want to code but are still developing your skills, there are many projects in need of assistance. These can give you a chance to participate, contribute, and deepen your knowledge. Help document a program, comment the routines, write the man page from scratch. Make the options available. When you feel strong enough to stand on your own code, you may have others coming to you seeking your advice, and then you will have the opportunity to repay those who helped you along the way.

Engage Your Primal Urge to Leave a Legacy

Stephen R. Covey, acclaimed author of *The 7 Habits of Highly Effective People* and many other successful titles, says one of the prime desires of a human is to leave a legacy (Covey, Merrill, and Merrill, 1994). His comments are validated every time you look at a memorial building, visit a monument to an individual, or recommend a book to a friend. That legacy, the passing on of something outside yourself that will outlast you, is a way of gaining significance. Not only do you feel important, but you also know you have contributed to life, and no matter what else happens, you have made something better than it was. Linux provides an arena in which to make that contribution.

However, consider this: In contributing to Linux, seldom will you have an opportunity to just pay some money and become famous. Even more outside the norm is that if you do have money, it's not nearly as important as in other sectors of society—except you tend to get stuck with the pizza bill. Instead of cash, your name and your reputation are the currencies with which transactions are made. When a program is written, generally the author also writes its documentation. This could be an online book or just a man page. Many pages tend to be bare-bones explanations of syntax and options. Each one tends to list the person who wrote the program and gives contact information for bug reports and potential improvements.

With these bits of documentation you can build a who's who in the Linux world. Some names are seen only once or twice; other names such as T. Ts'o (ext2fs), D. Becker (eth drivers), and L. Torvalds (general kernel hacker) appear more than once. Sometimes the chance to meet and thank the person on whom the code of your operation depends is a strong linking behavior between just being a user and appreciating the community.

Linux lets its community members transcend the drudgery of work because the opportunity for elegance is restored in the code. Since the solutions are so transparent, the code is open for comment and review by whomever wants to do so. This tends to foster a technical beauty not found in hidden code where no one will ever see your spaghetti.

Linux allows the technical person to demonstrate creativity in a bounded, but open, territory. The boundaries set are fairly simple: The code must work and meet a need. However, within those boundaries lies a wealth of opportunity to explore individual skills and tendencies. Although this may seem a business anomaly—parallel to giving the graphics arts section control of the budget—two strong guiding factors keep the code warrior fighting the right battles.

The first is the managerial guidance you give to the company's priorities, and the second, to increase profits and reduce total cost of ownership (TCO). Throughout this book, you are given the leadership role for your organization. You are expected to be able to make educated decisions about how to run your business and acknowledged for your prerogative to do so. Indeed, this book gives you demonstrations of technical solutions and explains the philosophy that motivates the solution. Most of the computer code here is easily readable, and it is done to show the simplicity of the resolution. Its technical merit is demonstrated in its function. In short, it is elegant because it clearly does what it needs to do, is understandable to those who need to see it, and does not attempt to do things not needed.

As a manager, you will have the chance to allow your systems administrators to produce such code. Nevertheless, they need your support and guidance. You must provide the tools for success. There are three essential resources you can allocate that will provide your systems administrators the technical expertise to provide solutions.

The first resource is time. If you have a human resources requirement for five bodies, and you staff with two, the systems administration will tend to be a bit haphazard and driven by crisis management. This is an invitation for disaster not only in the fragility of the system, but in the damage done to the workers. Such labor wears out those who otherwise could be long-term contributing members to your organization. Although a short-term personnel-level problem can be handled, fostering the illusion of profit gained through debilitating your employees will backfire when those two walk into better jobs elsewhere, and you have to staff a shaky system quickly.

The second resource is development. Whether through formal courses in-house or subsidized work-related education at a college, your systems administrators will return good profits when they have a good education. For example, if you want to help your folks get a good tool for success, provide them the resources to learn Perl. Even subscribing to magazines and joining professional organizations can provide benefits because they allow your workers to take advantage of the education of their peers.

The third resource is a sandbox to play in. Not quite the same type as at a child's playground, a *sandbox* is a testbed for new software and solutions. If your production environment needs to stay operational for long periods of time, a sandbox becomes a necessity. It allows the majority of bugs to be worked out before they have the opportunity to halt production and end someone's career.

What does providing these resources get you?

Primarily, you must set expectations aside. You have business needs—you must document them, allow the systems administrators to understand exactly what the necessary results are, and then find out what they need to give you the results you want. Note the emphasis on results and needs. What you want is an outcome, not a specific track delineating each step that must be followed. What you as a manager want to do is provide the list of results, and then receive them from the people you pay to produce those results.

The systems administrators have needs as well. Just as you have results-oriented needs, so do they. Systems administrators who feel the results are only part of the requirement, that the process must follow a certain methodology, which was written by people who don't maintain the systems, will often feel capable of providing only generic solutions and will have little desire to produce anything worthy of their profession. Systems administrators can produce solutions well above what most managers need because their job of systems administration demands both high skill levels and strong creativity.

If you ask for a report to be printed so you can have an administrative assistant deliver it to you each morning, you could easily get this from your systems administrator. If you focus on the results, that you want the data on last night's production run, including any deviation from performance statistics, likely your systems administrator could easily give you that information and also include an addendum if the same performance issues were a recurring item. In addition, of course, the report could be sent by e-mail, ready for you to summarize and brief on. This summary could also be automated, so that the systems administrator can get the same data and start working on solutions to those intermittent problems instead of just writing reports on them.

Go a bit further with this. Enterprise management systems, those tools that enable central management of a globally distributed network, are an emerging group of technologies and packages. You can buy off-the-shelf solutions that may meet your needs. However, there may be alternatives. There are already Simple Network Management Protocol (SNMP)–based tools for many data-gathering needs, and there are also hooks included for writing additional applications. The Linux model, based on Unix, is a set of many small but specific tools used in conjunction for large tasks. Your final solution could be a shrink-wrapped package. Or it could be a combination of SNMP tools, some Perl scripts to do the reporting, a database for data storage and retrieval, and some Web-based CGI (Common Gateway Interface) stuff to produce an easily read and digested overall graphic picture of the system's health. Of course, your shrink-wrapped package may be just the same thing with a larger price tag.

Also keep in mind that few packages off the shelf really fit your specific network needs. Most of the time there will be substantial amounts of configuration, ironing out of software and filesystem compatibility issues, and detailing of the system for it to monitor and report as you want it to. Either way, you'll have to get the systems administrators participating, and what better way to motivate them than to recognize their abilities in the first place?

Linux's Support Exceeds All Other Commercial Operating Systems

The Linux support infrastructure is more solid than most commercial products, has a documented faster response time, and provides better service at a substantially lower cost.

NOTE
For more information about Linux support and related links, check www.linux.org/business/support.html.

To see the strength of the Linux support infrastructure, you must have an entrepreneurial mind. You must be able to focus on success without being held down by dysfunctional process limitations that do not support the success model. Although there are some good bureaucratic reasons for a structured support model, such as accountability and quality verification, many strictures are counterproductive. The Linux support infrastructure is a multitiered system, with six easily definable layers.

As you develop the professionalism and skills of your systems administrators, you will be able to resolve most system needs in-house. This is a strength of Linux, because the tools exist, both in open Source software tools and written materials, for the systems administrators to develop superior levels of skill. Because the code is there, because the tools have been developed and contributed, many tasks can be resolved with just a little time and focus.

Sometimes there will be a need that isn't documented because of its newness or just that it's a result of a series of infrequently related factors. This is where the use of mailing lists and net news provides the next level of support. Your systems administrators will have access to their peers, and there is usually a good chance that someone somewhere else has experienced a similar difficulty. By utilizing these resources, your systems administrators can develop a deeper understanding of the system while resolving the need of the moment.

Often on the mailing lists for different packages will be people of varying skill levels for that package. However, the third sphere of support comes from the fact that the author of the package you are discussing often participates on the list. Linux has developed rapidly, and many of the same people who helped code it to its current level of superiority are still active. They are generally willing to explain esoteric features of the code and can often quickly provide a few leads for resolution.

Look back at these three areas for just a moment. In all of this, two threads give you significant opportunity for business advantage. The first is the lack of payment: Each of these methods is already paid for, such as your employee's time, or is free, such as the mailing lists or author's comments.

The other, more long-term advantage is that each of these solutions increases your ability to provide solutions for the next problem. This resource development means you can invest in your own future success. There are concerns about training systems administrators just enough for them to go to another job elsewhere. This topic is discussed in Appendix A, "The Care and Feeding of a Linux Systems Administrator."

You may develop a need that would dictate more than these avenues of support. For instance, a custom integration or a large-scale installation of a new network would be a bit much to expect from your in-house systems administrator. There are resources available to help with these sorts of needs.

There are commercial third-party support organizations available. Many companies are tooling up with Linux, and several major Unix packages are easily ported. You can find these integrators through distribution of a Request for Proposal (RFP) or through advertisements in professional journals and magazines. You can set the level of support needed, the performance benchmarks, and what functions you are willing to pay for. For diverse projects, you have the option of using a single larger company or smaller, focused teams.

If you need short-term use of specialized skill sets or experience times of increased production load, you can hire individual contractors to raise personnel levels temporarily. These contractors can be chosen for a specific task or can be used to develop certain software solutions. Here, you have the option of seeking a certain skill and requesting a portfolio demonstrating the deployment of that skill. Whether it's for a new C program or complex server architecture, consultants can often provide the short-term advantage you need.

The final level of support is the operating system vendor itself. Although most operating system vendors have some support functions available, Linux vendors tend to provide a higher level of service and a much more complete solution. Major distributors such as Red Hat, Caldera, and Debian have mailing lists with which to share information on package bugs and solutions; many of those solutions come from customers asking questions. As of this writing, both Red Hat and Caldera were building additional support functions for enterprise-level solutions, above the existing e-mail and telephone support available.

If you have a multinational company, Linux is even better for you. Linux support functions exist in many countries, and there is active development in the internationalization of Linux. Europe has a strong Linux support structure; one of the better distributions is by the German company S.u.S.E. Also, there are Japanese plug-ins for Linux.

Although there are so many levels of support available, there is another feature of Linux that must be mentioned in conjunction with the idea of support. Linux is transparent in how it works and in how the applications interact with the operating system. Because of this transparency, support functions have a significant advantage. Because the code is not hidden behind a compiled-only program or some multiple series of graphical menus, a support function can look directly at what is going on in the system and thus has a deeper understanding of it more quickly than those who have to muddle through the obfuscation.

This is why the Linux support infrastructure has such a high customer satisfaction rate and quick turnaround time. The openness of the system provides immediate access to the initial solution path.

Linux Power

Along with the technocratic influence comes the power to do your work. Linux provides the tools to let you do business, and it positions you for globalization and integration with external customers.

A Stable Solution for Information Technology

One of the biggest problems IT professionals face today is the need for 24/7 availability of system resources. A system that needs to be fixed every week becomes a drain on budget and work-hours. If your technical staff has to run around every day dealing with blue screens and system reboots, you're spending money and allocating workpower where it doesn't need to be. You need to begin resolving next week's issues today and planning next year's solutions in the calm of a well-run office. If your day is controlled by system faults, OS glitches, and recurrently inadequate resolutions, you're wasting your time and your company's money.

A stable platform allows you to run smoothly for uptime measured in months and years. If you need to upgrade the software, you can get the new version of each tool, upgrade it, and not have to take down the entire system for one single part. Even better, if you find the new version is not what you need, it's easy to back out without interrupting major system services.

A Customizable Solution

Another attribute IT professionals will appreciate in Linux is the ability to customize for specific tasks. Without having to completely migrate the entire network all at once, you can break off small sections and migrate them a piece at a time. You can also just plug Linux servers into most existing networks and start small by providing services from an added server. Linux can speak TCP/IP, IPX/SPX, and AppleTalk. It also integrates well with other OS filesystems, including Coherent, SYSV, SMB, and DOS.

Linux has all the history of Unix behind it when it comes to stability. Not only can the system stay operational for times measured in years, but it is actually multitasking—rarely will a hung process crash the entire machine.

Linux Puts You in Charge

There is a paradigm shift Linux provides that you may like. While your competitors function using shrink-wrapped software packages produced by other companies, and those other companies have many other clients so that your competitors have to wait in line for the next service pack or mega-patch, you have a different problem. You have an empire of your own to run.

When you start using Linux, you are going to have to make some significant decisions. Some questions will no longer need to be asked, such as, "Will the newest service pack fix the recurring system halts?" or "Will the network continue to run for another three months while we accumulate all the patches so we can upgrade everything at once?"

Once you start using Linux, you will have to ask such questions as, "Which free database package really meets my needs?" and "Since we've patched and tested the production kernel offline, do we want to take a 15-minute break and do all the upgrade reboots?" Probably the most frustrating question will be, "Since the rpm process is doing all the upgrade work, who is going to go for coffee?"

Imagine yourself facing the problems found in the building of a super-computer. Your project needs a supercomputer, and these big machines generally run over a million dollars. Instead, you get authorized for $200,000. Can it be done? Of course it can, with Linux. How about spending only $152,000, which leaves $48,000 for pizza and cool T-shirts?

Linux puts the decision making back into your capable hands. You are the person most knowledgeable about your work. You are the person held accountable if the system does not perform well. Your job is on the line every time a critical production halt loses the company big money. Why shouldn't you also be the one in charge of making the decisions about what is best for your department?

Linux provides tools without demanding a cut of the action. You have to be able to make leadership decisions, as you've never done before. The challenge isn't how to keep the system limping along until the vendor returns your call for support. Challenges are now how to plan for future needs, how to evaluate packages for what you want, and how to develop your group of tape jockeys into a professional team of solutions providers.

These are the leadership decisions that you need to begin making. These are the types of issues that let you sleep well at night and quit the regimen of antacids and stress medication. In short, these Linux-based decisions put you in command of your empire, and you get the control you were supposed to have in the first place.

Throughout this book you will be exposed to innovative solutions others have used, and you will be exposed to programs and code snippets that get you thinking of the possibilities. Put them to work! There is no dictatorial author's hand that will come after you with a lawsuit and say, "You got this from me! Give me money!" To tell the truth, this writing has been fueled by the work of others in the Linux and business community. You can benefit from this cross-generational idea flow by integrating those things that specifically apply to your environment.

Go to it! Somebody needs to run your empire, it might as well be you.

Multiple Licenses Are Free

The Linux licensing model provides some significant advantages. For example, a shop can easily distribute the software to all its employees for training purposes. If employees want to take copies home and work on related projects, they can. And, with Linux, they probably will because Linux provides the ability to run most functions and uses standard architectures. This is especially noticeable if you use an operating system that has unique hardware needs.

Linux lets you use most existing hardware platforms, so you can distribute Linux, use cheaper Intel architecture hardware for learning platforms, and then spend less time porting the solution to the production network. In addition, if your hardware is not state of the art, Linux can probably work just fine. In fact, this usage is very common for companies with hardware turnover. They let the systems folks have the antiquated machines, and the systems administrators put the boxes back to work with Linux. This is not to say they wouldn't appreciate larger, faster machines, but in a pinch, most anything will do.

Of course, the licensing issue has another effect: When a server needs replacement or a crisis demands additional servers to handle the load at 2 A.M. on Sunday morning, you can quickly add the machines without having to worry about whether the server will function with the number of licenses you purchased.

In-house Customization without Heavy Fees for the Code

You may likely have very specific needs for your environment. Such issues as integration with preexisting hardware, functionality for certain filesystem types, or network protocols demand an ability to integrate into the existing infrastructure. Linux allows this because you can compile the kernel and, if need be, edit the existing software to meet your needs. Indeed, this is where many Linux drivers (note-drivers) came from. People wanted to use Linux but they had hardware that was not yet supported. Therefore, with the open source code and some help from others, they wrote the drivers themselves.

The Linux kernel may have options you do not need, and you may have particular system space requirements that demand a smaller, tighter kernel. Because the source is open, you have a couple of options available. The first is to compile a custom kernel. This will eliminate many things you don't need and can reduce the kernel size. Alternatively, if you have significant space requirements, you can do a *code walk,* going through the source line by line and eliminating those things you do not need. This is particularly useful for embedded systems or robotics, where the kernel needs to do just a few things, but it needs to do them well and fast.

Linux can use legacy hardware for operational research and development (R&D), and training machines. Many companies that have existed for more than a couple years have legacy hardware that has been replaced by newer systems. Often Linux can give new life and a higher return on investment by allowing the reuse of these machines for limited service nodes. That is, you can use an older machine for the company mail server or perhaps as a file server for documentation. This allows production machines to be more focused on the mission-critical applications they are there for, and yet it allows you to provide the additional services you want.

Linux can also use older machines for research projects. Building a test bed and then trying out new scripts and programs to ensure the system will remain stable is always a good idea. Because Linux operates on such a wide variety of hardware, you can use it on machines that might otherwise be outmoded. You can also build training machines to provide places for new hires to work on site-specific skill requirements they might not have developed elsewhere.

Again, using a Linux platform allows you to reuse otherwise useless hardware that was just taking up storage space. In addition, if space is at a premium and the systems aren't going to be used for anything else, let your systems administrators take them home. You may never see the hardware again, but you have provided a retention hook for good systems folks and can benefit from their tinkering at home.

Craft

Many folks have their notions of what the 1960s were like. Long hair, tie-dyed clothes, and a lot of dynamic social change. The first efforts that became Linux were also then, in 1969.

The social change that bred political unrest in the 1960s also had consequences in the research field. Whether it was conscious or not, the Unix philosophy developed a very diverse collection of small, imminently configurable tools. Not only was each tool crafted for a specific purpose, but also it was built so that it could be put together with others in different ways, creating different solutions for each user.

Focus on this issue for just a moment, for it underlies every other bit of success (and most of the failures) you will have with Linux. Linux gives you the power to do whatever you want your system to do. Linux provides you with tools for every level of accomplishment you care to take.

For example, you are allowed to make multiple copies of files and to move them around easily. Every other operating system has these simple tools. However, with Linux, you have other tools. For example, you can take a file and count the words. (Maybe this is what teachers needed so many years ago, when they assigned 500-word essays.) Or, you can look at the file and see who owns it. Maybe you want to see how many copies of that file there are or the last time it was changed. Linux works with files in such an intense way; other operating systems don't have as many options.

Unix Started in Bell Labs in the Late 1960s and Early 1970s

During 1964 and 1965, Bell Labs, General Electric, and Massachusetts Institute of Technology (MIT) started on a project called Multiplexed Information and Computing Service (*Multics*, for short). After a while, Multics no longer captured the interest of the world, but a couple of folks from Bell Labs, Dennis Richie and Ken Thompson, considered it. They had some thoughts which then turned into Unix, but not nearly the powerhouse in use today.

What happened was the growth of a system from a working idea which focused on a small set of tasks into a large, diverse group of tools able to function together and perform significant tasks. The developers were technically competent and developed tools for use by competent people. The tendency was to experience a need and then to develop a simple, compact tool to meet that need.

In some cases, complex tasks were encountered. What then would happen is that the task was broken down into its respective smaller component tasks, and existing tools were used together to resolve each small task. Then, if no tool was found that met the needs, a tool could be quickly developed for that subtask. The new tool was also shared with the other developers, and comments for improvements or suggestions for further use were developed, keeping the basic focus of the tool in mind.

This usage of small tools has created a successfully scalable server concept. From the early flashing-lights machines of the 1970s to the modern office server under a desk, the way users physically relate to computers has changed. But the basic idea remains, and because Linux uses this same small-tool philosophy, it allows for customization of the tools for the project at hand.

Using many small tools for complex tasks is also what makes Linux systems administration a craft instead of a button-clicking automation. Some tools, such as **cp**, can be used fairly easily.

```
cp <source file> <new file>
```

This copies one file to a new destination, with the same or a different name, your choice. However, if you want to make archive copies of files, you can use **cpio**, which has over 50 options and parameters available. **cpio** is, by the way, one of the most hated, yet loved tools in Linux.

Use of small tools is made easy because much of the coding between the Linux operating system itself and the programming languages in daily use are related. For example, Linux is written mostly in C. C was also the language Unix was rewritten into; some of the folks who wrote the original Unix also wrote C.

Most of the programs you use today are written in C, from word processors and spreadsheets to other vendors' operating systems. Linux is in C, the source code is open, and C has a long and pervasive history of development by programmers. Finding someone who can code a specific tool or solution for you tends to be easier than for some systems in which the code is hidden and you must start writing code to figure out what is going on before you write code to do what you want to do. C is also a contributing parent to many scripting languages. Perl is written in C and uses some of the same syntax and command structures. But unlike C, Perl code is in text form, so going through a Perl program is easier.

When you buy into the Linux solution, you break out of the mold. Current graphically based systems restrict your ability to make the system perform the way you want. You have certain possibilities presented on the screen, and you must choose one of the few given options. If these choices don't meet the need you have, you're out of luck unless you are willing to wait for the next release to be developed and stabilized. On the other hand, you could pay for another product to give you another set of buttons. This leads to spending money until you happen along on the right button to push.

Alternatively, if you are tired of looking for the mythical one-size-fits-all operating system, sit down with your Linux systems administrators. Create the list of functions you want your network to have, then let them write just the right buttons. Take control of your network once again, and reaffirm the leadership prerogative that you are paid to exercise.

Linux's Technical Specifications

Linux is a robust, high-performance, multitasking, multiuser, 32-bit, network-capable, fully featured operating system that runs on the Intel x86, the Digital Alpha, the Sparc, and the Motorola 6800 hardware platforms. Linux has a well-developed support model and a wide variety of software packages available for it.

Linux gains robustness by using processes for program completion. A process that errors out or causes problems can be fixed without taking down the entire system.

High performance is gained by having the option of a command-line interface, allowing more system resources to be allocated to production activity. Further performance gains are realized by the customizability of Linux and its kernel to the specific machine it's on and the mission that machine serves.

A *multitasking* system allows the system to run more than one task at a time. If you remember the old DOS days, you recall that you had to run a program and end it before you went on to the next program. With Linux, as with all versions of Unix, you can run multiple programs concurrently. Any speed or numeric slowdown will come from the hardware limitations imposed by the platform. Currently, symmetric multiprocessing (SMP) is being stabilized, so industrial load servers are a very real possibility in the near future.

A *multiuser* system is an extension of multitasking, with some added security features. Linux filesystems allow tracking of the ownership of a file or directory, and the owning user and group can have certain restrictions placed on file access and execution. For example, marketing personnel could not accidentally delete financial reports in a properly set up Linux network because they likely would not have full access to the financials of the company.

Actually, on some architectures, Linux is a full 64-bit operating system. For those stuck with Intel-based machines, it is only 32-bit, but that's still better than the 8-bit standard of just a few years ago. Linux is capable of operating on an ISA, VESA, Personal Computer Interface (PCI), and Small Computer System Interface (SCSI) bus. Most hardware works with Linux, either through generic or through vendor-supplied drivers. Linux fully implements the Transmission Control Protocol/Internet Protocol (TCP/IP) suite and is fully Internet-capable. There are many Linux-based Internet sites, and Linux fully runs such standards as Apache (the Web server), sendmail, news, firewalls, DNS/BIND, Netscape Communicator, PPP dial-up connections, modems, Ethernet, ISDN, and both the IPX and AppleTalk protocols.

Linux provides a feature-rich server environment, allowing database applications, network transport functions, file and printer services, multilanguage program development, enterprise management, performance monitoring, multilevel security, data backup and integrity, and server-client programming.

Linux also provides desktop capabilities with office application suites, Internet workstations, graphical user interface (GUI)–based applications, local printing, connectivity to other workstations, and, of course, a lot of cool games.

There are business applications for Linux, including financial packages and major database applications, such as Oracle, Sybase, and Informix. Word processors such as Corel's WordPerfect, Applixware, and StarOffice allow documents and spreadsheets to be handled nicely. The first four chapters of this book were drafted in Linux before being sent out to the printing process, from a Linux platform.

Because of its open source nature, Linux has been ported to more hardware platforms than any other. There are also current projects to port Linux to the 286 chip, to embed Linux in flight-monitoring systems, and to develop Linux as a point of sale (POS) system. Linux-based solutions have a much shorter development time because you start with a full system and can toss out the bits you don't need. Late in 1998, Intel announced its investment in Red Hat software, fueling the fire for making Linux even more powerful on that platform. Linux support comes in a wide range. (This topic is discussed in further detail in subsequent chapters.) Keep in mind that the general consensus for customer satisfaction among network operating system vendors rates Linux highest of all. And, yes, actually, there is concrete evidence for this.

Further, Linux provides incremental upgrade capability with such things as the Red Hat Package Manager (RPM). Although originally developed by Red Hat Software (a popular Linux vendor), RPM has been made open-source and has become a standard with many Linux distributions. RPM files allow for the safe upgrade of specific packages because the upgrade procedures are handled in one structured file. Instead of spending several hours to configure a certain server setup repeatedly, a couple of short commands will send RPM on its way to do the boring stuff for you.

One of the features of the Linux development movement is the File System Standard (FSSTND). This is a feature to keep the distributions building file hierarchies in a set pattern. A system configuration file that resides in the /etc/directory should be there in every distribution. Although vendor-specific additions are allowed, the basic programs and files should be in standardized places.

TIP

If interested in getting the Linux official Penguin, you can download it from www.isc .tamu.edu/~lewing/Linux/.

Linux community members tend to write for enjoyment, and there are usually jokes scattered here and there in any Linux manuscript. Since many of the Linux originators are academics, this further compounds the oddity of humor found in the average Linux manual, book, or magazine. If you start laughing while reading a book on the internal workings of the Linux kernel, you are in deep trouble.

REFERENCES

Covey, Stephen, Roger Merrill, and Rebecca Merrill. 1994. *First Things First.* New York: Simon & Schuster.

CHAPTER 2

Under the Hood of Linux

"The constant temptation of every organization is safe mediocrity."

—PETER F. DRUCKER

Although Peter Drucker's comment was opening a section on poor management, he has fairly well described the operating parameters used by most corporations in software selection. They have degenerated to mediocrity in the name of simplicity and have provided competitors overwhelming opportunities to take larger market shares. Your industry is not unique in exercising the options to choose default settings on programs and operating systems. However, doing so gives the competition a significant business advantage. Whatever your industry, your work has site-specific needs and tasks, and you need the ability to use tools that can leverage your work to a higher profit margin. Linux is that tool.

Any tool that you bring into the office must meet two criteria:

- It must work.
- It must provide a good cost-to-benefit ratio.

Although seemingly silly statements, these two criteria are not met by most commercial software on the market. Indeed, the current paradigm is that you buy software and must then conform your organization to the functions its programmers thought your operations section should run. And if, perchance, you operate from a different position, you're out of luck. Conform or die. That's the current choice.

What this does is violate the first rule of a good tool. Instead of a tool that works for you, the tool becomes the master and you are the servant that must conform. This is one of the most asinine assumptions in existence, but multibillion dollar software companies were built this way. The basic assumption you must adopt is that one size does *not* fit all.

The second rule simply extends the first. A software solution should perform its work, and you should be able to configure it to meet your needs. If you recurrently have to buy new licenses and hardware to scale to your business needs, you've violated the cost-to-benefit ratio logic. Bad choice, and a potential career limiting move (CLM).

It is time to change. Linux is the tool. You are the implementer. This chapter provides an in-depth look at how Linux operates and how you can learn how to make the decision on where and when to deploy Linux to improve your bottom line and increase market share.

An Overview of the Linux Kernel

The Linux kernel uses processes to manipulate files. This is one of the most profitable issues here. The kernel is a grouping of threads, streams, system calls, and network routines that does the work of Linux. What makes this important is the separation of the kernel from the user-level interactions and the technical makeup of the kernel itself.

NOTE
For more information about the Linux kernel and how it works, check http://sunsite.unc.edu/LDP/LDP/tlk/tlk.html.

The Linux kernel may be defined by its behavior. Randolph Bentson used to say that "in broad terms, a system kernel must maximize processor availability, protect users from mishap and attack, and provide interactive response and background processing" (Bentson, 1996).

The Linux kernel provides three major services for the system. First, it schedules CPU activity. Rather like a well-run mass transit system (assuming you've ever experienced one that runs well), the scheduler keeps multiple operations functioning at the same time. This means that the system activity can flow in segmented but smooth paths, and that processing activities are capable of handling large internal transactions over a long time span.

This is significant because Linux is by definition a multiuser system, and the smoothness of the kernel scheduling is noticeable in system availability. A kernel that does not schedule well takes inordinate amounts of time to do simple operations. Scheduling is controlled in the kernel because the input and output (I/O) speeds of most peripherals are much slower than the CPU. Thus, several users can request transactions, and the CPU can handle them because the schedule allows processing while the data is coming in or going out.

Supporting this is the synchronization of the systems transactions. In a workstation environment, this isn't much of a problem, because the user is just doing a few data transactions and is seldom changing the same data in different ways simultaneously. But in a server arena, especially with corporate database applications and financials, several people may be interacting with the same database section, and the resulting computations must be run in proper sequence. Failure to do so would potentially damage customers' files, opening the company to liability issues and quality-of-service complaints.

Scheduling and synchronization provide high availability of the CPU and trustworthiness of the system. For mission-critical operations, you can see why the ability to read the source code and understand exactly what is going on is a significant business advantage. Interactive response, dealing with the shell or applications, relies on the ability to do background processing. Although you could function with each process acting in time with your responses, it would be like writing a memo and not being able to do anything until the memo was delivered, read, and responded to, which also ties up recipients of memos who must now wait for your comments on their responses.

Background processing uses scheduling and synchronization to allow users to process their work and then move on to something else whether the process is actually finished. For example, a print server would receive requests for printing, and each one would be put in line (spooled). Since printing generally takes some time, the user can go on to another transaction while waiting on the print job.

These functions provide the user with an ability to access resources as needed, and yet do not require a significant amount of knowledge of the kernel or system internals. Although a programmer needs to understand the kernel and its internal workings, most users don't.

Although the kernel runs on every Linux machine, you will never see it. Instead you will interact with a shell that takes your commands and sends them to the kernel, which then does its work and deals with the files as you've told it to. You may make entries in the company database, schedule an appointment, or write e-mail to a customer. All these activities go through the kernel in some fashion, yet you don't have to know how to specifically make the kernel do what it's supposed to do. The shell takes your commands, and then the work is done.

This is similar to a manufacturing plant operation. You receive an order for 100 units of product, the order is processed down through the midlevel managers, and then the machine workers produce the required product. Shipping prepares the product for transport and it is delivered without you or the customer having to actually go down to the level of raw materials to craft the product by hand. Keep this image in mind throughout the chapter, because it very well demonstrates the power of Linux.

Start at the heart of the operation, the machine that produces product. The product is information, and you are the CEO. Down on the manufacturing floor, you need product made. It must be in line with customer requests, it must be crafted well, and it must meet rigorous performance and quality standards. These issues are central to the Linux kernel philosophy.

In the development of the Linux kernel, the standards-based measurement is technical quality. No changes are made that are not hashed out by many developers, and improvements are made only when the developers have tested the changes on other platforms and understand the process and how it improves function. This becomes a business advantage to you immediately because you know the machine producing your product is the result of stringent development standards and expert craftsmanship.

You've probably been subjected to market hype before. Read the charts provided at the following URL for objective proof, and then you can get serious about turning these pictures into profit for you.

TIP

▬▬▬ **For objective information on the major network operating systems and their satisfaction levels, check www.redhat.com/redhat/datapro.html.**

There are more benefits programmed into the Linux machine. One of the most important in terms of performance needs is the modularity of the kernel. This complex issue has proponents on both sides. Following is an explanation of both, and then details on why Linux modularity is better.

The first option is a kernel with everything programmed in. This allows plug-and-play functionality, as well as a wide range of hardware and software plug-ins without having to change the kernel. This option uses a standardized kernel on every machine. It simplifies configuration by removing many options and disallows optimal performance. Most personal computer (PC) desktop operating systems use this sort of functionality, and it provides benefits to the small user who doesn't have the capability or desire to derive maximum functionality from the tools. It allows for global marketing of the OS because every possible option has been programmed in.

If you've made purchase decisions for more than a couple years, you've probably noticed the minimum hardware requirements for PC operating systems, and the attendant programs have been growing rapidly. Indeed, a top-of-the-line PC from five years ago will barely run most desktop systems now, much less allocate resources for user programs. This is caused by the desire to program such a wide variety of possible configurations into the machine that the system is bogged down by being ready for possibilities that will never materialize. Modularity solves this problem.

A configurable kernel lets you decide what you want a server to run. For example, you could build your standard desktop PC with support for CD-ROM, Ethernet, and connectivity to a Netware IPX server. You might not need ISDN, FDDI, IP-Multicasting, or tunneling support. These are functions for routing servers and network interconnectivity machines. By using this configuration, you can conserve system resources for the desktop and spend them where they are needed—on the desktop.

The same applies to your Internet connectivity server. You can configure in the network connectivity functions and tools you need and save resources by eliminating sound-card support, printer support, and connection types you do not use.

But Linux takes this functionality a big step further. By using a modular kernel, you can deal with the possibility that you may need a service, but either not right now or not all the time. For example, you could compile a server's kernel with modular support for CD-ROMs. When you need to load a program, the module activates and allows the function. When you are through, the resources are reallocated to some other function. This is enhanced by load on demand.

Load on demand allows the kernel to handle the request for a modular service and bring it online just by your request for the work. This is similar to a limited production run for a short-term need. The machines would be set up, configured, and the products made. When quotas are met, the machines are removed, and floor space, personnel, and power requirements are allocated to other production needs. When Linux does this with a modular service, you get the product without the long-term overhead of having those particular machines geared up and staffed full-time.

The use of a modular kernel provides direct business advantage by allowing you to keep a standard OS for uniformity, yet allows you to build site-specific and even server-specific functionality into your OS. Modularity is similar to the business use of skilled temporary workers. For example, if you need to negotiate a short-term agreement with a foreign partner, you could temporarily hire translators to work with the legal staff to draft the document you wanted. When the project is completed, the temporary workers are no longer an expenditure, and you are not encumbered with severance costs. A kernel module works the same way. When it's needed, it can be specifically or automatically called up. It will work as if it were compiled into the kernel, and when it's no longer needed, its resources can be allocated elsewhere.

Using Linux allows you to utilize more hardware platforms in a standardized system. Linux works on x86 processors such as Intel, AMD, and Cyrix. It also works on Sun Sparcstation, DEC Alpha processors, and Motorola 6800 processors. Linux has been used for embedded systems, and the modularity and ability to compile a system-specific kernel provides more opportunities for this, especially in the areas of automated manufacturing and isolated systems such as aircraft.

Linux Kernel

The kernel is a moving target! There is a dual track for the kernel, although we speak of a single kernel for our production purposes. As new CPUs and hardware are developed, we need to develop new capabilities in our operating systems. We also must take advantage of research in performance issues, such as the development of Symmetric Multi-Processing (SMP) and internal security. These needs, however, should not interfere with a stable system. To manage this amount of change, Linux uses a parallel kernel track. The *production* kernel is made available, and its capabilities are pretty stable. The only changes made are those that fix (patch) minor problems in the system; no significantly new thoughts are introduced. However, the parallel track is the *development* kernel. This is where new thoughts are tested, peer review of ideas is made, and new code is implemented.

Although you must get the kernel for your specific platform, all kernels are covered under the same license. The directory trees are kept as congruent as possible, and kernel development is returned to all current platforms.

So far, this chapter has discussed the kernel, compiling or rolling your own, and other functions of the deep, dark system internals. More in-depth information is freely available. As you lead your systems administrators into providing solutions, you'll want to find resources. Probably the first and best read would be the *Linux Kernel Hackers Guide* by Michael K. Johnson. Johnson wrote the *KHG* early on and has continued to work in the Linux business field. He currently works for Red Hat Software.

If you need to develop in-house solutions, *Linux Application Development (LAD)* translates how Linux functions into how your development department can utilize your existing servers. Written by Michael Johnson and Erik Troan, *LAD* assumes a knowledge of C programming, yet does not require a Linux- or Unix-specific background. A significant amount of the book is spent detailing the tools provided for programming.

Processes and Files: Midlevel Management

The Linux boot process is done in stages, and the configurability of each stage is an immediate business advantage. When a server first powers up, the hardware is configured to check itself and can be made to pause on errors. These instances should be rare, but having the recourse to do a self-test is a good tool to keep handy.

After the hardware checks and configures itself, it goes to predefined locations to search for a bootable operating system. This step provides you with a *hook*, a place to control the system the way you want to. There are three major options here; each one works with Linux and provides its own advantages.

The first is the normal hard drive boot. Most servers are configured this way, and so are most desktops. This provides a system to run in *stand-alone* mode, that is, if the network is not available, you can still perform work, although the network functionality will not be there. If the network is up, then you can connect fully.

However, because the hardware looks at certain sectors on the hard drive for boot instructions, you can put an option there to boot your system the way you want. For example, if there are tools you need to use for both Linux and non-Linux platforms, you can use **LILO**, the Linux loader. **LILO** lets you boot a machine, and it lets you have more than one operating system available for the boot. Although you could not have two different operating systems active at the same time, you could choose to boot into Linux, Windows 95, or OS/2. Each of these operating systems can reside on the same machine, and you then have options to work the way you want.

A further refinement, which is the second option, is the ability to boot different Linux kernels. This is commonly used when a new compile is being tested. You can set up **LILO** to boot with either the production kernel, the new kernel, or to use new parameters for either. This gives you the ability to back out of a change if things don't work as seamlessly as they were supposed to. If you do choose to have multiple kernels, keep in mind that they would still use the same directory tree, and all your other configurations and site-specific modifications would still be in place. **LILO** also adds the ability to pass certain configuration information to the system as it's booting, thus allowing you to really control your machines, even if your site has fairly unique needs.

LILO comes with the ability to set a default boot process. Another track to consider is the ability to have restrictions and passwords on the reboot process. **LILO** provides these because for some very secure servers, you don't want unattended reboots. The configuration information can be found in the **LILO** documentation, and setting the options is as easy as editing the file /etc/lilo.conf and then running **LILO** as root.

The third option is to boot from a floppy disk. Although rarer for servers, there are some situations where the ability to boot from a floppy can be a career saver. Probably the most significant is in case of a system crash, in which the kernel itself is damaged. In this case, you can have a boot floppy handy, boot the system into single-user mode (sometimes called *maintenance mode*) from the diskette, and begin the troubleshooting process. It's advisable to have a boot disk handy just for safety's sake. This rescue ability is made possible because the kernel can be compressed small enough to fit onto the floppy diskette.

Another reason for booting from a floppy is security. Once the system boots, the kernel is loaded into memory and is not removed. A server that must be kept secure could be built with no kernel loaded. It would need the floppy for the initial boot, and then the floppy is removed, making attacks on unattended reboots nearly impossible.

Once the kernel is loaded into memory, the system proceeds through a series of configuration scripts found in the /etc/rc.d directory. These scripts provide the first step in exacting system control. There are a series of run levels and each one has appropriate scripts. A *run level* is a state of service availability. For example, run level 3 is the normal full-services state. Run level 1 is single-user mode, used for maintaining the system. A major difference is that while run level 3 includes network operations, run level 1 does not. Each run level has its own series of scripts that bring up certain services.

Further customization is found in the naming of scripts. The first letter is a capital, and either *S* or *K*. These are the start and kill scripts, called when the service needs to be initialized or cut off. The *S* or *K* is followed by a number. This number allows you to specify the order that services are brought up. For example, on a specific system, S30syslogd gets started before S85httpd. This means that since the logging service syslog gets started first, it's available if the Web server httpd has an error. The user can then check the logs and see what happened. Another use is the S99local script, which makes any specific system messages or changes on that particular server.

Having a K script is important for system stability. Many services use a process identification number (PID) logfile that locks a service. If the

PID (in /var/run) exists, it prevents another instance of that service from starting, thus helping prevent system conflicts. If a process is killed inappropriately, then the PID lock still exists and can cause problems. Using the K scripts closes the service and removes the PID lock, allowing for a cleaner system.

NOTE

S and K scripts are symlinks to files in /etc/rc.d/init.d. Also, the S and K names, in and of themselves, do not cause services to be started or stopped; this is done by passing the script a start or stop parameter. The init process simply calls all S names in order, passing start to each one. Same with the K, except it passes stop. Most people will do something like /etc/rc.d/init.d/foo start.

Processes

Understanding what a process is can be considered the initiation into the deep magic of Linux. The use of processes is an essential ingredient in providing the stability for which Linux servers are known. Although it would be easy to just consider a process as a program, there are sufficient reasons not to do so.

Consider a process to be the Linux equivalent of a specific step in a manufacturing production action. For example, a car engine is a complex machine. To assemble an engine requires a large number of specific tasks to be performed in a certain order. These tasks must be tightly controlled or else the engine will not function. Indeed, if a major task has even slight misalignment or is mistimed, catastrophic damage could occur not only to the engine, but to the manufacturing machinery and nearby materials and workers.

The level of control exercised in building a car engine provides the ability to examine each task and build metrics relevant to that task. It also allows overall evaluation of the system, in an effort to find a better arrangement of the task sequence or combinations of tasks. There is even the ability to work two or more tasks simultaneously.

Again, this level of performance is only possible because of the level of control exercised. Linux provides this level of control for the system. By using processes, systems administrators can examine the processes currently active on the server. Each process has a unique identifier, called a *process ID* (PID). Administrative tools such as **top** allow the use of metrics to see how much of the systems resources the process is actually using.

Processes that are low priority but that demand significant system resource allocation, such as data backups, can be scheduled during low-usage times. Processes can be arranged by priority, allowing time-critical work to supersede routine data processing. A process that has run into an error and starts causing problems can be gently shut down (kill –1 <PID>) or terminated immediately (kill –9 <PID>). Processes are also linked to users, so an administrator can determine if a single person is tying up the system. In fact, the use of process tracing is a major advantage in tracking and halting intruder actions.

When the server boots and you get a login prompt, you are using a shell process. If you start a program such as **top,** the shell will **fork,** that is, it will create a copy of itself, and then the copy will execute (**exec**) the **top** command, taking any parameters passed to it during the **fork.** This is called a **fork and exec** and allows multiple tasks to run because the shell, once forked, is then available for the user.

CAUTION

There is an attack called a **fork bomb. It** causes the system to repeatedly **fork for new processes, tying up resources. The systems administrators can easily handle the symptom and knowing the attack method helps them track and deal with the source problem. Also, a buggy software program may create this problem unintentionally, and the systems administrators can deal with restoring the system and then working out the issues with the software itself.**

A final benefit of using processes is the ability to base resource allocation on the properties passed to the process. This means that a user can run an application, and the processes forked by that application can do all the work they are supposed to do. The processes carry the user ID (UID) and group ID (GID) of the person running the application. There are instances in which a user is not allowed to access certain resources, such as the system management programs used to shut down the system and reboot.

These could create a lot of damage if used by someone who does not understand how they work. If a user reboots the system, that would kill all the services. Since this is not a good idea, the reboot commands do not let users shut down the system. The way this is controlled is by the permissions set on the program. If a user process asks to run **shutdown**, the process authorities are compared to those needed to run the program. If the process has insufficient authority, based on the UID and GID, the user cannot run the program. This level of control is a security measure against both inadvertent mistakes and malicious intruders.

Expanding to the Network Level

After the server loads the kernel and starts running through the rc scripts, network connections can be established, and services can be shared and used across the entire company. The following discusses some ideas on distributed computing.

There are significant advantages to running multiple servers with low-end hardware. One is cost. As production systems are upgraded and new servers brought online, the storage of older servers and desktops can become a problem. By building, a network using distributed services, you can reutilize hardware and scale the server to the intended need.

Look at some examples. Many companies today need to share files across departments and across time schedules. Using a centralized file server allows control over access, lets you focus backup and recovery procedures on a specific area, and helps negate accidental user damage by taking the server out of the area of mainstream desktop functions. To convert a networked desktop PC into a file server, you load Linux, install and configure the specific connectivity suite for your site, and then you're up and running. The only hardware considerations might be to have available a large hard drive to store the files and a tape drive for backups.

If you use an intranet Web server such as Apache, you can turn an older desktop PC into a Web site. Again, once Linux and the connectivity suite for your site is installed, you can set up the specific services and use minimal system resources for other programs. For this server, the only major hardware considerations are to have enough drive space for the Web pages and enough random-access memory (RAM) to be able to keep a good cache and serve pages quickly.

Another server might be used for dial-up connectivity. The reasoning behind using a specific server is to have both a strong security model on this server and provide limited dial-up access into the network. The hardware issue here would be to have an adequate modem or router connection. These services would need to be configured for the system, including secure shells, IP monitoring, and other access control measures. Since this would likely be the first line of defense against an external intruder, the fewer critical resources on this server the better. This topic is covered in more detail in Chapter 4.

Linux Applications

No matter how technically superior the Linux kernel and design structure is, there is no business benefit if it does not let you do your work, your way, at your speed, and in your existing environment. Although it would be nice to get budget approval to completely reinstall the information infrastructure at your company, it's not likely. What is more likely is that you will have a need for a project, and there will be insufficient funding to buy a top-of-the-line, shrink-wrapped solution complete with documentation, training, and a sandbox for development.

Going back to the production plant example, you must be able to integrate new machines and functions without completely shutting down the product output. The ability to integrate into the existing network requires compliance with industry and international standards. It also requires scalability—if the project needs to grow, it can without a completely new system install.

Other desirable benefits are licensing issues. If you need to bring a service online quickly, having to wait for budgetary and managerial approval as well as the purchase process can add to the frustration level. Add the need for stable yet up-to-date development of the solution and reasonable upgrade procedures to the simulation.

Fortunately, this is exactly what Linux does. Linux is standards-compliant. It integrates a superset of the POSIX standards. This means that the programmers who write for Linux know what system calls they can use and how things work. It means there aren't volumes of "It only works with Linux" books that must be digested before a programmer can start producing useful code. Such books as *Linux Applications Development* (Johnson and Troan, 1998) provide the transition for experienced Unix and C programmers. However, because Linux is standards-compliant, those same programmers can quickly learn the few system-specific differences that Linux uses. There is no great need to completely overhaul the knowledge base.

Linux is written almost exclusively in C, the de facto standard in Unix and Linux programs worldwide. The parts that aren't in C are in assembler. Assembler is a language giving detailed control, is reserved only for the most hardware-specific tasks, and, as such, comprises a small percentage of the total kernel.

By using these standard tools, Linux makes itself available to the existing body of C and Unix programmers. The power and diversity of C enables it to be used for simple one-line programs to complete operating systems and network tools.

This makes finding trained workers fairly easy. Most college computer science curricula provide assembler and Unix instruction and almost every one offers several C courses. There is no need to develop a completely new training program internally, and the professional development you offer in the company will be a strong draw for potential new employees.

Another advantage of standards compliance is the documentation available. Unix and C have more than a 30-year history of research and design manuals available. Because of this, a well-developed model of how things work has been established. Many potentially disastrous errors can be avoided simply by being aware of what has been done before. Reports of previous experiments can be reviewed for possible new ideas, and the record of difficulties encountered can prepare the development team for similar problems. This means that the team starts off several steps ahead and can more clearly map out future areas in need of attention.

A quaint but useful thought is about the age of Linux, Unix, and C. Although they've been around long enough to seem old, most of the original developers are still involved with some related project or other. If your development team runs into significant trouble and gets completely bogged down, a politely worded message to one of the old-timers can often result in a dialogue that helps solve the problem. Note that in this case, an attitude of abject obeisance and appreciatory awe is in order, combined with free pizza.

Linux Standards Compliance

Standards compliance also includes other operating systems. Linux developers have made interoperability an issue and have made Linux able to connect to every other major networked operating system. Linux includes support for AppleTalk, which allows Linux to network with Apple and Macintosh machines. Linux also includes Samba, support for the Server Message Block (SMB) protocol. This allows Linux to function as a server in a Windows environment. SMB is also called LanManager or Netbios protocol. If you have an existing Novell-based network, you can use Linux support for IPX/SPX, the native Novell network transport protocol.

Linux provides an extremely high level of functionality with other desktop operating systems and with other network operating systems. Linux also provides TCP/IP network connectivity; that is, Linux allows you to connect to any service that follows the international protocol standards. This allows you to make incremental server insertions into your existing infrastructure. You do not need to commit to a multiyear budgetary reallocation. You simply find an older machine, figure out which services you want to add, and then load and configure Linux for it. Although there will undoubtedly be some configuration settings that need to be tweaked, if your existing network is standards-compliant, then Linux will connect to it. If you need help, search the newsgroups (comp.os.linux.*) or mailing lists for others doing what your network does. They will more than likely be glad to help.

Advanced Remote System Administration Tools

Linux also provides for enterprise network solutions. Enterprise management is a technology still in its infancy, yet Linux has the tools to grow as the model grows. Such tools as Simple Network Management Protocol (SNMP) and the suite of TCP/IP network diagnostics (TCP/IP is covered in more detail in Chapter 4) provide standards-based, mature functionality. Linux tools cover standard Ethernet networks and can also be used for dial-up connections and remote-site connectivity.

A Linux network management station can provide extra benefits for your infrastructure. Using standard connectivity tools such as Telnet, rlogin, rsh, rcp, and FTP, you can monitor and administer diverse wide area networks (WANs) from a central location. Although few sites can go without some human intervention, an operations center function can standardize procedures, focus skill pools, and build integrated networks.

There has long been a perceived opposition between corporate management and network systems administration. Although both groups want the best for the system, for the higher good of the corporation, there are often differences in opinions about how to manage that desire together. Enterprise management allows the systems administrators and the managers to be relatively colocated. This lets the managers see the struggles involved in managing a significant network in which "everything goes as planned" is not a motto. However, this also lets the systems administrators participate in the managerial functions of the corporate decision process. Although an open-ended budget is a systems administrator's dream, once he or she tries to work such a budget through the corporate jungle, a new appreciation of the managers' activities may develop. On the other hand, if the systems administrator does get it through, so much the better for the manager in question; time to ride the wave.

In most cases, however, the collocation will help both groups integrate their visions and missions into something the other can understand and support.

Managing Strategic Use of Product

Linux follows industry standards, except where it leads them!

There is one problem with commercial support that encapsulates customer frustrations. The simple fact is that the software vendor is a separate company with its own business interests and priorities. It does not regard your priorities and needs as nearly as importantly as you do. This is especially true of large software companies. If they lose your business, they can absorb the loss while fueling their marketing departments for more ads and their sales departments for more revenue.

The way to successfully overcome this stranglehold on your business is to build relationships with the software providers in a way that lets you control the pace and depth of support. Open source software is ideal for this because you have the code you need to take to any third-party support function and get a solution. You are not bound to one vendor, nor are you required to try to obtain proprietary source code at outrageous, if not impossible, costs just so your systems administrators can start work on a solution.

Indeed, Linux provides significant advantages in support solutions because the layers between the user and the system are fewer, and they are more transparent. You have graphical user interface (GUI) buttons and representations for when things are going normally, and if something happens you can look at exactly how the system is performing a test and fix what's needed.

Since the code is not nearly so abstracted, you don't have to pay support to go through hoops and trails to find the solution.

Enabling Linux To Provide Maximum Benefit

Linux provides support levels that exceed levels of almost every commercial vendor currently in existence. Linux provides six areas of support.

In-house Solutions

If you have a systems administration staff, you probably have at least some level of professional development. You also have people dedicated to your system needs and whose work is to make your priorities theirs. This gives you, as the manager, the position of discerning corporate network needs and then providing the systems administrators the resources needed to meet those needs. This does mean a commitment on your part to supporting the professional position of the systems administrators.

However, it also means they're tasked to provide solutions. A skilled systems administration pool can provide a wealth of solutions based on prior experience, available manuals, and thorough research. Nevertheless, the key factor in the in-house solution track is priority management.

In fact, the issue of priority management is one key point of dissatisfaction in the customer base. Your ability to function may depend on an external source. Although not all vendors create difficulties, some do. Having an in-house staff skilled in the solutions you need means your production department can more easily stay on track no matter what the problem.

To be in a position to use in-house resources means a commitment to the development of the internal staff. The collocation of systems management and corporate managers was previously mentioned; this proximity to the source of solutions can aid you in gauging the professional development needs of the individuals in question. You will have a closer understanding of the personalities involved and will be given the opportunity to assess the possible promotion potential for each worker. You will also be able to sit down and get a personal, detailed explanation of why some problem or other exists, and you can use your managerial skills to focus on providing the resources that are needed.

Mail Lists and Net News

If your in-house resources need to be supplemented, you have access to mailing lists and net news information. These vary from mailing lists on deep development issues (Linux-kernel@vger.rutgers.edu) to net news advocacy issues (comp.os.linux.advocacy). The level of readership provides the business advantage these lists have.

Many systems administrators can debug and make operational the programs that they install. This body of knowledge is joined by the knowledge contained in various mailing lists, and few problems are new. Most lists that have been around for a while have a Frequently Asked Questions (FAQs) list, where they post the recurring questions and the steps to solve the problems. Your systems administrators can use these lists to not only research solutions needed now, but to find information on the value and function of products before they are purchased. This gives you a chance to evade market hype and those profit-minded sales types and to connect with people who have already taken the course of action you are contemplating.

Linux development has its origins in the early net news days of 1991. Its author, Linus Torvalds, discussed some concepts on comp.os.minix. His original question dealt with the memory management of the 386 chip. Shortly thereafter, he posted the availability of a new kernel with very rudimentary functionalities. What he did next, however, changed the course of server history. Instead of hoarding the profit potential in his new operating system, Linus posted it openly and let others make suggestions on improvements. This usage of net news allowed rapid inclusion of new ideas, new functionalities, and new developers into the project.

Surprised at the acceptance the operating system got, Linus realized the intellectual potential gained from brainstorming. The participation in the discussion naturally weeded out those who weren't interested in providing solutions, and it nurtured those who had tremendous skills ready to be tapped.

Direct Contact with the Software Author

Was Linus's choice a good one? At this writing, there were an estimated 6 to 10 million machines running Linux. Not only does this demonstrate the ability of net news to help proliferate a good solution, but also many of the same developers who started with the original preproduction kernel are still active.

There are personal issues at stake when someone writes software that is open source. If you report a bug, it's often the author who will be the first to say thanks and start to work on a solution. A professionally worded explanation of the problem, including attempts at resolution and inputs from other sources will generally present a challenge that the developer tends to savor.

However, here is a problem. The commercial paradigm is to pay for support rendered. In fact, few Unix developers are independently wealthy. But if you are going to operate in this entrepreneurial environment, you must accept the fact that the world does not always live up to your expectations. Most developers who answer e-mail or net news inquiries don't charge for their comments. Yet those same comments may be preventing system downtime and its attendant revenue losses. The people who provide these solutions do not always operate within the same paradigm as the rest of the corporate world.

The Linux culture is divergent from the business norm. That is, a person's status in the group is not determined by things possessed, but by intellectual and professional respect gained. Your systems administrators represent you in this culture, and they will define the questions to be asked and the solutions needed. Then, when the problem is fixed, they will be expected to document and make available the solution. This is the cost of working with professional open source developers. You must participate in the building of the culture.

How about it? Are you ready to work with a culture that's not like your corporate one? In following sections, the benefits other corporations have reaped from this interaction are discussed. Mark Twain once said, "I knew a man who grabbed a cat by the tail and learned forty percent more about cats than the man who didn't." Are you willing to risk improving your bottom line by 40 percent?

Commercial Third-Party Support

Is there support for long-term custom-designed solutions? Of course! Not only are there major software companies such as Netscape, Computer Associates, Informix, Sybase, and Corel writing industrial solutions for Linux, there are many smaller independent companies that know Linux and C and can write or port custom applications for whatever your need is.

Mentioned briefly earlier, there are significant benefits to using Linux when you need a custom application written. Because the source is open, a programmer can get detailed information about how to interact with the operating system. You can gain significant performance benefits from the ability to custom tune the software to the system. Further, since Linux uses C, you have a body of developers that has been training for 25 years. This provides you with the breadth of skill sets needed to find just the right provider for a solution. Indeed, there are multiple avenues of finding programs, from reading *Sys Admin* magazine and *Linux Journal,* to viewing Web pages for the types of products you want.

Contract Support

There may be times when you need a short-term project done. You don't want to bring in a full-time employee, nor do you want to make a corporate contract. What fits the bill is a contract consultant—fixed length, defined parameters, easy ending point.

This is another area where Linux outperforms the competition. Because Linux uses the same internal philosophies as Unix, most consultants have found it very easy to add Linux to their list of skills. They can work on what you need and can use the other methods of support. They also tend to have their own professional network contacts if there are problems they are unsure of.

Another advantage is the ability to find a consultant for exactly what you need. There are those who provide skills over a wide area, and those who have focused specifically on certain issues, knowing them in a much more detailed fashion. What separates Linux consultants from other operating systems consultants is the ability to learn the specific task down to the program level. You can find consultants who have a deep familiarity with your type of setup, and they can provide the boost you need to clear certain hurdles.

If your problem is significant enough, you can sometimes contract the author of the program you are using to customize it for your needs. A significant advantage of this is that the author knows the internal workings of the software and may be able to create a solution fairly quickly.

Operating System Vendor Support

Three companies sell Linux distributions and provide installation support. Caldera, Red Hat, and S.u.S.E have created professional-grade software packages and have made enormous efforts in making the installation and configuration of Linux an easy task. With each of these distributions, you can pop in the CD-ROM, boot from it or a diskette, and follow the installation instructions. As Linux is installed, you can also configure printers, video displays, and even networking.

When you get past the installation, you have access to e-mail support and telephone support. As of this writing, all three companies were building commercial support structures to provide for those customers who want contractual agreements. Check with each vendor before you commit to a specific version, and see what supports arrangements it has available.

Support Philosophy

There are some background comments on Linux support that will provide you with a level of comfort not available with other operating systems. These apply to all vendors of Linux.

Linux server applications are scalable. The Internet, with about 30 million users as of this writing, runs off the same services that Linux provides. TCP/IP connections run providing Domain Name Service (DNS). Sendmail tosses mail worldwide. Point-to-Point Protocol (PPP) provides dial-up access between remote sites and the central hub. Web pages are served with HyperText Transfer Protocol (HTTP) regardless of whether the request originated from the next room or the next continent. Although throughput issues are a consideration, the ability of the basic services to provide solutions for every level of client base is proven.

If you need to build support for a global mail service, you can develop your staff with sendmail seminars. Whether the site has 50 clients or 5000, sendmail can provide what you need. If you want each department to have a Web site for document availability, you build the server once, train the systems administrator, and then replicate that for each department. There is no need to buy extra licenses or learn new software to scale from one size to the next.

Reboot on Your Schedule

There are few reasons to reboot a Linux server. If a certain process is having difficulty, you can kill it or just reinitialize it so it restarts in working order. Even for cases in which the server is making significant errors, a methodical pruning of processes will more than likely solve the problem. Every so often, an upgrade of the kernel and a test of the server failure procedures are needed. This scheduled outage lets you forewarn customers on that server, and you can prepare for the event by having the necessary software and possibly extra support available.

Global Support

The progenitors of Linux software are a global community. This community can provide locale-specific information for your global corporate needs. If you need a short-term field site consultant in Europe or the Middle East, there are Linux experts there. Because of the open source nature of Linux, it has been allowed to develop where economic conditions prevent other, more costly operating systems from building a local base of expertise.

Competitive Solutions

Linux provides the open source to build a broad network of available experts. This allows you to define reasonable guidelines for hiring outside expertise and having a group to choose from. Not only does this give you some leverage with the competition, but you can look for someone who has the specific expertise you need.

Often the availability of solutions requires a selection on your part. There have been quite a few folks writing software for Linux for several years; unless you have a customized need, there will likely be a variety of possible answers. It remains for you to pick the one that most meets your business and support needs.

This competition gives you further leverage when time lines are considered. You have business needs that are mandated by your production schedule. Most of the time you do not have the luxury of waiting for your solutions provider to finish with other commitments before handling your priorities. This is especially evident when dealing with larger vendors whose multibillion dollar revenues allow them to pick and choose what support they provide and where.

By using competitive bidding and open source software, you have the ability to find a pool of talent that can get into the heart of the matter quickly and is motivated to put your priorities on the front burner. This need for solutions-provider responsiveness can lead to faster production, lowered costs, and more options available for the specific solutions you need.

A further benefit is the general lack of competitive business interests a solutions provider has with your company. Unless you are also in the software development business, the solutions provider will not have controlling market share in a business that is in competition with yours.

This benefit is strengthened by the transparency of solutions provided. Since the source code for the operating system is provided, the developers are more able to link closer to the system. Conversely, you don't have to build multiple layers trying to integrate an operating system that no one really knows well.

You Are Solutions Provider

In cases where the solution you need can be shared with the Linux community without hurting your business interests, you have the opportunity to become a contributing member of a technocracy.

Indeed, in the summer of 1998, IBM joined the ranks of open source contributors by providing the Apache Group with bug fixes and improvements for the Apache Web server. Since over half the Web sites in the world run Apache, this was no small contribution. Not only did IBM perform a marketing coup, but it also found one of the few forms of currency in the technocracy—contributions to the community.

IBM wanted to use the Apache server for its business advantage but had to abide by the strictures of the open source licensing agreement. Further, it had to buy the rights from the group to market the product. Instead of succumbing to the struggles of understanding a new paradigm, IBM took advantage. It grabbed hold of the cat's tail and didn't let go until it had its 40 percent. If a founding member of the computer industry can make it in the new information technology world, doesn't that mean leaner, more entrepreneurial companies can do so much more? Open source encourages others to feed back to the development tree, thus providing software development for lower costs.

Providing Feedback to Development Trees

This makes your decision to support open source software easier. You not only benefit from the efforts of your own developers, but you also have access to the talents of many other professional programmers and network developers. Although some of your competitors may be using Linux for business advantage, most won't be.

You will have to decide how much to share and on what schedule. However, the contributionary field becomes another marketing tool. Lack of participation is failure. It also becomes a significant hiring point when you need to add skills to your team. Although many companies claim to hire the best and brightest, few demonstrate the capabilities of their best. It becomes more like "the best we could find in the market who had some semblance of the skills we require and would accept the package we offered." Companies that tend to do open source seem to be much more entrepreneurial and dynamic. These are the places the best and brightest want to go.

Linux provides business advantage in its choice of functionalities and its technical superiority. It is written for large-scale servers (covered in more detail in Chapter 3) and for providing network services (covered in more detail in Chapter 4). The kernel's interaction with the system is built to provide extreme functionality, yet specific modules can be loaded on demand and used only as needed. In Chapter 3, the server and how to administer it is discussed.

References

Bentson, Randolph. 1996. *Inside Linux: A Look at Operating Systems Development.* Seattle, Washington: SSC.

Drucker, Peter F. 1974. *Management: Tasks, Responsibilities, Practices.* New York: Harper & Row.

Johnson, Michael, and Erik Troan. 1998. *Linux Application Development.* Reading, Massachusetts: Addison-Wesley.

CHAPTER 3

Managing and Administering a Linux Server

The key to any successful business is a strong control model over all the resources. This chapter discusses some of the basic capabilities of the Linux server, examines a few of the ideas behind the model, and takes a glance at some of the tool sets made available to systems administrators.

Take a moment to examine the systems administrator's (SA) role in your business model. As an IT professional, you need to provide the SAs with the resources they need, yet, at the same time, they must buy into the corporate mission. The selection of a systems administrator will significantly affect your network (for more information, see Appendix A, "The Care and Feeding of a Linux Systems Administrator"). However, for now, look at the SA as a craftsperson.

In medieval times, skilled work needed to be done, but often there weren't many around who knew how to do work such as stone masonry, high-temper metalworking, or shipbuilding for sailing the rough seas. The idea of a craft, filled with persons able to learn such skilled work, nurtured a sense of responsibility and accomplishment in those who had earned their way into the ranks of the masters. Although you can easily find people who title themselves masters, you can only judge real masters by the work they do.

Systems administration is such a craft, and no amount of book learning will fix your network at 2:37 A.M. Sunday morning. It takes a master in the craft of systems administration to be able to analyze the problem, look for the documentation, select just the right tools for the work, and carefully build a solution without doing more damage to the already frail network.

The term *systems administrator* refers to those who take pride in their ability to provide crafted solutions for you, not to those who want to throw money around, hoping a problem goes away. It is this level of mastery of the craft that lets you sleep well at night, knowing the network is tucked in as well.

IT departments have long struggled with being able to provide data resources to their customers. Hardware can be expensive for small operations, and the budget approval process can be a struggle as well. Massive updates that force the department to structure its work hours around downtimes for the system cause problems, and if the upgrade doesn't perform well, then the problems are multiplied.

Further, the inability to see what should happen in an upgrade is compounded by hidden code and a support organization that does not know how your systems run. What is needed is the opportunity to put the control into the hands of the technicians who know the local network best and give them the information they need prior to the migration so they can prepare. Additionally, being able to migrate incrementally lets you schedule work in accordance with your other business needs, preventing department fragmentation and schedule conflicts.

This is a built-in strength of Linux since most of the people involved to date have been developers and systems administrators. They build the tools they need to do the work. This chapter discusses how to develop and maintain a Linux server. Almost every tool discussed here comes with a standard Linux distribution or is freely available in the resource community. In addition, of course, it's been honed for the past 25 years, which puts well-crafted tools in the toolbox.

This chapter looks at the Linux server as an independent component of your integrated system. You want to focus on building the server in just the way you want it. Craft it to your needs, and set it up in such a way that it does the work you need. Chapter 4 then places this component into the broader framework of your network and shows how it can serve.

Linux performs well as a server, giving you the standard Unix tools to do the daily work:

- Deal with files
- Manage user and group accounts
- Monitor system resources
- Write scripts for recurring tasks
- Add filesystems
- Perform backups
- Network printers
- Handle e-mail, net news, and chat
- Set up Internet workstation services
- Man pages
- GUI/X-Windows

Additionally, Linux gives you a strong set of development tools to resolve specific performance and configuration issues:

- Configure the server to meet mission parameters
- Control and audit system resource availability
- Set up specific hardware for unique situations with other networks (IPX, AppleTalk, and so on)
- File security models to meet your specific needs
- Build system start-up routines for a bullet-proof network
- Monitor critical configuration, password, and resource files for security
- Provide advanced server administration tools to automate many high-level tasks
- Customize applications in every major language

Linux as a Self-Sustaining Server

Linux has a history rooted in communal development and access to some of the best minds in computing today. One of the many side effects of this access is a wealth of tools for doing systems administration. Many of the people who originally contributed to Linux are still active in its development and often can be counted on to help resolve particularly sticky problems.

Linux Applications

Linux runs every major type of application, from communications, graphics manipulation, database engines, and word processing and office suites, to network monitoring. There are a significant number of applications available; however, more are added too quickly for a printed book to keep current.

For up-to-date information, stay current with the major vendors' Web sites such as Red Hat at www.redhat.com and Caldera at www.caldera.com. In addition, bookmark http://unc.sunsite.edu for ftp downloads and application archives. Of course, for general information and links to a world of resources, try www.linux.org.

Basic Linux Administration

Linux works most system tasks using text-based configuration files. The advantage in this is the ability to easily read what the configuration is supposed to do and to edit it if it deviates. Since all standard Linux commands manipulate text, systems administrators have the ability to quickly build a sequence of piped commands that can do various things with the configuration files. For example, the standard password file is /etc/passwd. This is a plaintext, human-readable file. Although the passwords themselves are encrypted,* the rest of the file has lines like this:

```
joeuser:D9eiYD43vFx8M:514:100:Joe Q. User:/home/joeuser:/bin/bash
```

This gives the user name, encrypted password, user ID, group ID, real name, home directory, and shell of Joe Q. User. A systems administrator could easily edit this file and change the shell or any other information.

---

*Actually, it is strongly suggested that you use shadow passwords. This makes it much more difficult for intruders to get access to your passwords and run a program such as Crack on it to try to determine weak passwords or unprotected accounts. The reason you can't do this with the regular /etc/passwd file is that many programs need minimal but vital access to it. For example, some services need to check whether such a user exists on the system but don't need to log in.

There are many edit tools available for Linux systems; probably the most used are **vi** and Emacs. In translation to the business world, **vi** would equate to older-style secretaries, who were highly skilled in writing letters, taking specific instructions and dictation, and answering the telephone. Emacs, on the other hand, aspires to more. It can do text editing, formatting, work with directories, do mail, spell check, drop to the operating system for a quick command, and, in general, execute most user functions. Indeed, there was an effort sometime ago to make Emacs the operator platform of choice. Although unsuited for the task in today's graphical environment, Emacs does do many larger text tasks well.

TIP

For additional information on Linux systems administration, check the guide (and other electronic books) available at www.ldp.org.

vi is a very compact editor found on most Unix systems. Small enough to fit onto a single floppy disk, it is used everyday for quick, focused tasks. Although not as well suited for long file editing and text formatting, **vi** excels in quickly finding specific text and editing key sections of long configuration files. For example, if your sendmail configuration file (sendmail.cf) needs the official domain name changed, instead of going through the entire file trying to find it and stop on the specific line, Dj$w, in this case, you just use

```
vi +/Dj$w /etc/sendmail.cf
```

This lets **vi** open the file sendmail.cf and take you straight to the specific line you need to change. This gives you the ability to focus your work, use minimal system resources, and control the system as you wish.

Emacs has a much different nature. One common example is that you could read your mail, and get a note discussing an interesting command. Without leaving Emacs, you could start a Unix shell, run the command, and if you liked it, open another buffer and add the command to your personal start-up scripts. Weighing in at over 20 M, Emacs has a rich variety of possibilities. Indeed, one major book on it chooses to focus on basic commands and then on showing readers how to edit the environment to suit their particular needs. In fact, this part of this book was written in GNU Emacs.

Managing User and Group Accounts

Networked systems must allow multiple users access to system resources. In fact, this is one of the prime enabling strategies for modern business—to give the workers the ability to access what they need to do the job. As the network system grows past the small office, however, there are significant issues that arise in the areas of who has what access. For example, a hierarchical organization would have an introductory level for workers, an unofficial level for trusted workers, and one or more managerial levels. Often these levels are blended or less than clear-cut, but generally each person has a defined amount of access to proprietary company data.

Imagine Jane is in the marketing department, as a trusted employee. Her new position entails writing initial performance evaluations on the more junior-level employees and writing interdepartmental coordination memos to people in her level. Further, she writes initial in-house notices on new products and services; these get sent to all employees so they can be aware of changes and upgrades in the product line.

It is clear that some of this information is open to the entire organization, some made available to Jane's peers, and some must be kept closely guarded and only shared with Jane's immediate supervisor. This becomes difficult when the data is electronic, since there is no physical barrier on a network that prevents other network users from accessing the data.

What is needed is a sense of appropriateness, and Linux provides this. Jane is a user, and thus has her login, *janeuser*. When she writes a memo, a file is created and ownership of that file is assigned to Jane. Since Jane is in the marketing department, she needs to have access to general departmental information, so a group is created called *marketing*, and Jane is assigned as a member of that group. For security and auditing purposes, each user should have only a single account. However, employees may be members of as many groups as needed.

In the example, Jane has to write company memos that anyone who has access to the system can read. Since most users on a system are members of the group called *users*, Jane can write the memo and then assign it to the group *users*. For example, the note on the new network system is called "Linux Network Sweeps Company." She writes the memo in Emacs, drops to the shell and runs:

```
chmod 640 "Linux Network Sweeps Company" chgrp users "Linux Network
Sweeps Company"
```

Now, the file has the permission set 640, meaning Jane can read and write it, all members of the group *users* can read it but they cannot change it, and no one else can do anything with it. You may wonder why this last bit is noted, and it's important in the global networking mindset. Often a company will build an alliance with another organization and want to share some information but not all. In this example, a different group could be created to which these external customers belonged, and they could have the appropriate access to information they need to build the alliance. The same process occurs with the peer memos. Jane writes them, assigns them to the group *informal*, and lets everyone know they are available.

The last instance is a bit different. What can be done here is to create a new group called *new-evals* and create a directory that allows only Jane and members of the group *new-evals* to use that directory. This lets Jane have a safer place to put her evaluation notes, her manager can easily be put into the group *new-evals*, and no other user on the system can get to it without a compromise in the system.

How difficult is this group management process? Not very, when you look at it. The most involved part will be to develop the access model, and only you can do that. You must ensure those who need information have access to it, and those that need to stay outside the loop, do. Creating a group is as simple as editing the file /etc/group and adding a line similar to the following:

```
new-evals::150:janeuser,marketmanager
```

This creates the group *new-evals*, skips the password for the group, assigns group ID number (GID) 150 to the group, and authorizes *janeuser* and her boss *marketmanager* to access this group's permissions. The next time they log in, Jane and her boss will be members of this group.

Monitoring System Resources

Monitoring system resources is another critical issue in server management, and Linux provides many resources to monitor the system, as shown in Table 3.1. Of the commands listed in Table 3.1, **top** is one of the most interesting. It provides a running evaluation of many

Table 3.1 Command Resources to Monitor Linux Systems

df	Show amount of filesystem space and usage levels
dmesg	Help print out boot messages for troubleshooting
du	Summarize disk usage
free	Show memory and swap space usage
ifconfig	Show and change network Interface configurations
last	Show listing of last logged-in users
logger	Add an entry into the system log
netstat	Display network connections, routing tables, and interface statistics
procinfo	Show system data gathered from /proc filesystem
ps	List processes by process ID (did) and user
route	Show or change the IP routing table
syslog	Generate a running log of system events
top	Show a running compilation of system usage
uptime	Show how long the system has been operational
utmp/wtmp	Show system login records
w	Show who is logged in and what those users are doing
who	Show who is logged in

facets of the system and repolls at a specified interval. See Figure 3.1 for a snapshot of the results when **top** is run on a system.

The first line in the figure is the same as the results of **uptime**; it shows system time, how long the system has been operational, how many users are currently logged on, and some load averages. The second and third lines show the number of processes and some statistics on the CPU usage; as this is a separate workstation, the CPU is not taxed heavily. Lines four and five show the same results as for the command **free,** which displays the memory and swap space available and used.

The last section in Figure 3.1 shows the breakdown of the most intense users of system resources. Focus on columns 1, 2, 10, 11, and 13. Column 1 shows the process ID, a unique number for each system process. As you seek control over these resource-monitoring tools, the PID is the key. (Remember the discussion in Chapter 2 of how each process has an individual tracking number that allows you to control its priority, whether it lives or dies, and so on.) Column 2 shows the

```
3:46pm  up 27 min,   2 users,   load average: 0.04, 0.03, 0.00
22 processes: 21 sleeping, 1 running, 0 zombie, 0 stopped
CPU states:  2.7% user,   3.6% system,   0.0% nice, 93.6% idle
Mem:   13816K av,  12300K used,    1516K free,    8944K shrd,    1172K buff
Swap:  96280K av,      0K used,   96280K free                    7196K cached
  PID USER     PRI  NI  SIZE  RSS SHARE STAT  LIB %CPU %MEM   TIME COMMAND
  572 root      10   0   564  564   444 R       0  6.4  4.0   0:00 top
    1 root       0   0   392  392   324 S       0  0.0  2.8   0:03 init
    2 root       0   0     0    0     0 SW      0  0.0  0.0   0:00 kflushd
    3 root     -12 -12     0    0     0 SW<     0  0.0  0.0   0:00 kswapd
  271 gershom    0   0   772  772   620 S       0  0.0  5.5   0:00 bash
  263 root       0   0   924  924   556 S       0  0.0  6.6   0:00 login
  285 gershom    9   0  2300 2300  1556 S       0  0.0 16.6   0:01 emacs
   23 root       0   0   348  348   296 S       0  0.0  2.5   0:00 kerneld
  162 root       0   0   444  444   372 S       0  0.0  3.2   0:00 syslogd
  171 root       0   0   412  412   328 S       0  0.0  2.9   0:00 klogd
  182 daemon     0   0   412  412   336 S       0  0.0  2.9   0:00 atd
  193 root       0   0   488  488   404 S       0  0.0  3.5   0:00 crond
  204 bin        0   0   332  332   268 S       0  0.0  2.4   0:00 portmap
  226 root       0   0   416  416   344 S       0  0.0  3.0   0:00 inetd
  240 root       0   0   944  944   704 S       0  0.0  6.8   0:00 sendmail
  264 gershom    0   0   752  752   540 S       0  0.0  5.4   0:00 login
  265 root       0   0   312  312   260 S       0  0.0  2.2   0:00 mingetty
  266 root       0   0   312  312   260 S       0  0.0  2.2   0:00 mingetty
```

Figure 3.1   Results of the command **top**.

user who created that process. This allows you to monitor users who are placing too high a demand on the system and to perhaps get clues as to potential new departments to which to add servers, giving you a chance to lighten the server load and increase performance for everyone else; this is a prime budget documentation tool. Columns 10 and 11 show the usage of CPU and memory. Again, this is a workstation, so the resources aren't taxed heavily. The last column, 13, shows the actual command being run. This is important to note in conjunction with the PID and user, because if the same command is being run by two different users, then there are two PIDs. Even if the same user is running two instances of the same program, there are still two completely separate PIDs. This will again help you justify budgets based on system usage and needed services.

Figures 3.2, 3.3, and 3.4 are from the main server at Red Hat Software, a major supplier of commercially supported Linux for servers, clustered servers, and workstations. Red Hat also maintains a large Web presence and File Transfer Protocol (FTP) site for most Linux software. Some of the most intense usage comes from ypserv, a Name Interface Server (NIS) server. Using resources are sendmail, the Internet standard mail transport agent, and rpc.nfsd, the remote procedure call for NFS.

```
 3:40pm  up 2 days,  3:51, 25 users,  load average: 0.83, 0.57, 0.47
 121 processes: 117 sleeping, 4 running, 0 zombie, 0 stopped
 CPU states: 15.2% user, 13.7% system,  0.0% nice, 71.3% idle
 Mem:   63160K av,  61552K used,   1608K free,  35612K shrd,    3096K buff
 Swap: 104384K av,  15244K used,  89140K free                  11408K cached

  PID USER     PRI  NI  SIZE  RSS SHARE STAT  LIB %CPU %MEM    TIME COMMAND
  386 root       9   0   828  776   324 R       0 10.6  1.2   44:38 rpc.nfsd
16524 ed        12   0   624  624   468 R       0  9.9  0.9    0:00 top
16528 root      12   0  1076 1064   788 R       0  5.3  1.6    0:00 sendmail
  410 root       4   0  3248 1504   232 S       0  2.2  2.3 139:06 ypserv
  238 root       0   0   268  236   184 S       0  0.7  0.3   12:13 syslogd
    1 root       0   0   180  144   108 S       0  0.0  0.2    0:08 init
    2 root       0   0     0    0     0 SW       0  0.0  0.0    0:04 kflushd
    3 root     -12 -12     0    0     0 SW<      0  0.0  0.0    0:00 kswapd
14501 root       0   0   516  516   428 S       0  0.0  0.8    0:00 mgetty
  422 root       0   0   192  160   128 S       0  0.0  0.2    0:00 ypbind
   26 root       0   0   112   56    44 S       0  0.0  0.0    0:00 kerneld
  247 root       0   0   360  184   140 S       0  0.0  0.2    0:00 klogd
  258 root     -12 -12   384  364   232 S <     0  0.0  0.5    0:02 xntpd
  269 daemon     0   0   168  136    92 S       0  0.0  0.2    0:00 atd
  281 root       0   0   216  176   128 S       0  0.0  0.2    0:00 crond
  336 root       0   0   396  336   256 S       0  0.0  0.5    0:39 sshd
  292 bin        0   0   240  220   164 S       0  0.0  0.3    0:38 portmap
```

Figure 3.2   Results of the command **top** on Red Hat's server.

Note the services that are listed but do not have many resources allocated. These, following the Unix pattern, are started when the system boots. (Recall that discussion from Chapter 2.) The services are actually running, but are sleeping until there is an actual need for them. This gives a quick response time to requests for services without having system resources taxed unnecessarily.

Writing Scripts for Recurring Tasks

As the discussion moves into shell scripts and task automation, think about ideas on how to improve the system. Chapter 2 discusses the boot sequence, which is actually a shell script. Because it's in plaintext format, and there are editors, you can modify the scripts to boot the computer the way you want. You can write scripts to back up files, to set reminders, and to do general tasks a specific way so you don't have to remember each configuration option every time you run the script.

On most Linux systems, you have a variety of shells to choose from. There are a few that are worth extra note. The most basic is the Bourne shell *sh*, a very standard shell that allows you to work with the kernel. *sh* allows you to use input/output redirection, wildcard characters, and gives you the ability to set environment variables. Many users have their default shells set to *bash*. This is set in the /etc/passwd file. *bash* is a superset of *sh*, it keeps compatibility while offering quite a

```
3:40pm  up 2 days,  3:51, 25 users,  load average: 0.84, 0.58, 0.47
123 processes: 120 sleeping, 3 running, 0 zombie, 0 stopped
CPU states: 18.0% user, 25.7% system,  0.0% nice, 56.9% idle
Mem:   63160K av,  62180K used,    980K free,  35520K shrd,    3084K buff
Swap: 104384K av,  15244K used,  89140K free                  11660K cached

  PID USER      PRI  NI  SIZE  RSS SHARE STAT LIB %CPU %MEM    TIME COMMAND
  410 root       19   0  3248 1504   232 R      0 17.4  2.3 139:06 ypserv
16533 root       16   0  1112 1104   784 R      0  8.7  1.7   0:00 sendmail
  386 root        4   0   828  776   324 S      0  6.0  1.2  44:38 rpc.nfsd
16528 root       13   0  1116 1104   804 S      0  3.6  1.7   0:00 sendmail
16524 ed          8   0   624  624   468 R      0  2.9  0.9   0:00 top
16534 root       18   0   588  588   476 S      0  2.1  0.9   0:00 procmail
  324 nobody      1   0  9376 9184   456 S      0  0.7 14.5  20:07 named
16531 jrb         4   0   832  832   580 S      0  0.7  1.3   0:00 show
16532 jrb         5   0   472  472   368 S      0  0.5  0.7   0:00 more
  238 root        1   0   268  236   184 S      0  0.3  0.3  12:13 syslogd
  484 root        0   0    52   24    12 S      0  0.1  0.0   0:29 update
23848 jrb         3   0   948  948   656 S      0  0.1  1.5   0:00 tcsh
    1 root        0   0   180  144   108 S      0  0.0  0.2   0:08 init
    2 root        0   0     0    0     0 SW     0  0.0  0.0   0:04 kflushd
    3 root      -12 -12     0    0     0 SW<    0  0.0  0.0   0:00 kswapd
14501 root        0   0   516  516   428 S      0  0.0  0.8   0:00 mgetty
  422 root        0   0   192  160   128 S      0  0.0  0.2   0:00 ypbind
```

Figure 3.3 A second screen shot of the results of the command **top** on Red Hat's server.

few improvements, such as command history, command-line editing, and command completion. These allow you to run the same long command more than once simply by pressing the up arrow key. Note that for Unix commands, since they can be rather powerful and very specific, this not only saves time but files as well.

The C shell *csh* is good for C programmers or those otherwise comfortable with that syntax. There are many similarities between *csh* and C,

```
3:40pm  up 2 days,  3:51, 25 users,  load average: 0.77, 0.57, 0.47
122 processes: 120 sleeping, 2 running, 0 zombie, 0 stopped
CPU states: 17.0% user, 15.8% system,  0.0% nice, 68.1% idle
Mem:   63160K av,  61940K used,   1220K free,  34944K shrd,    3068K buff
Swap: 104384K av,  15244K used,  89140K free                  11668K cached

  PID USER      PRI  NI  SIZE  RSS SHARE STAT LIB %CPU %MEM    TIME COMMAND
  410 root        5   0  3248 1504   232 S      0 12.3  2.3 139:07 ypserv
16533 root        3   0  1168 1160   804 S      0  6.7  1.8   0:00 sendmail
16535 raster      2   0   852  852   684 S      0  4.8  1.3   0:00 ipop3d
16524 ed          7   0   624  624   468 R      0  2.9  0.9   0:00 top
  324 nobody      3   0  9376 9184   456 S      0  1.3 14.5  20:07 named
  386 root        2   0   828  776   324 S      0  1.1  1.2  44:38 rpc.nfsd
16538 jrb        10   0   832  832   580 S      0  1.1  1.3   0:00 next
  238 root        1   0   268  236   184 S      0  0.9  0.3  12:13 syslogd
16539 jrb        11   0   472  472   368 R      0  0.3  0.7   0:00 more
  292 bin         1   0   240  220   164 S      0  0.1  0.3   0:38 portmap
  315 root        3   0   164  116    80 S      0  0.1  0.1   0:19 inetd
23841 root        1   0   724  724   540 S      0  0.1  1.1   0:00 in.telnetd
  484 root        0   0    52   24    12 S      0  0.1  0.0   0:29 update
23848 jrb         9   0   948  948   656 S      0  0.1  1.5   0:00 tcsh
    1 root        0   0   180  144   108 S      0  0.0  0.2   0:08 init
    2 root        0   0     0    0     0 SW     0  0.0  0.0   0:04 kflushd
    3 root      -12 -12     0    0     0 SW<    0  0.0  0.0   0:00 kswapd
```

Figure 3.4 By watching the changes on a server for a period of time, you can assess the status of that server.

and thus the learning curve is less steep. There is the added advantage that a larger shell script can more easily then be turned into a small C program. Note, however, that most users who are not programmers will get less from *csh* because most of the improvements went into C. There is an improved version called *tcsh* that adds some of the features of *bash* and *ksh*.

The Korn shell *ksh* is another shell that has had a bit of recent development and offers compatibility with *sh*. For the most part, *sh* is the most basic shell that generally all the system functions need. In fact, system-level stuff should *only* use *sh,* as it is guaranteed to run under any circumstances. C programmers may want to use the *csh* for familiarity's sake, but most users will use *bash* or *ksh*.

One of the more useful languages for routine systems administration is Perl. Although there are a lot of things to be said about Perl, the first introduction comes from its name. Two explanations for the acronym exist, both supported by Perl's author Larry Wall as equally valid and correct. The first, Practical Extraction and Reporting Language, does indicate its use in manipulating text files and providing information on the files and their contents. The second explanation goes more to the heart of Perl: Pathologically Eclectic Rubbish Lister. Larry Wall is a linguist by training, and one of his major goals in writing Perl was to break away from the very artificial thought pattern indoctrinations needed for most computer programming languages. Indeed, the Perl motto is "There's more than one way to do it!" (TMTOWTDI—pronounced by the faithful as *tim toe di*). Perl is available for most Unix platforms and is currently in operation on 32-bit Windows platforms as well.

Probably the best way to explain Perl is to focus on its market. If you consider very basic shell commands on one end, and C-based programming on the other, Perl fits well in between both. It provides the usefulness of a shell and can replace many of the commands with custom versions. In most areas, you would have to go into application-level software to exceed Perl's capabilities.

Apache, the open source Web server that runs about half the world's Web sites, has modules for additional Perl functionality. Majordomo, a very common mailing list manager, is written entirely in Perl. Perl is very culturally appropriate for Linux, since much of its syntax draws heavily from various and sundry Linux commands.

TIP

For more information on Perl for Linux, check the Comprehensive Perl Archive Network at www.cpan.com.

Adding Hardware

Adding new resources to a Linux server is relatively easy. Of course, for safety reasons, this operation requires a system shutdown. However, the downtime is minimal—only what is required to physically install the hardware. Once this is done, you can reboot and let the system integrate the new hardware.

Some things are automatically configured, such as RAM and a more powerful CPU. Other hardware issues, such as hard disk drives, CD-ROM, and network interfaces, need to be physically installed and then the system must be configured to recognize the resource. However, this is rarely difficult. A new hard drive requires the creation of partitions using **fdisk** (Format DISK), and then the filesystem needs to be mapped out. This is done with the **mkfs** tools, with different types for different filesystem setups. Finally, the new partition needs to be assigned a mount point on the existing system. Assuming that the mount point doesn't exist and somebody must create one, a total of four commands are involved in this process.

For example, add a hard drive for Jane User to store all the new company manuals on. Jane creates the directory /home/janeuser/manuals. Once the server has the hard drive installed and is operational, the systems administrator runs:

```
fdisk /dev/hdb # create a single partition, /dev/hdb1
mke2fs /dev/hdb1 # map the Second Extended File System (ext2)
mount -t ext2 /dev/hdb1 /documents/manuals # link the physical drive
to the created directory
```

Depending on the size of the drive and the CPU speed, it probably takes less than half an hour to install and the server can still be running other operations. Again, keep in mind that the only server outage is the actual time to install the hard drive itself.

Some advantages are fairly obvious. First, system downtime is minimized. Often the instance can be combined with other server or network maintenance. The installation of tape drives and other removable storage media is similar. Note that this procedure is pretty much standard whether the system is workstation-class hardware or SCSI peripherals on a RISC processor. The only difference is in the custom configuration of the kernel. If you need SCSI capability, you can compile the kernel with it. If not, you can make the kernel leaner by culling the excess.

Another clear advantage to this sort of setup is the capability to focus finite resources to maximum effect. Instead of another server in marketing, you can settle for a quick upgrade of disk space and an easy solution. This is another example of the Linux philosophy in action, "Specific tools crafting custom solutions."

If you use Name File Server (NFS) in your network, it's even easier because the physically added hard drive space can be almost anywhere in the system, yet users can treat it as if it were local.

As mentioned earlier in this chapter, the command **ifconfig** is used to show and change network interface configurations. This is usually used when you add a network card to set the parameters. You can also use the command for debugging, to see if something has gone wrong. For instance, if the NIC died, you would need to install a new one and configure it. If you use the same brand and model, the kernel is already set up for it and you just need to run basic configuration numbers including IP address, broadcast address, network, netmask, and such. Again, minimal time is spent. If you are using a custom kernel and your IT department uses more than one brand of NIC, you can easily compile in the specific few you use. The system overhead is minimal, and it will save you the time of a compile. Another possibility is to make the selection of NICs modular and only activate the modules in the kernel as needed. This saves the base kernel space by minimizing overhead, yet makes the quick upgrade possible.

Performing Backups

Critical to any successful business is the wisdom to know that not everything works as it should. A regular system of backups is vital to good business, and developing and training on restoration techniques and plans is a chance to test the validity of the process. No matter who's fault it really is, few things will get you fired faster than losing all of last week's financial transactions. An essential allocation area for resources is in backup system hardware, software, and training. This vital area is easier for managers to sign off on because they seldom want even partial responsibility for lost data when they could have helped in the proactive solution.

Backup hardware needs to be standard, multiply redundant, and worked often. It is possible to have a perfect backup tape, yet have no access to data because the only server with that particular model of tape drive is the one that crashed! Although tape drives are the standard backup media, modern removable disks are another possibility. Also, use of RAID systems is advised for data that has significant changes from one minute to the next.

Because of the nature of the problem, backup software comes in many forms. Linux gives the standards of **tar** and **cpio. tar** puts several files into a single archive, retaining the permissions and other information. **cpio** does the same thing, but has better recovery capability if the medium is damaged or corrupted. There is also **dump** and **restore.** These let you back up and restore just a few files or the entire archive. Again, because these are Linux tools, you have the ability to design a custom shell script that lets you identify key files that have changed since the last backup and pipe them into an archive.

However, depending on the cost severity of a potential data loss, you may be well advised to also check into software that may have technical improvements or provide guarantees.

Network Printers

Linux supports three general types of printer; local, remote, and SMB. You can have multiple printers accessible. Local printers are those connected to the printer port on the local machine, remote printers are connected to other machines, and SMB printers are connected to SMB servers. This is useful when you have a printer connected to a Windows box or one running Samba software. You need to provide unique printer names, and your printer vendor should be able to supply you with any particular information needed to bring its equipment online.

Printing under Linux provides several controls. Specific programs include the following:

- **lp**—the actual devices, /dev/lp0, and so on
- **lpc**—used to disable/enable the printer or its queues, rearrange the order of jobs, and find the status of printers, their queues, and the printer daemons

- **lpd**—the actual spooler daemon that controls the printer
- **lpq**—examines the printer spool queue, giving information on users and jobs
- **lpr**—controls printing offline, sending the print job when the resource becomes available
- **lprm**—allows removal of print jobs from the print queue
- **pr**—allows some conversion of text files to be printed
- **printcap**—the file that details how the printers are set up, what they are called, and what special handling tools are used

Handling E-mail, Net News, and Chat

Linux provides many communications capabilities. Native to Linux is **mail**, which handles internal system mail easily. For larger sites, **sendmail** is the Internet standard, scalable to any organization. There are supporting programs such as **fetchmail** for getting mail from remote servers, **elm** and **pine** for reading mail, and others.

Electronic mail requires several connected parts to be useful. First, there must be a mail user agent, a program such as **pine** or **elm** that lets you read and write the messages. These are then picked up by a mail transport agent (MTA) such as **sendmail** or **qmail.** MTAs are used to carry the mail between systems and have rulesets for handling different situations. For example, you may have a mail server for your internal network and set up the rulesets accordingly.

However, for security reasons, you want the mail traveling between your network and the Internet to be passed through the security line; you could set up the transport model to allow this. One very desirable security feature that actually simplifies life for most people is *aliasing*. Jane Q. User has the marketing department server (market.company .com) set up to handle the marketing mail. However, without aliasing, someone would have to send mail to Jane as janeuser@marketing .company.com.

Using aliasing means someone can send mail to janeuser@company .com, the mail gets forwarded to the specific machine that handles Jane's mail, and the outside world does not need to know or have access to internal company information. Indeed, the rules can also be set up so that any mail Jane sends will come from company.com, again hiding the internal network setup from potential intruders.

Mail programs work in close parallel to their nonelectronic counterparts. You would write postal mail and address it in ascending order of general delivery areas. Mail sent to Jane would have her name and title. The second line would have her department, and the third the company name. After that, the street address or post office box, the city, state, and zip code. When mail is delivered, it goes to the state, then to the city. The city mail handlers sort mail by street, and then carry it to the company. Inside the company, the mail gets sorted by department and then individual.

There are additional mail programs, such as **procmail. procmail** provides filtering for messages, so a user can sort mail and preplace it in folders by topic. There are many possible ways to filter mail, and your systems administrator can help build the model that provides the most value.

There has been mention made about security problems in **sendmail.** Many stories are true; however, most are old stories rehashed long after the problem is fixed. Security is discussed later in this chapter.

Net news, a very early form of Internet communication, is still going strong. Indeed, news is one of the places many systems administrators hang out to stay absolutely on top of the latest solutions and where they can seek first-tier support. Often a news response will solve a problem within 15 minutes, and if it doesn't, there are more resources available.

Chat is an even more interactive form of communication, although today it has been regarded as more the teenage hangout medium than any real useful business resource. However, chat has significant advantages to the systems administrator. Imagine being able to communicate in real time with the developer of the software you are running. Or being able to interactively obtain technical support from your software vendor. Or get live instructions, with feedback, for application installation. Another usage is as an internal training mechanism, allowing the systems administrator to teach a user-level topic to widely dispersed subunits, and giving the students a chance to ask questions and have live classroom participation not hindered by separation of several thousand miles or a few time zones.

Linux was developed, in large part, on the net news platform. Many of the initial notes and announcements came out on news, and the building of Linux-specific newsgroups, mailing lists, and chat areas has kept the developers of Linux in close contact. These programs have helped make Linux the self-sustaining business resource it is and are used to ensure Linux stays near to the needs of the market.

Netscape, the Internet Workstation

Probably the most visually advanced Internet application is Netscape Communicator, an integration of Netscape's Navigator with regular mail-handling needs. It can be set up to retrieve mail from POP3 or IMAP servers. POP3 (Post Office Protocol, version 3) and IMAP (Internet Message Access Protocol) can read mail, net news, and Web pages in a common environment.

Netscape also has Java, Java Script, Secure Sockets Layer (SSL), Certificate, and Cascading Style Sheet (CSS) capability. Netscape also comes with an authoring tool to allow you to write internal and external Web resources and allows internationalization with 56 languages and dialects to choose from.

This gives businesses access to current Web technology and the ability to grow an electronic presence. *Intranets,* internal networks using Internet technologies, are able to be quickly set up to start production. Users have the ability to provide company content and the tools are available to learn and cut training costs.

Netscape Corporation is one of the leaders in the new open source wave. Releasing the source to the Web browser in mid-1998, resolutions to challenge areas have been fairly quick, with Linux response time being one of the fastest. As the products grow in capabilities, companies are better able to customize their environments to meet internal needs. Larger vendors, such as Netscape, can then focus on enterprise-level support.

Man Pages

Another strong point of Linux is the documentation available. These are referred to as *man pages,* the term coming from *manual.* Man pages are divided into nine sections:

1. User commands
2. System calls
3. Functions and library routines
4. Special files, device drivers, and hardware
5. Configuration files and file formats
6. Games and demos
7. Miscellaneous: character sets, filesystem types, data types
8. Systems administration and maintenance commands
9. Reserved

If systems administrators need detailed information on a command's syntax or options, they can enter

```
man <command>
```

and get the information.

Sometimes there are several instances of certain keywords, and the systems administrator can specify the section

```
man 8 <command>
```

which would go specifically to section 8 of the man pages and look for that specific command.

Another value of the man pages is their cross referencing; most have notes to refer users to other related commands. Many man pages are currently being transferred into HyperText Markup Language (HTML) format, allowing a server to provide command information across the network regardless of workstation platform.

GUI/X-Windows

People are mostly visually based, and the trend toward providing graphical user interfaces has promoted a sense of familiarity and ease with computers. Although the GUI is a positive accomplishment, there is a point where it becomes a loss. When the interface prevents the systems administrator from keeping fine controls on the system resources, it creates a dependency on invisible things that cannot be controlled.

Linux has a GUI, generally referred to as the *X-Windows system.* However, the GUI supplements the command line skills systems administrators have developed, and there is no need to adjust the system to use the command line. You simply open another window and run the command.

Core to the concept of a Linux GUI is the idea of a Window manager (**wm**). Most Linux GUIs are customizable for the individual user; indeed, multiple users on the system can have different GUIs and each one remains highly functional relative to its user's personality.

The major differences in **wm**s are how the windows and background are controlled. For example, AfterStep uses an attractive set of graphics on a sidebar control panel with a good mix of colors and borders to clearly delineate active and inactive windows without creating a disorderly visual image. On the other extreme, there's 9wm. Created to duplicate the feel of the **wm** for Plan 9 (currently under development at Bell Labs), the GUI is almost nonexistent, with each window created and individually sized as needed. Although dissimilar to the visual experience of AfterStep, it gives a systems administrator the ability to focus on several tasks that require attention to detail.

Some significant tools provided by GUIs are system resource usage meters, which are scrolling displays having 1, 4, or even 16 different virtual window screens available at once. This is done with a window control panel that indicates which window you are currently in and lets you click to another window.

For example, you could have an application running an editing tool in one window, and you could have it cover the full real screen so you can review several lines of code at once. After each minor modification, you could switch to another window and run the program to see how the changes affect it. In another window, you could have **top** running to evaluate the resources consumed by the program, and yet another window could have mail being monitored. Of course, you can designate a complete window for Web browsing and keep one with a family picture just for encouragement.

However, the Linux GUI just starts here. You can have dual-headed displays; there are several different window packages you can choose from to suit your corporate needs, and each one comes highly customizable for individual tastes. Further, you can run remote X-Windows commands as if they were native. In Linux, the GUI is an enabling tool, and like almost everything else, it comes with the source code and is completely modifiable. X is very networkable. There's no need for a PCAnywhere kind of application; if you have an X app, it can run almost anywhere. An SA can have an xload (graphic display of system resource usage) from each of the main servers displayed along the bottom of the screen.

It must be admitted that the basic window manager for Linux has room for improvement. Such features as drag and drop between windows are still being hashed out; however, there are two projects that are operational now and are expected to develop more fully. The first is the GNU Network Object Model Environment, or gnome.

For more information about the gnome project, check the home site at www.gnome.org.

Another project is the K Desktop Environment (KDE), a work to simplify systems administration and interact well with the server's environment.

More on System Configuration

Other system configuration tools are provided with Linux. For example, a very useful tool is **linuxconf,** which lets you control many system resources. User configuration allows the adding, deleting, and control of users and groups. There are boot and net configuration tools provided for network information such as name servers.

For more information about linuxconf, check www.solucorp.qc.ca/linuxconf/.

Note that these tools are not only in the graphical user environment. Each one acts as a front end for modifying the actual text files, something you can do by hand if you choose. The GUI just saves time and lets the systems administrator do more.

Advanced Linux Administration and GNU Tools

GNU's Not Unix (GNU) has a wealth of software available for free. Although, historically, free software has been associated with low quality, this is not the case with GNU. Many commercial vendors are including GNU software, and professional SAs generally consider the GNU versions to be more robust and have a greater variety of options.

For more information on GNU check www.gnu.org.

Configuring Servers for Mission-Critical Applications

Earlier in this chapter, upgrading hardware and having to compile the kernel to meet different needs was discussed. Although there are different stages on the continuum between a completely customized, server-specific kernel and a bloated, monolithic kernel, most systems administrators will find balance a good determiner in deciding where to build.

For example, if you are committed to a certain vendor for network cards, then you can save system resources by compiling the kernel for those specific cards. Or, even if you use a few different brands, the kernel can still benefit. Another example is AX.25, a protocol used to connect computers and amateur radios. Although a technological wonder, most find no need for it in the kernel.

On the other hand, as you incrementally migrate your network services to Linux, you may need to build a firewall. This is a specific server type, requiring that specific options be compiled in and enhancing security if everything else is compiled out. Specifically, you would need to compile in support for networking, TCP/IP, IP forwarding/gatewaying (for IP filtering), firewalling, firewall packet logging, accounting, dropping source-routed frames, network devices, dummy net drivers, general Ethernet, and your specific cards. You need to deny masquerading, tunneling, aliasing, PC/TCP, and reverse Asynchronous Routing Protocol (ARP). There are some specific instances in which you could use extra services or deny the regular ones, but that is a decision only you could make for your specific organization. There is a wide range of options for other hardware and software from which to choose in a case by case basis. You can focus system resources where you need them. This level of system control is what Linux provides—the tools necessary to build a customized system.

Building File Security Models to Meet Specific Needs

One of the strengths of Linux is the ability to build a comprehensive security model using file permissions and user access. Modern business has a need to keep internal information available to authorized parties and unavailable to others. The use of a good security model based on groups can provide this level of comfort.

By using user ownership, you maintain accountability. Users, except root, are not allowed to change ownership of files. This gives you the ability to track system resource usage by user. This also applies to groups: a user cannot change group ownership of a file to another group. You can create groups by department, by functional task, or for short- or long-term projects, and users can easily be added to or deleted from groups. One useful advantage is for writing multidepartmental reports. Each department assigns a person to assist in the task, a group is created, and the specific members added. Now each person in that group can allow others in the group to review documents relevant to the task, without endangering any other data.

There has been a good deal of comparison of operating systems, especially in the area of relative security. Later in this chapter, security is discussed in more detail. For now, think about this model. It is a management task to determine just what information you are responsible for, and to balance the availability to those who need it while still preventing access to those who don't. This can be a difficult task, made more so by the requests of users in each department for more access to company information, while managers are daily faced with employees leaving the job who have had access to vital company secrets.

The security model you choose must be understood by the workers. Informal networks of people can easily destroy any security plan, and the enthusiasm of the systems administrators in adhering to the plan will depend in great part on your ability to listen to what is needed, compromise on things that are unessential, yet firmly maintain corporate data responsibility. Although any security system can be cracked, a good security model takes care of the mundane details and allows you to create the model you need for your business.

Building Systems for a Bullet-Proof Network

One of the big trouble spots in many networks is the unreliability of system resources. There is always a chance that a system may lose contact with a remote disk server or that a software package requires certain functionalities. Linux does not claim to resolve every nuance of every problem, but there are plenty of tools available for you to have the custom network you want and to make it as bullet-proof as you feel is critical.

Stable systems, with stability measured in uptime of over a year, require the ability to configure for unique hardware needs, to audit resources, and to interface with other networks. Linux provides these resources in a variety of ways, most often upon users' requests on the Internet.

Sometimes a developer is using the hardware and makes drivers available. Tools are written by professional-level network administrators to keep their networks going. Or, someone has a heterogeneous network and needs capabilities not normally provided in a commercial application. Keep in mind that large software firms require a sizable interest in the customer base to profit from a software package. If you have a need that is transient or relatively unique, the chances of finding an off-the-shelf package that meets your needs are slim. However, as you have the tools available in Linux, you can write the solution yourself. Or you can outsource a short-term contract to get the results just to your specifications.

Linux provides the ability to build heterogeneous networks that interact well together. Your concern in this is simple, the network should be available. If it isn't, the company loses money. Linux provides the tools to build a bullet-proof network and the ability to fix problems collectively before they surface.

Some of the specific tools available are **make** and **rpm**. **make** automatically determines which parts of a large program need to be recompiled and it does that without breaking other parts. One of the most common uses of **make** is in the kernel compile. **rpm**, the Red Hat Package Manager, helps control upgrades to programs and manages the version control sections to ensure all parts of the program go to the right places and that conflicts with older software are avoided.

Consider a kernel compile from the top. First, obtain the source code, either on CD-ROM or by FTP. If you use CD-ROM, you can always have the ability to build systems without Internet access. This example uses the Red Hat distribution and runs through the entire process.

To upgrade the kernel, use **rpm** to install the source files. Using files on the CD-ROM, issue the following commands:

```
cd /mnt/cdrom/RedHat/RPMS
rpm -Uvh kernel-headers-2.0.35-2.i386.rpm
rpm -Uvh kernel-source-2.0.35-2.i386.rpm
```

These install the source and the headers into the directory /usr/src/linux. You then change the directory (CD) and run the *make* commands as shown here:

```
make mrproper   # cleans out old compiling files
make config   # set up the particular configuration you want
make dep   # sets file dependencies
make clean   # gets rid of excess files and notes
bzImage   # builds the compressed image
make modules # builds the modules for your system
make modules_install   # installs the modules you configured
```

After this, the kernel is ready. You still need to do a bit of housekeeping, but the system hasn't had to go down yet, and you can polish off the last bits quickly. First, you must get rid of the old modules, then set up the system to reboot with the new kernel:

```
rm -rf /lib/modules/2.0.34-old
mv /lib/modules/2.0.35 /lib/modules/2.0.35-old
cp arch/i386/boot/bzImage /boot
```

Finally, you need to edit /etc/lilo.conf to add a stanza to boot the new kernel, and then install the configuration onto the master boot record. Add a stanza, specific to your machine but similar to the following:

```
image=/boot/bzImage
label=new
root=/dev/hda1
read-only
```

Save this file, run **LILO** to install it, and then boot using the new label. The purpose of this is reliability. If the new kernel does not work, you just reboot the server and return to the old configuration. This provides the ability to safely back out of an upgrade at any time. As you run the new kernel, you can test its capabilities to run your existing applications and monitor it for any potential problems. After a good period of burn in, you can change the /etc/lilo.conf stanza to make the new kernel the default and rerun **LILO**. Note that you don't need to reboot; this just sets you up for the next boot.

In this entire process, the server remained active, able to service user requests and provide resources. The only downtime was the reboot, and that can be scheduled at your department's convenience. Indeed, until the reboot, you were able to back out during the entire process, allowing you to take each step and ensure you were doing exactly what was necessary.

Also in this process, the tools you needed were provided by other professionals. The shared corporate needs of developers builds the tool sets used in common. You will use exactly the same tools in your network as the developers use in theirs, and thus the linkage is stronger. Developers also require various tools to be configurable, and you have the exact same access to those configurations. **gcc**, the GNU C compiler, has a few options you can choose from. Try the following:

```
man gcc
```

and see how long it takes you to read all the options you are provided! (Believe that a document with over 17,000 words does give you some information. In fact, this entire chapter has only about 10,000!)

Building Custom Applications in Every Major Language

Which languages are spoken in your development department? Most likely C/C++, possibly Cobol, Java, and maybe FORTRAN. To make this work, you need compilers, and Linux gives them to you, as well as Pascal, ADA, Basic, and Assembler. There are other scripting languages as well, such as Perl, expect, python, and more shell scripting languages including ash, zsh, tcl, and tk. There are newer development libraries supplied with many languages that allow you to utilize work from other minds.

Keep in mind that Linux has been a developer's platform since it began. It draws people who can make a difference, contribute to performance issues, resolve code problems, and find better ways to model different processes. It does so in an open environment, so you can find someone who has probably already started on a resolution for the issue you just discovered. The turnaround time for development tools in Linux is extremely quick, not only because of the number of people involved with each aspect, but because there are plenty of aspects that give different avenues of approach to most problems.

Further benefits come from various mailing lists and newsgroups. Linux is still a hot developer's platform, and many new capabilities are surfacing, including Linux versions that work on the PowerPC-based Macintosh systems and one that works on a 286 processor, embedded systems, and soft real-time kernels. Again, going back to the open source model, corporate benefits may be gained by having the source code available. Whatever the specific need, you can start with a stable base and then develop it to meet your unique needs.

Linux also provides advanced programming tools such as Electric Fence, **gdb**, and **rcs**. Electric Fence is a debugger for memory allocation processes. **gdb**, the GNU DeBugger, can check C, C++, and Modula-2. It can help you step through a program and search for bugs by setting breakpoints, then steps through each line after that. **gdb** can also be used to examine core files, those dumped after a program crashes to see what caused the problem. A core file is just a dump of the memory image of the process when it crashed. You can use **gdb** to get a clearer picture of exactly what happened. This is just one of the powerful tools Linux systems administrators have put in your hands.

rcs is a revision control system, keeping software revisions controlled by using access lists, change logs, and tracking multiple revisions of text. It can use **cvs** as a front end to allow more active yet concurrent development of programs.

Security Resources

The *Linux Security Administrators Guide,* published by CERT, goes into detail about how to secure a network server for reliable operation. Consider, for a moment, the power of Linux security.

TIP

For more information about Linux security, check www.geekgirl.com/bugtraq or CERT Announces at www.cert.org.

First, note that there really aren't that many viruses around that can affect a Linux system. The basis of this strength is in the user concept: no user can affect another user's process. Only the *superuser* can affect system resources. If Joe User brings in a floppy disk that has some intrusive program on it, the damage will be limited to Joe's machine, data, and reputation. Jane's data is running and will continue to do so.

The one weakness in this concept is the root user, or the superuser. root has access to the entire system, and problems introduced at the root level usually mean a compromised system. This is one of the major reasons Linux systems administrators keep their own accounts separate and only log in as root to do specific system maintenance tasks. Performing routine work while logged in as root is an open invitation for disaster.

There are many general security resources for systems administration, and many of them can apply to Linux. For example, there is the Bug-traq list, the CERT Advisory List, and specific lists by vendor, such as redhat-announce-list. There are also newsgroups that deal with security issues specific to Linux and those that deal with computer system security in general. Monitor several of these, especially your vendor's list, Bugtraq, and CERT. There will be a bit of duplication, but your vendor's list will offer detailed solutions while the general lists will help keep you informed about trends in problems and solutions if you have an heterogeneous network.

This chapter discusses many issues, the most basic of which is the ability to make a Linux server function as you need it to. The tool sets are available for you to implement custom solutions for whatever issues you may have. Further, the nature of Linux attracts developers and you will have the availability to draw on external resources to help resolve issues. This multiplies the effect of your in-house development staff, effectively giving a significant added value to using an open source platform.

PART TWO

Linux for Business Applications

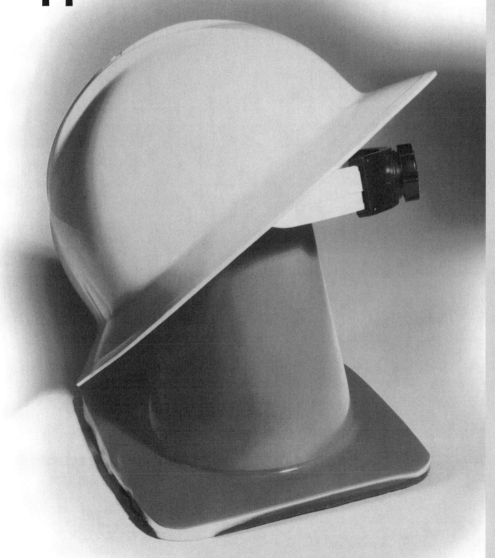

CHAPTER 4

Linux for Internet Applications

L inux functions as a network server, providing standard TCP/IP services. Here is a short indoctrination to networks. Network connections are based on logic, that is, the connection only exists as long as both machines agree that it exists. Thus, either machine can terminate the connection, or issues outside the machines can terminate the connection, such as a loose or broken wire, a power outage, or an essential intermediary server going down. This last is one of the strengths of TCP/IP; it can survive the loss of certain intermediary machines if there is an alternate route.

Using Linux for Internet Applications

The machines build the connection based on data packets. These packets come in a couple of different varieties, but they are fairly standard worldwide. Protocols determine how the packets are set up, dealt with by intermediary machines, and resolved once they reach their destinations. The primary protocol suite to be aware of is TCP/IP. Following is an explanation of a few of the technical issues and why they are important to your business.

In dealing with TCP/IP, you must recognize that there's actually two different major protocols involved. Transmission Control Protocol (TCP) is a reliable, ordered, two-way transmission stream involving handshaking and acknowledgments. What this means is you can be relatively sure a TCP packet will reach its destination or let you know that it didn't. This is especially important for critical data traveling long distances. In general, the longer the distance, the more intermediary machines there are, and thus the more links in a possibly breakable chain.

This is where the Internet Protocol (IP) comes in. IP deals with the routing of packets in large networks and the Internet. Hence, the name. Since it works on the current worldwide network, you can assume it's scalable to your organization. (If not, please contact the author of this book; he would be interested in helping you resolve distant end routing issues.)

You're probably familiar with most of the common services run on TCP/IP though their formal names aren't used as often. But daily, you use things such as Web servers (HTTP), Simple Mail Transfer Protocol (SMTP) which deals with how e-mail is handled between mail servers, and File Transfer Protocol (FTP) which lets you download files from other organizations.

There are other less well known but relatively important services. Post Office Protocol version 3 (POP3) verifies user name and password, then transfers the user's mail from the mail server to the user's local machine. POP2 is also still used in some places, but most systems administrators have gone to POP3. Another essential service is Telnet, which allows you to work on another machine as if it were your own. This is how many systems administrators do remote maintenance by logging into the distant server, fixing the problem, and then logging out.

Another protocol, used much like TCP, is User Datagram Protocol (UDP). It's not reliable, that is, there is no guarantee the packets will reach the destination, nor is there any notification if they don't. UDP lets the applications themselves ensure the data flow necessary. Some applications use the lost data flow for network information gathering, others just request another transmission. However, in a LAN environment, packet loss is generally negligible, and UDP is used for services that don't have to have 100 percent reliability. Lest you look down on UDP, following are some of its advantages and uses.

For example, the network file system (NFS) and the network information system (NIS) both use UDP. Routing information is also generally done with Routing Information Protocol (RIP) over UDP. The logic is that the information is requested until an answer arrives; thus, you don't need to know if a particular route works, you just keep transmitting until you find a good one. The main benefit of UDP is the lowered overhead. Often a UDP packet can perform its work ten times as fast as a similar TCP packet.

Internet Protocol

IP gives you a world of possibilities. Although seldom used in plain sight, most are familiar with the *dotted quad* addresses of early Internet history. Such things as 152.2.22.81 and 128.214.6.100 have been replaced with sunsite.unc.edu and nic.funet.fi. However, don't disparage UDP because of its unreliability; remember, you couldn't use names without the Domain Name System (DNS), which runs on UDP.

IP addresses are broken down into subsections, and each of the four numbers can go from 0 to 255. Based on organizational size, IP addresses are divided into Class A, B, and C networks. Class A networks are huge, allowing about 1.6 million IP addresses for each network.

Most small to midsized companies have a Class C address, allowing 254 host machines. This can be further managed by using *subnetting*. This means using the IP numbers in groups, so five company departments could divide up the 254 addresses as needed, perhaps just using blocks of 50. However, as discussed in Chapter 3, you can do aliasing and masquerading to funnel service requests through certain servers. When you add another concept, private network addresses, your network can grow fairly large, well in excess of the amount of IP numbers you have.

Private network addresses are reserved dotted quad numbers that are never assigned to any network. For Class A needs, network 10.0.0.0 is reserved; for Class B networks, 172.16.0.0 to 172.31.0.0; and for Class C, there's 192.168.0.0 to 192.168.254.0. Note that these numbers can be reused in your organization, so if you want to have several separated networks, you could use IP address 192.168.0.23 in each network. There is a safety factor here as well. Generally, if a packet does escape the network, no other machine can readily respond to it, so the packet will quickly die. These addresses cannot be directly connected to the Internet, but you can use Linux tools to link your intranet to the Internet.

There is one last bit to mention before discussing specific services. The current incarnation of IP is version 4, referred to as IPv4. There is a new emerging standard, IP Next Generation (IPng). Or, for the science-fictionally challenged, IP version 6 (IPv6). IPng brings several solutions to the table, namely more addresses, high-performance networks, more security features, autoconfiguration, and improved routes. Please don't hop on the IPng bandwagon just yet. It's still in the beta stage, and unless your organization is in the technology development business, you don't need to spend resources just yet. But do keep an eye out, and start the migration strategy now. Buy products that are IPng-ready, and ensure any connectivity relationships you have are posed to step forward when the time comes.

Linux provides servers for Internet applications. Following is a look at a common Internet server that handles each function under Linux.

First, the workers need to be in contact with their peers, so they use e-mail to keep up on the latest techniques for their particular function. When their workstation client contacts the server, it transfers mail using something such as fetchmail or qmail. It sends messages out using sendmail or smail. When the mail gets to the server, it is queued and forwarded using sendmail and either handled internally or sent outside. Mail can be handled on the server using Netscape's Communicator, or Pine, or even just **mail.** Each has benefits, although there is the constant trade-off between ease of use and system resources consumed. sendmail does tremendous work, yet only takes just over 250K of disk space. Netscape Communicator 4.5 is over 13M. Both do great work, but the ease of use for Netscape is nice sometimes.

sendmail

Systems administrators have a dynamic relationship with sendmail (www.sendmail.org). Often cited as a gross frustration to install, it provides one of the most important connectivity functions—it lets us communicate globally. sendmail can handle routing mail for local systems, UUCP, and Simple Mail Transfer Protocol (SMTP) mail. sendmail can also provide mail aliases, which help create mailing lists.

Although sendmail can run with just a couple modifications in its configuration file (sendmail.cf), much of the power comes from understanding what options are available and what your SAS can do for you. For example, you could refer mail to a certain department, and the systems administrator could change that label as needed. This functionality is provided by creating an alias for the department, running the database rebuild through **newaliases**, and you're ready to go. For example, edit the /etc/aliases file to create the managers list. Use **vi** or Emacs to open it up, then add the following:

```
marketing: janeuser
```

There are some things to note. This expects a user on the system to be identified as *janeuser*. Any mail sent to the marketing department would be sent to Jane, and she would handle it or pass it on as needed. There are other options with sendmail; for example, if you have a small intranet that connects to a larger network, you can configure the smaller sendmail to use the larger network as the smart host, that is, it does all the major work and you just pass stuff to it.

If you would like to build an internal mailing list, you can use sendmail in combination with majordomo. *Majordomo* is written in Perl and runs many existing Internet mailing lists worldwide. Again, it is open source, and you are provided the information to configure it to meet your needs.

Before ending this discussion on sendmail, here's another warning. Over the years, sendmail has been reputed to have many security holes. A significant part of the problem has been that the power of sendmail requires substantial authority on the system, and, thus, if the configuration is not tightly maintained, there are openings to do damage. But sendmail is another work that is being constantly improved. Its original author, Eric Allman, is reinvesting time and corporate resources in a commercial support function for sendmail. For example, recent versions of sendmail contain antispam hooks, which allow more control in bouncing unwanted mail that uses system resources.

Web Browsing with HyperText Transport Protocol Daemon (HTTPD)

Browse the Web for current news related to your business. When you do this on the client side, you have access to Netscape's Web browser. You can also use Mosaic or Lynx, a text-based browser. If you choose a full Web-enabled browser environment such as Netscape, you have access to Java, JavaScript, graphics, and the secure connections needed for business transactions. On the server side, it's an entirely different ball game, but one that Linux handles just as well.

First, remember the Web protocol is the HyperText Transfer Protocol (HTTP). A Web server handles client requests. The Web server of IBM and over half the Internet Web sites worldwide is Apache (www .apache.org). Maintained and developed by the Apache Group, Apache is a full-featured, stable, extensible Web server. It answers requests for information from all HTTP 1.1–compliant browsers, giving them the content they request in a format they are configured to receive. For example, Lynx browsers will not receive text images, but Netscape Navigator users can. Note that all current major browsers support HTTP 1.1, including Netscape Navigator, Microsoft's Internet Explorer, Sun's HotJava, and NCSA Mosaic. The use of this standard is an important tool in global connectivity.

A Patchy Server, err . . . , Apache Server

Apache supports secure transactions and can authenticate users for certain areas of the Web server. This gives you the ability to create sections of your information infrastructure that are restricted, as you need. For example, you could have a section of your site deliver internal memos to employees and have this section restricted to those with an internal level of access. You could further provide information to close business partners, for example, a material-tracking log that your suppliers could check to ensure you received what they sent you. Alternatively, you can make a proposed product line available to existing suppliers, soliciting their bids for the materials contracts. The key issue is the ability to provide information where it needs to be, without spreading it where it does not need to go.

A strong advantage in the business use of Apache is its ability to link to databases, both serving information and to upload incoming data. For example, think back to your suppliers. If you have a contract that requires the maintenance of certain levels of supply for stock and prohibits overages, then the supplier could view your Web site, log into its area, and see what your current stock levels are. If the supplier's materials take some time to produce, the contract can specify triggers for certain requirements. These are facilitated by the use of shared data.

Here's another example. The manager of a plant that runs 24 hours a day, 7 days a week would like to come in each morning and see what happened since yesterday. Connecting to the Web page, the manager can have data translated into a visual accounting of production levels, stock levels, and whatever else is pertinent to company success. Like any report, this data is written in a specific format and delivered to the manager. The difference is that its automated nature reduces typographical errors, delivers it exactly when the manager requests it, and keeps it as current as that moment—and its dissemination is restricted to those who really need to know.

Apache uses Common Gateway Interface (CGI) scripting to provide these services. CGI gives Apache the ability to interact with other parts of the server to run scripts and commands as needed. There is a downside, however. Please keep in mind that running such scripts in a poorly maintained environment can breach any security standards your server may have. This is one reason many companies place the Internet-accessible Web servers outside the network security area. Then, any breaches to the server tend to have less effect on the rest of the network. Secure transactions are possible through a well-configured CGI setup, but electronic commerce is a specialized, developing subject.

Finally, Apache is under constant improvement. Web services are constantly demanding more capabilities, tools, and configuration options. Apache, with over 50 percent market share, is the current standard for the Internet, and the Apache Group is working to ensure servers' functionality for tomorrow's HTTP needs.

Perl

When you consider training courses for your systems administration staff, invest heavily in Perl. Not only does it provide superior systems administration shell-scripting type functions, but its power lets it automate many tasks that drain resources. Additionally, Perl can be used to augment your Web site; there are many Apache/Perl combinations that can give you more for the corporate dollar. Perl also performs many Internet tasks. One commonly used example is majordomo, a widely used mailing list manager. If you've ever sent a subscription e-mail to majordomo@somelist.net, then you've tasted one small piece of the Perl pie.

Probably the best conclusion to this section is a simple note. Everything discussed so far comes with most standard Linux distributions, at no extra costs, with no extra licensing fees or any legal issues to deal with. Often the software can be updated to the most current version via the Internet, and you can generally find support mailing lists and other resources when you visit the site that sponsors the program. This is just one more way Linux excels.

Bandwidth Issues, Ethernet, Fast Ethernet, Asynchronous Transfer Mode, and Frame Relay

In order for any computer to interact with other computers, it must be able to network with them. Today's networks consist of a varying array of topologies, network media, various interfaces, and transmission speeds.

Since the very early versions of Linux, networking with other computers has been possible. The evolution of Linux includes the capability to communicate with today's most popular networking types, as well as some of the less popular. What follows is a description of the methods of connectivity that Linux supports. Local area networking, as well as wide area networking, is fully implemented on Linux and capable of being used in a production environment.

Serial Line Protocols: Point-to-Point Protocol and Serial Line Interface Protocol

The Point-to-Point and Serial Line Interface Protocols are fully supported on Linux and have been since the very early days. SLIP (Serial Line Interface Protocol) and PPP (Point-to-Point Protocol) are used for TCP/IP networking over serial lines such as the telephone via modem or a local cable between two machines. Typically, speeds equivalent to the modem's maximum speed are supported, but direct serial-to-serial speeds are much greater.

Ethernet, Fast Ethernet, and Gigabit Ethernet

Ethernet is a 10 megabits/second baseband local area network specification developed by Xerox, Intel, and Digital Equipment Corporation several years ago. This technology was later extended to provide 100 megabits/second. The interface cards are relatively inexpensive, as is the cable necessary to connect them.

Full support for nearly all 10 and 100 Mbit Ethernet cards is available for Linux and is by far the most common method for networking local computers together. Internal interface cards as well as laptop Personal Computer Memory Card Interface Adapter (PCMCIA) cards are also fully supported.

Gigabit Ethernet is also supported for several cards under Linux. Gigabit Ethernet is 1000 megabits/second and is available for use over existing wiring. Gigabit Ethernet is still a highly developmental technology, and the Linux developers are watching it very closely.

Additionally, multiple Ethernet cards in the same computer are fully supported, allowing a Linux server to be configured as a router on your network.

Integrated Services Digital Network

Integrated Services Digital Networks (ISDN) is a suite of internationally adopted standards for end-to-end digital communication over the public telephone network. Normal end-user ISDN service requires an ISDN device, much like a normal modem, to enable speeds of 64 or 128K. ISDN provides a clean, error-free connection that can ensure reliable transmission worldwide. ISDN is a digital technology, unlike normal analog modems, and can transfer data nearly five times faster than ordinary modems. ISDN is suitable for connectivity from the home network to an Internet Service Provider (ISP) or the small office.

ISDN support for Linux is well established, and several vendors make internal ISDN interface cards for Linux. An external interface can be connected to the computer's serial port with no trouble at all.

Frame Relay

Frame relay is a method of transferring data that is low overhead and high capacity with low delay over existing public networks. It is largely designed to be a public service for interconnecting private local area networks, although private networks can be built. Frame relay is generally considered able to provide service at speeds up to 2.048Mbps, although some service providers claim that they are able to squeeze out 45Mbps. Public frame relay carriers have rolled out frame relay services in the increments of 56Kbps, fractional T-1, and full T-1. Several commercial companies offer drivers and frame relay products for use with Linux.

Asynchronous Transfer Mode

Asynchronous Transfer Mode (ATM) is a method of transmitting, switching, and combining multiple streams of data on a single circuit. ATM supports (or will support) optical fiber and coaxial cable at throughputs as high as 155Mbps, although the speed of ATM can be extended as far as the market's ability to pay for it. Two gigabit/second speeds are currently possible.

The ATM Forum has chosen to adopt existing physical layer standards wherever it can. Potential future standards may include 52Mbps over Category-3 (or higher) UTP, 155Mbps over Category-5 UTP, and 1.544Mbps for T-1 (or DS1) lines.

It is with fair certainty that ATM will be the most important networking technology in the early twenty-first century. ATM allows users to control the volume of traffic through virtual circuits. Using these features, ATM will allow you to use one protocol from the local desktop machine to the most remote machine.

ATM development on Linux is also advancing rapidly. While still in alpha development phase, several network devices are currently supported. Other networking systems can act as bandwidth translators between the ATM connection and the Linux servers.

Miscellaneous Protocols

Various other protocols and networking types are available under Linux as well. These include Amateur Radio, or AX.25; AppleTalk/EtherTalk, for connectivity to Apple computers; wireless networking, for mobile communications; ARCNET, which is the predecessor to Ethernet; and PLIP, for connectivity for parallel port networking.

Intranet and Extranet Business Models

Linux provides the scalability needed in today's global markets. Although intranet and Internet are spoken of as two different entities, for technological purposes, they are almost exactly the same. An intranet uses Internet technologies and protocols for a more localized use. The following looks at some of the areas your business might need to link in with an heterogeneous network or protocol.

Apache may be used to serve Web documents to your internal customers and, to some degree, your external customers as well. There are other communications tools, such as newsgroups, mailing lists, and shared files, that allow data to be disseminated. But upper management has the coordination skills and authority to take this open data to a higher level of interactive success.

Consider your company again, and introduce a new idea. Say management wants to introduce flextime to the workforce, but there are a lot of needs and the diversity of internal customers makes a one-size-fits-all policy useless. Also, some managers would suffer in productivity if they disallowed flextime while other managers implemented it. Such lack of equality in the workforce causes problems and decreases worker satisfaction.

However, management also has the responsibility to keep the company moving forward, and work must be done. The problem is one of information flow. Workers must keep the company mission and needs a priority, yet management wants to open the workplace up to some quality of life issues.

What could be done is this: Set up an internal Web page, which lists the corporate mission, vision, and goals. Include data showing the completion level of the goals and what yet needs to be taken care of. Create a mailing list that all employees can receive, and let it be used to disseminate updated information. Third, create an internal newsgroup, allowing employees the ability to discuss topics and interact without schedule and location conflicts.

As employees get used to the technology, open the question of flextime. Explain the concerns of management, the limitations perceived, and ask for feedback. Certain employees need the adjustable schedules, yet certain production line–based activities cannot easily give any workers leeway because the process is so integrated. These problems, along with possible solutions from the employees themselves, will be aired in an electronic forum that does not intrude on anyone's schedule. Workers can respond to queries during downtime or when they have a few extra minutes. These building blocks of group collaboration extend the idea of business hours to a global, time-irrelevant model.

If there is a need for real-time interaction, Internet Relay Chat (IRC) can provide the opportunity for conversationally based interaction without having to be in the same physical location. This is the infamous chat room; however, there are many uses to which the technology can be put. It provides interaction as fast as you can type, and you can build ideas and have conversations as you brainstorm during the session.

You can also consider a technological improvement a major internal process. Several areas need to coordinate data, schedules need to be shared, requirements for materials are made, budgets are adjusted, and a tremendous amount of coordinated communication must be done. Using the same network tools, you can provide the electronic bridge to communication that many companies desperately need. How many organizations that have failed have complained of too much coordination?

The ability to eliminate many meetings, yet increase the amount of communication can give your organization a market edge over a less technologically inclined competitor. Indeed, although the capability to do these tasks electronically has existed for some time, how many organizations use these technologies to their fullest extent? How many companies need resources that are on hand, yet that are unused?

W. Edwards Deming suggested many things, one of which was to "break down barriers between staff areas" (Walton, 1986). Is there any doubt, if you concede to the productivity increases possible with the Deming method, that the technologies exist to significantly negate many barriers? By using e-mail, a message can accurately be transmitted, including supporting files and graphics. The recipient can read the message, consider the information, then ask for clarification if needed or share the thoughts with another colleague or reply directly to the original author.

Even mass mailings can be handled, with each recipient getting exactly the same data, with no garbling from interpersonal translations or poorly scribbled notes taken by someone else while you were out of the office. Indeed, a single thought could be mutually built into a well-developed plan using inputs garnered from each sectional manager involved. Not only would you be able to utilize the expertise of each manager, but also every person would feel knowledgeable and part of the project. This level of buy-in helps increase the amount of focus on the issue, gaining higher odds of success.

One big issue for total communication is interoperability. Linux tools provide significant solutions for this because they are standards-compliant. For example, a Web page that is HTML 3.2–compliant will be readable in any HTML 3.2–compliant browser, this means Sun's HotJava, Netscape's Navigator, or Microsoft's Internet Explorer.

The only difficulties come when there are no standard add-ons that are browser-specific. Fortunately, Web authors are getting newer standards in HTML 4.0, which gives more options that are standardized and eliminates some of the incompatibility issues. News articles can be read with any standards-based newsreader, and e-mail clients can be based on any platform and can be as remote as the farthest part of your organization.

This issue of standardization is one the Linux community feels strongly about, and it is the basis for many other internal standards. When you use Linux for an information server, you know that the data you need made available is open to those who are allowed to access it.

This section concludes with a note. If you've been in management for any length of time, you know that there is not a technological solution for every problem. On the other hand, some problems have technological solutions that no one ever uses. This is a matter of personality, of the user's level of familiarity with computer technology, and of the user's background experiences in using technology to implement change. Linux cannot change a person's mind if that mind is closed. However, it can provide all the possibilities needed to convince a thinking person that its advantages deserve significant investigation. Indeed, once you start bringing Linux into your organization, those who are able to handle change and want to improve the corporate standing will be able to help you define needs for which Linux provides the solutions. It is this level of enthusiasm you must foster in workers: the willingness to think, the desire to improve, and the ability to translate new technology into successful corporate goal achievements. Linux can't do it without your leadership.

Linux as a Secure Server

Linux provides the security, strength, and reliability needed today. Current technologies that provide system power for business applications can also provide intruders with the keys to your network. This section discusses some security issues from a network server standpoint and provides details of how Linux can provide a cost-effective solution for many security needs.

As with any discussion on security implementation, please read all appropriate documentation for your systems and always work from a proactive defensive posture. Security in the enterprise requires a delicate balance between making data available and keeping information secret. In the continuum between these two possibilities, you must choose a policy, provide resources, and staff the security administrator positions. Such work must be developed in line with the current business model used in your organization. Contrary to most security marketing and sales brochures, there is no solely technological solution that covers all possible breaches of your system. Indeed, security professionals and intruders agree on at least one point—the weakest part of any system is the human factor. Humans tend to make lousy password choices, leave written passwords out, or leave systems unattended.

One solution is to build a technological tool that helps minimize the human potential for error, while helping workers build solid security habits. Although training your workers is beyond the scope of this book, it can give you the technological tools to get the first part done.

Security is enhanced by making it more difficult for someone to break into your systems. For example, to get to your office, you may have to pass by a receptionist and security staff member, open a cipher or electronically sealed door, and then unlock your office. Further, your desk may have certain papers you want to keep private, and there may be other security measures taken at highly sensitive facilities.

What these measures do is build a series of hurdles for intruders to have to deal with before they could read the private files in your desk. None of the hurdles is solely responsible or even capable of preventing the intruder, but taken in combination with the other parts, it makes it much more difficult for someone outside your work to get to those documents.

Network security works with the same philosophy. The only completely secure network is the one nobody can access, and thus is useless as a business resource. The following sections discuss some solutions in detail and cover some more thoughts and give pointers to other information you may need to pursue, depending on your organizational needs. First, the most common defense between an internal network and the Internet is a firewall.

Setting Up a Firewall

A *firewall,** in computer terms, is a system that protects your internal network from the outside world. It can also be set up to delineate internal subnetworks, which provide extra security for such highly sensitive areas as payroll and company-proprietary information. Firewalls work in several ways but most simply block certain types of data packets. A firewall must be connected to both networks, the protected network and whatever that network connects to, be it the Internet, the company intranet, or another internal network.

Since there are different services needed on different types of networks, and since the systems administrators control the network addresses and the internal security model, firewalls can have some simple characteristics. For example, if there is no need for a user to Telnet from the internal network to the Internet, then you can simply disable the Telnet service. The same goes for Web browsing and other services. A firewall allows you to control inbound and outbound services, determining who can come and go where.

However, what if the model needs to provide some services to some users and not to others? This is where firewall configuration becomes a management issue, because a poorly modeled and resourced firewall can not only make your network more open, but it can give you a completely unreal sense of security.

The following discusses a general firewall first, and then goes into some of the more specialized versions. Most networks use TCP/IP; this focuses on the IP, Internet Protocol. This protocol details how a packet is handled as it travels the Internet. Each packet has the source address, where it came from, and the destination address, where it's bound. If the source and destination are on the same network, then the packet quickly finds its way. However, if the destination is on a completely different network, the packet must be routed through other servers, and eventually it will arrive at the destination.

Although this is a great way to share information and is what has built the Internet, it causes problems when intruders target your system.

---

*For a detailed discussion of the need for and the implementation of firewalls, see *Firewalls Complete* (McGraw-Hill) or *Protecting Your Web Site with Firewalls* (Prentice Hall/PTR), both written by Marcus Goncalves.

For example, it's possible for them to capture packets from your internal network and to try to find such things as user names and passwords. Even the packets themselves can give information on the structure of your network.

IP firewalls can filter at the packet level based on the source, destination, port, and packet type. Note that there is little to do to filter the actual data inside the packet, but there are other measures that can be taken in order to secure data. It is rather like a concerned father screening boys before they take his daughter out on a date. The father can make judgments based on the boys' reputations (source), where they plan on going (destination), what they plan on doing that evening (port), and the general image he gets of each boy (packet type).

Firewalls can do other things as well. A firewall can provide a focal point to the security decisions made by management. It is to this single perceived choke point that most decisions can be linked. This allows the creation of a security mission statement and has it directly linked to the machine providing firewall services.

A site that has one or more firewalls actively in place and that has funneled all activity through the firewall line presents a much thinner target to a potential intruder. Some industries, such as finance, defense, or innovative technology, present highly desirable targets to intruders. Data that can be obtained can be marketed outside the organization, either for monetary gain or for status.

This is something of which managers do need to be aware. Many system intrusions with external origins are done for the thrill and prestige that the successful intruder gains among peers. This means that high-visibility targets such as financial organizations, those with classified information, or those that would be perceived as antithetical to the cracker's culture including governmental agencies can expect to be hit more often.

However, there is another layer of desirability, and that is the stepping stone. Even if your site is not on the most-prestigious list, your site can be cracked for a number of reasons. First, there is always the concept of counting cou, that is, intruders showing off the sheer number of systems they have cracked. Another one is that information in your system may prove useful in cracking the intruder's real target. Finally, the more steps intruders have between them and the target, the more difficult it is for law enforcement agencies to track them down. This is where detailed logging helps, since it can assist in providing prosecutable evidence should you seek legal recourse for intrusion.

There is a limit to what a firewall can do, and it's often caused more by poor management than technical wizardry. Some systems actively support this problem, and it's difficult to resolve the issue without full cooperation from all concerned. It's the placing of entry portals that bypass the firewall. One network that hired a security consultant had a modem connected to the PC containing most of the financial data and another modem directly connected to the server so the software vendor could log in and provide support. Needless to say this level of insecurity became a recurring item in discussion, because the consultant wanted to provide the client with a good network. Most of the issues were resolved through education and a bit of compromise on everyone's part.

But many networks have some sort of backdoor vulnerability for which there is no resolution because relationships between systems administrators, functional managers, and end users are so strained that no one wants to compromise and gain resolution. However, this point must be dealt with. No firewall can provide protection for channels that bypass the firewall entirely.

Another benefit of an active firewall and attendant security policy is in the ability to provide a central control area for enforcement of the corporate security model. By linking the model directly to the machine, you have more control over the activities, and that control is in a central place. This also mandates that any mutually shared firewall be as secure as the highest need. That is, if one section wants a loose network but another needs higher security, defaults will lean toward the higher-security network, thus providing tighter security for all concerned.

Firewalls also provide logging of activity, thus giving you information on usage, requests, and potential data on possible intruders. Keep in mind that these logs can be altered if they are in an insecure area, so they need to be duplicated and secured for later use.

Following are some weaknesses of firewalls. The basis of a firewall is that it protects your network from intruders outside your network. However, if the intruder is an insider, a firewall by itself can do little.

It's a common sentiment that most problems stemming from data loss, damage, or compromise come from insiders. This is one main reason for multiple internal firewalls. Giving each critical section the defense tools to prevent anyone from outside that particular section from doing damage can significantly lower problems. Not only do potential troublemakers know they are limited to systems they have access to, but sufficient logging and a solid firewall scheme can give vital clues for identifying intruders and providing legitimate grounds for disciplinary or legal action.

Firewalls use rule sets to defend against known attack avenues. This is good, because most intruders don't know the systems they are trying to crack, they just have notes gleaned from other intruders or scripts that exploit known bugs in older software. However, some intruders are capable of finding and exploiting system bugs that have not been noted before. This tends to be much rarer, because the intelligence required to find and exploit a bug generally precludes such childish behavior. But not always. A firewall cannot protect against intrusions that are outside its programming.

One way to extend this defense is to keep the firewall OS and software current, especially by tracking new bugs listed in the advisories. Such lists as CERT and Bug traq as well as the particular Linux distributor and the firewall software providers' lists can help you stay on top of the situation without having to dedicate full-time staff to the coding of new firewall software.

Linux as a Bastion Host

One of the most common firewall arrangements is to use a *bastion host*. This is a machine that serves as the focal point in controlling entrance to your network and controls what can go outside. A bastion host is a firewall, and it can do packet filtering, logging, and most of the other firewall activities previously discussed. Nevertheless, some design considerations can help make this a more defensible option. Please note that this is a managerial introduction to the setup of a bastion host. It covers policies and training items and is not a detailed technical analysis of the process of bastion host configuration.

The first point to consider is that the bastion host will be the most vulnerable system on your network because it will be exposed to the Internet and possibly to your internal users. This threat level requires managerial support to keep the mission focus on the bastion hosts as clear-cut and regulated as possible. This is a case where it's almost impossible to be too restrictive, and the systems administrator will appreciate every bit of support you give.

The bastion host should be as simple as possible, to keep program interactions and possible loopholes and bugs to a minimum. What this entails is loading minimal amounts of software and pruning each loaded program to ensure it has either a needed purpose or is removed.

One way to do this is to load just what you think you need, then go through the boot-up scripts and track each one line by line, checking what it does and commenting it out if it's not absolutely essential. It's a good practice to do a few lines, reboot the machine, and then see if it runs. If not, back up a bit and see what you commented out that was necessary. If the machine works well without the lines, delete them, noting in a comment as to why. After the system has been thoroughly tested, delete any extra program executables whose start-up scripts were commented out or deleted. This helps prevent someone from just starting the executable even though its start-up script is gone. The point here is to remove anything that is not absolutely essential.

The next consideration is to assume, at some time, the bastion host will be compromised. To minimize the impact of this requires a few good habits. The first is to not allow any trust relationships to be established between the bastion host and any machine in the network. This is another reason to trim all unnecessary services from the bastion host—any added capabilities may be desired by the users and removing them helps remove the temptation for users to start using and trusting the bastion host more than they should. Assume the bastion host will be compromised at some time, and you can not only avoid your corporate pride being hurt by recognizing the inevitable, but, if the bastion host is properly configured and monitored, its demise will only marginally threaten the internal network. Thus, any intruders will be confronted with another complete exercise before they can get any useful information.

This brings up another point. The bastion host should be as lean as possible both in software and in hardware. There is no need for a faster processor than necessary, since few computations are being performed. What is needed is a good bit of RAM to allow for a cache to build and enough file storage space for your logs. But having lower-end processors benefits the defense by preventing the speed of compromise if the intruder has broken into the bastion host and is trying to use it to get into your internal network. You will need enough power to handle the traffic, but no more.

One prime network consideration is to place the bastion host on the topology so that it does not receive normal interior traffic. Since most Ethernet connections can be used to sniff data packets for network troubleshooting, they can also be used to gain unauthorized access to the network. For this reason, you would be safer if there was a router between the bastion host and the internal network.

This could easily be another Linux machine, again, specifically configured to provide certain services and not others. It would be a dual-homed host, that is, having two completely separate connections between the networks. For example, it would have two Ethernet cards, one configured to talk to the bastion host and the other to communicate with the internal network. As long as internal packets did not cross the router, then the network would be relatively safe.

NOTE

If Tripwire did not come with your Linux distribution, you can find it at ftp://coast .cs.purdue.edu/pub/COAST/Tripwire.

You need good logging facilities on the bastion host, yet most normal logging schemes are susceptible to compromise. Some things that are possible include attaching another small PC to a serial connection, and having the logs sent there for storage. This also provides for electronic review and analysis, something printed logs are less useful for. There are some logging software packages that can supplement the normal Linux packages, such as the Computer Oracle and Password System (COPS), Tiger, and Tripwire. These help deal with known security holes and can perform *checksum databasing*. This is a technique of sampling data from each file and periodically comparing that log to the current file to check if the file has been modified.

NOTE

One last note on logging. There is a great program called Swatch that can monitor system logs and perform certain notifications or actions when specified criteria are met. The main drawback is that it runs in Perl, and you really don't want Perl on the bastion host. Swatch and Perl would be very useful on the PC linked at the serial

port, however. This would allow you to use the full functionality of both without compromising the bastion host quite so much.

One standard program for recurring file checking is Tripwire, by Gene Kim and Gene Spafford. Tripwire gives a highly configurable list of options to the systems administrator, allowing options to be determined for each file or file group.

NOTE

Swatch either comes with your distribution or can be found at ftp://ftp.stanford.edu/general/security-tools/swatch.

Once the bastion host is secured, cleaned of unnecessary files and programs, and plugged into the network, you need to develop usage profiles for the system. Monitor processes with **ps** and **top** to try to build a graph of typical daily usage. Build an understanding of what the system should be doing so you are aware of times it's doing something different. Track the logs to see if there are any unusual logins or other activity. Especially, investigate system reboots and crashes; they may indicate an intruder is trying to reconfigure the system or has altered files.

Other Security Servers

Don't think that a single firewall and a bastion host will take care of all your corporate security needs. If you've got the itch to defend your stuff, there are a few more services you should be aware of.

First, there are proxy servers. A *proxy server* lets your internal network be screened from the outside by channeling all questions and queries through it. However, it does so in a very transparent manner. For example, a proxy server will let an external host send mail to the internal network.

Nevertheless, the proxy will function as the network. This keeps the insides safe while giving the appearance of total access. Also, a proxy server can be configured to let internal hosts get external resources, but it does so in a more secure fashion. For example, Jane wants to see a certain Web page to get financial data on a potential client. Her Web browser has been configured for proxying, so when she connects, the browser links to the proxy server. Then the proxy server goes to the Internet, gets the page, and serves it to Jane just as if she had gone there directly. Indeed, proxies have an additional advantage. If several people need the same Web page, they will build up a cache, or reserve, for that Web page in the proxy.

Therefore, anyone connecting after the first will get the cached page, and the page will only have to travel the distance from the proxy server to the user. This greatly increases speed on some transactions, though you will need to provide enough memory for the proxy to store the pages. In today's visual environment, much space will be consumed by graphics, so proxying has begun to be less of a benefit.

TCP Wrappers are another service provided for security. A *wrapper* provides a secure environment in which to run services. They control user and host access to specific services, as well as provide additional logging capabilities useful for information gathering. They do this by intercepting the incoming connection, checking its characteristics against your well-defined security policy, then passing the authenticated connection onto the real server for that service.

References

Walton, Mary. 1986. *The Deming Management Method.* New York: Perigee.

CHAPTER 5

Linux for Business Advantage

L inux not only is proving itself as a great server operating system (OS), but it's turning out to be a reliable desktop OS as well. It is certainly more crash-proof than Windows 98 and much cheaper, too, as you can download Linux for free from many sites on the Internet, which actually is mainly responsible for the fast proliferation of Linux in the past year and a half.

Although the Linux business model is often misunderstood, which contributes to the skepticism of many, it is actually a simple one. Many decisionmakers in corporate America and throughout the world hesitate in considering Linux as a reliable and cost-saving business solution because they cannot understand how vendors, such as Red Hat, Caldera, and S.u.S.E., can survive and provide prime support to an OS that is free.

Paraphrasing Robert Young, Red Hat's president and CEO, Linux is looked at (and should be looked at!) as a commodity. The key is to create a demand for the product. Once you have this demand, you then create a brand and provide quality service and reliability. Sure as Dunkin' Donuts makes millions every year selling 10-cent doughnuts, Linux can be seen as the doughnut every business needs to be successful.

The simplicity of a doughnut allows it to be customized any way the customer wants, without adding prohibitive costs. The Linux model works the same way. You can add cinnamon to it (or Internet tools) without dramatically increasing its cost. Actually, for the most part, many implementations are also free or carry a very nominal fee.

Expanding the doughnut example, the doughnut's cost is so low that in reality it could even be free. What the customers pay for is the convenience of having a variety of flavors to choose from and the ability to add on a variety of other ingredients (or components), all on the fly, without cumbersome operations and long waits. Linux is free, its source is open, and there are thousands of doughnut makers out there willing to add a new spice, a new flavor, to a Linux implementation that makes it very tasty for business advantage and enjoyment. It works. Just look at the many Dunkin' Donuts stores around the world!

As pointed out by Young, an operating system is a highly technical tool. Most people don't want to get involved in downloading the tool off the Internet and take the full responsibility for it themselves. Corporations want to work with a trusted partner, and although certain products such as Microsoft's Windows NT have their merits (the author is an NT professional from its birth!) and strengths, through the years it has become unclear how much trust you can deposit in a company's products and business model.

In today's competitive global market, a corporation can no longer afford to just decide "where do you want to go today?" but must try to accurately define "where do you want to go (or need to be) tomorrow?" It's comforting to know, from the business perspective, that the Linux kernel is what it is and will not change or be revised any time soon, especially not three-quarters of it, as has Windows 2000 Server (former Windows NT 5.0). It's comforting to know that the goal of the OS implementors is to provide a bug-free kernel and stable implementations, rather than to fashionably revamp it every so often, introducing new bells and whistles at the cost of a new "blue screen of death."

Selling Linux to Corporations

Clearly, as Cliff Seruntine (asacs7@uaa.alaska.edu), from the University of Alaska, points out (on the Usenet),

Linux is not what it was, but what it came to be. Born of an idea by Linus Torvalds, evolving from infancy as an OS just powerful enough to control a disk drive, it grew into a very powerful, Unix-like operating system with the capability to meet the needs of such demanding users as medical centers, theoretical physicists and communication corporations, as well as the more modest needs of businessmen and end users. Linux offers you the power to accomplish whatever task you may have at hand with unparalleled stability and reasonable ease of operation. Software is abundant, help is as close as the Internet, and the potential is limited only by your imagination and computing skill. The bottom line is, this incredibly flexible and powerful OS is free.

This section is an adaptation of Seruntine's article, fully available at www.linuxresources.com/business/2499.html. The importance of this article when discussing Linux for business applications is the fact that, as Seruntine describes, everything you can say about Linux is the absolute truth. Discussing Linux for business enables you to present it without the need for embellishment in order to score support from upper management or decisionmakers at the corporation.

In promoting Linux for business applications, the whole truth about it is more than enough, and nothing else. The most important thing is to listen to the company's or client's needs and design a Linux system tailored to meet them.

For instance, tucked into a spare bedroom (corporate America doesn't like to hear this), Seruntine's small consulting business, cybertronics, is not a Microsoft-sized operation by any means. You would think that in this day and age of big conglomerates taking over the technology industry, small businesses like his would be shoved rapidly out of the way or swallowed up—but Linux is an asset that has allowed him to remain competitive. He offers a useful, powerful product. The open source code allows this OS to be customized for whatever specific uses a client might have. And, the fact that it is free allows his prices to remain extremely competitive.

Small businesses like cybertronics, which account for almost 80 percent of U.S. business, can achieve great business advantage by specializing in Linux systems. As Linux continues to evolve, now at a crossroads and experiencing the associated growing pains, two opposing sides can be seen arguing over the way Linux should go in the future.

On the one side, those opposed to the simplification of Linux usage to expand mass appeal argue the OS should remain complex to force the user to learn something and ensure that only dedicated computer hobbyists and aficionados will use it. At the other extreme are those who would have the development of Linux take it down a road of utter ease so that it resembles Windows 95.

Linux is a powerful OS. It has been so for a long time. But it is only recently, due to advances made largely by Red Hat and Caldera in making Linux more user-friendly, that it has become a truly marketable product to a diversified client base. The growth of Linux and related software depends on the mass acceptance of the OS. The more users there are, the more people and companies there will be turning out applications and making improvements.

The option of simplification is a good thing, as long as Linux is left with all the complexities of making the full power of the OS available for those users who desire or demand that kind of control. It is also desirable to leave in that power and intimate control capability, right down to manipulation of the source code, to maintain the unique flavor and spirit of Linux.

Linux is now at this very place. Simplification has been added so the end user can use the system, while full control can be accessed by the experienced user for the ultimate control and enhancement of the OS. This is what makes Linux different and marketable at the current time to a broad range of clients. Linux can be adopted by (or sold to) an average end user who simply wants a good, inexpensive system to balance the books, do word processing, or surf the Net—and this represents the majority of computer users—because it has become relatively easy to use. It can also be sold to a client that must maintain a huge database of corporate records or run a powerful Web server because its power is also easily accessible. Because Linux currently maintains a healthy balance of end-user simplicity and ultimate user control, it is a highly attractive product to a wide range of people.

The second feature of Linux that should be strongly emphasized to clients is the incredible stability of the system. At cybertronics, the three servers, (an AMD-based system, a Cyrix-based system, and an older Intel) have never crashed with Linux. On a couple of occasions, according to Seruntine, applications have closed down, but this always turned out to be the result of a poorly programmed application, a user error, or that the program was using some new, experimental aspect of Linux that hadn't yet been tested and proven. But never, in all the time the company has used Linux, has it seen it crash due to an instability problem.

For businesses that believe time is money, stability is a major advantage. When computers crash, they lose not only the un-backed-up data on the system, but also the time paid to the employees while they wait for the system to come back online. If a network server crashes or becomes unstable, it can cost many thousands of dollars, as computers throughout the company are affected. Worse, customers tend to have little tolerance for businesses with faulty equipment; they will take their business elsewhere, sometimes for good.

A third and extremely important point in selling Linux is that all of the software is available, and most of it is free. The list is always growing and changing. There is just so much software out there, much of it is good yet hard to find, that creating a comprehensive list is almost impossible. This brings up another important point.

From the standpoint of business, professional software that is designed and sold commercially for Linux is extremely affordable. For example, office suites are sold by Caldera and Red Hat, Star Office and Applixware, respectively. Often, for less than a thousand dollars, a company can purchase and outfit an entire network with professional-quality productivity software that takes advantage of the full networking, stability, and processing power of Linux.

This selling point is truly great. The trouble is, it sounds too good to be true for corporations. There's an old adage "You never get something for nothing." Well, businesspeople tend to be very cautious with money (especially the small to midsized businesses) and they become dubious at hearing how Linux can offer so much for so little. This point in the pitch is a good place to have references and demo software available, and an especially important place to understand the business behind Linux that makes all this so affordable.

The Linux OS is free and freely developed by computer enthusiasts around the world. Therefore, there are no royalties to be paid and development costs are cut to almost nothing.

Companies producing Linux software for profit are engaged in hard competition with the software giant, Microsoft, and are turning out superb products to give them an edge where they cannot compete in financial and advertising resources. Although Microsoft is desperately looking for a competitor these days (otherwise the Department of Justice would be right about Microsoft being a monopoly), Linux does not really compete with the Windows 2000 series. Linux delivers benefits to users that Microsoft's operating systems just don't offer. As a result, Linux will succeed in the OS marketplace, regardless of Microsoft. To me, the so called Halloween memos don't really add anything to this issue, it just flatters the Linux OS and its community!

The spirit of free software is shared even in the businesses involved with Linux. While those businesses are not running charities, they help promote the growth of Linux by making their products more widely available with reasonable prices—and anyone familiar with the Unix business knows that the price tag behind that OS and its software has nearly ended its service in the consumer market (a sad way for such a fine OS to go).

The only possible downside is that for the private consumer who wants a more powerful computer system, professional Linux software is often too expensive. More competitively priced similar items are available for Windows—but this is changing. Caldera makes Star Office available free for private users. Also, you can find a number of practical, good applications available at more reasonable prices within the last year—everything from Web design software to data backup tools.

Moving on, it is important to note in selling Linux that there are many less obvious reasons for a corporation to turn to a Linux system:

- The way Linux manages memory is advantageous. No more worrying about high memory and low memory. Linux uses it all.

- Linux's ability to communicate with other operating systems enhances its flexibility.

- Linux's efficient and powerful programming enhances its speed.

- Source code availability allows Linux to be entirely customized to fit the needs of the user.

- A good distribution of Linux comes with so much free software that a business can often find a great deal of what it needs right there on the Linux CD-ROM.

The target market for Linux is very broad. You would think that with the broad potential for client usage previously described, anyone who uses a computer would be a potential Linux user. Actually, this is true. Many casual end users who want more power than an old DOS-based system has to offer are potential Linux users.

Now, Seruntine is very clever when he asserts that Linux is not an OS for gamers. Yes, there are a lot of games out there for Linux. Unfortunately, most of them are reminiscent of the earlier days of computing when two-dimensional arcade-style games such as "Asteroids" and "Space Invaders" were the rage. There are some other, more advanced games, such as "Quake." But Linux is really lacking in the intense, power-demanding, multimedia games that are available elsewhere these days. Currently Linux is too demanding for the needs of someone who only wants a super-gaming machine, which, in a way is too bad, because Linux has so much power and stability to offer. On other platforms, games crash or move jerkily; both are frustrating. Linux harnessed for such applications would make the ultimate gamer's computer.

In addition, Linux is not the first choice for the end user who wants as little to do with the computer as possible. Linux, like any OS, has a learning curve, and for most amateurs, the Linux learning curve may still be too high. Until a shell for Linux is created that greatly simplifies its usage for the least-demanding of end users, Linux will not appeal to this market.

Linux's primary users are probably those who want a system strictly for some form of business, be it personal bookkeeping, writing, or running small businesses. The stability to insure against not losing time or work is one of the biggest selling points for Linux. Linux is for mission-critical applications, just like Unix, but free. Linux is also for applications that require stability, which ensures that the jobs will be done in the least amount of time, so users can move on to other projects.

For larger companies, the power of Linux is a factor that should be emphasized. Knowing that they can take this OS and put it to serious work, and thereby save their companies thousands of dollars by not buying commercial operating systems such as Windows NT or a Unix flavor is very impressive. Of course, the stability of Linux is also appealing to them. It is like icing on an already delicious cake.

Certainly, there are many other people for whom Linux could prove a useful and desirable product. Later in this chapter, there is a list of influential companies already using Linux, such as Mercedes-Benz, Sony, Cisco Systems, Roger Cable, and both the U.S. Navy and Army.

NOTE

▬▬▬ The previous section was based on an article written by Cliff Seruntine, who owns and operates cybertronics, a computer and electronics service center, from his home in Anchorage, Alaska. He's currently affiliated with the University of Alaska in Anchorage and can be reached via e-mail at asacs7@uaa.alaska.edu.

Integration with Heterogeneous Platforms

Most businesses today are running a mix of computer types and computer operating systems to get their work done. For example, Intel Pentium and equivalent computer systems running Windows 95 are very common on office desktops, but other types of computers may be used for graphic arts work, point of sale systems, or connectivity to the Internet. In fact, it is very possible that you are not even aware of what type of computer hardware and operating system is contained in a dedicated system performing a specific function for your company.

The right mix of computers offering the necessary interoperability is almost always a better choice than selecting one type of computer and operating system and then attempting to make it fit all tasks. The latter choice would be similar to requiring all employees to have the same type of workspace—for secretaries, computer programmers, or warehouse managers.

This is not to say that you should not dictate standards when appropriate. For example, you will most likely want to select one word processor that will be used by everyone. This decision, however, should really be based on interoperability rather than an arbitrary edict. Table 5.1 shows a quick OS feature comparison.

In-House Solutions: A Case Study Approach

The following is a list of companies already using Linux for many of their everyday business needs. Some companies provide more information than others, but all the information directly reflects actual use of Linux for business applications.

Table 5.1 Operating Systems Feature Comparison

OSS	CONNECTIVITY	STABILITY	SCALABILITY	MULTI-USER	MULTI-PLATFORM	POSIX	NON-PROPRIETARY	AVERAGE PRICE
Legacy System	Poor	Good	Medium–huge	Yes	No	No	No	$50,000
MS-DOS	None	Poor	Small	No	No	No	No	$100
Windows 3.x	Poor	Poor	Small	No	No	No	No	$100
Windows 95	SMB only	Fair	Small	Insecure	No	No	No	$100
Windows NT	SMB+	Fair	Small–Medium	Yes	Yes, 2	Some	No	$500
Unix	Excellent	Excellent	Small–Huge	Yes	Yes, many	Yes	No	$5,000
*BSD	Good	Excellent	Small–Large	Yes	No	Yes	Yes	$50
Linux	Excellent	Excellent	Small–Huge	Yes	Yes, many	Yes	Yes	$50

Mercedes-Benz AG

Mercedes-Benz AG is using Linux for the development of new electronic systems for Mercedes cars such as ESP (Electronic Stability Program). It uses Linux as a stable platform for all kinds of software development and office work.

One of its main projects is to create new controller software with Matlab/Simulink (under Linux). In addition, Mercedes-Benz AG uses Linux for the following functions:

X-Windows

- X-Windows server (runs applications, possibly exports display)

Network file server

- NFS server for other PCs and Unix systems

Print server

- Print spooler using Line Printer daemon (lpd) (Unix, NFS clients)

Office productivity software

- Document preparation with TeX, LaTeX, and derivatives
- Spreadsheets created with Wingz
- Other document management

Network services provided to local users

- HTTP (World Wide Web) server or cache
- Accepts Telnet connections
- Services finger requests

Software development tools

- C and/or C++
- Perl
- Bourne, Korn, C, or another shell; using **sed, awk, grep,** and similar tools
- Others

NOTE
For more information, contact Reinhold Schoeb, at Mercedes-Benz AG by telephone at +49 711 17 42147 or fax at +49 711 17 42096. You can also e-mail him at schoeba @str.daimler-benz.com.

Sony Worldwide Networks

Sony Worldwide Networks is a radio network division of Sony. Linux is being used for various business tasks, which include the following:

- Web server for internal company intranet
- FTP server for worldwide contacts to send files, which are then transferred to the internal Novell LAN.
- Mail server for entire company (formally done by Sun box)

Sony decided to adopt Linux for several reasons:

- It's free.
- It has the best support (questions are answered via the Internet in hours time).
- There is plenty of online documentation.
- Many industry-related professionals use Linux in production environments, so it was easier for Sony systems group to obtain plenty of hints and information.
- It is reliable, robust, and efficient. Under tests, the company's systems administrator overloaded Linux with a multitude of applications, and the system still ran flawlessly.

Sony Worldwide Networks uses Linux for the following functions:

Network file server

- File server for other types of clients
- Internet client software—mail
- Pine
- Other mail clients

Electronic mail server

- POP3 server
- SMTP server (sendmail, others)
- Network services provided to local users
- HTTP (World Wide Web) server or cache

NOTE
For more information on how Sony is using Linux for business advantage, contact Kevin Borowsky via e-mail at borowsky@swnetworks.com.

Deja News

Deja News archives the full text of Usenet news and provides Internet users with a powerful search engine to locate postings of interest. The archive and search engines run on high-end Intel-based hardware, with Linux as the operating system.

iConnect Corporation

iConnect Corporation uses Linux for the following functions:

X-Windows

- X-Windows terminal (display, keyboard, mouse—applications run elsewhere)

Network file server

- NFS server for other PCs and Unix systems

Print server

- Print spooler using lpd (Unix, NFS clients)

Modem communications

- Server answers the phone, provides PPP, SLIP, or term logins

Office productivity software

- Document preparation with LyX
- Document preparation with TeX, LaTeX, and derivatives
- Internet client software—WWW
- NCSA Mosaic
- Lynx
- Internet client software—mail
- Pine
- Mail
- Other mail clients

Network management

- Internet or WAN router
- Electronic mail server
- POP3 server
- SMTP server (sendmail, others)

Network services provided to local users

- HTTP (World Wide Web) server or cache
- News server or cache
- Accepts Telnet connections
- Accepts secure-shell (ssh) connections
- Services finger requests
- Runs one or more database servers
- Other services

Network services provided to remote users over dial-up or the Internet

- HTTP (World Wide Web) serv_remoteer or cache
- News serv_remoteer or cache
- Accepts Telnet connections
- Accepts secure-shell (ssh) connections
- Services finger requests
- Runs one or more database serv_remoteers
- Other serv_remoteices

Software development tools

- C and/or C++
- Perl
- Bourne, Korn, C, or another shell; using **sed, awk, grep,** and similar tools
- Others

NOTE

For additional information, contact Michael Neuffer at (503) 641-8774, fax (503) 641-7648, or via e-mail at sales@i-connect.net.

Rogers Cable

Rogers Cable, the biggest Canadian cable company, uses Linux/Apache although it does not advertise that fact. In some areas of Canada, Rogers is already providing cable net access using Linux boxes as routers and gateways.

Realtime Software Solutions

Realtime produces real-time embedded/nonembedded networked imaging solutions and also develops Web sites. The company uses Linux for the following functions:

X-Windows

- X-Windows terminal (display, keyboard, mouse—applications run elsewhere)
- X-Windows server (runs applications, possibly exports display)

Network file server

- Samba server for a network of PCs
- NFS server for other PCs and Unix systems

Print server

- Print spooler using lpd (Unix, NFS clients)
- Print spooler using Samba (PC clients)
- Office productivity software
- Document preparation with ApplixWare
- Internet client software—mail
- Pine
- Electronic mail server
- POP3 server
- SMTP server (sendmail, others)

Network services provided to local users

- HTTP (World Wide Web) server or cache
- Accepts Telnet connections
- Network services provided to remote users over dial-up or the Internet
- HTTP (World Wide Web) serv_remoteer or cache

Software development tools

- C and/or C++
- Java
- Perl

NOTE

For more information about Realtime's use of Linux, contact Thomas A. Bond at (716) 467-8889 or via e-mail at tom@realtime1.com.

Pacific Digital Interactive

Pacific Digital combines the latest technology with creative front-end design to deliver powerful interactive marketing solutions across all forms of new media. The company uses Linux for the following functions:

X-Windows

- X-Windows terminal (display, keyboard, mouse—applications run elsewhere)
- X-Windows server (runs applications, possibly exports display)

Network file server

- Samba server for a network of PCs
- NFS server for other PCs and Unix systems
- File server for other types of clients

Print server

- Print spooler using lpd (Unix, NFS clients)
- Print spooler using Samba (PC clients)

Office productivity software

- Other document management
- Internet client software—WWW
- Lynx
- Other browsers
- Internet client software—mail
- Pine
- Other mail clients

Electronic mail server

- POP3 server
- IMAP server

- SMTP server (sendmail, others)
- SMTP mail router

Network services provided to local users

- HTTP (World Wide Web) server or cache
- Accepts secure-shell (ssh) connections
- Runs one or more database servers
- Other services

Network services provided to remote users over dial-up or the Internet

- HTTP (World Wide Web) serv_remoteer or cache
- Accepts secure-shell (ssh) connections

Software development tools

- C and/or C++
- Java
- Perl
- Bourne, Korn, C, or another shell; using **sed**, **awk**, **grep**, and similar tools
- Others

Cisco Systems: Linux Print System at Cisco

Cisco runs a redundant system of 50 print servers using Linux, Samba, and NetAtalk. The system can be thought of as a distributed machine, printing to approximately 1600 printers worldwide, serving 10,000 Unix and Windows 95 users, some of which are in mission-critical environments.

Introduction

In your office, can you print to the printer that is closest to you or do you have to use a printer that is set up for your desktop machine? If you wanted to send a job to a printer in another department or in another office, could you do it as easily as you can send it to your local printer? In most large companies, the answer to both of these questions is *no.*

If you mention a printing problem to systems administrators, they will probably freeze like deer caught in headlights, insist this is not their responsibility, and tell you that you had better find someone else. However, there is rarely a single someone else to whom you can turn. In most companies, there is no centralized control over printing.

In desperation, you try to fix the problem yourself, only to be told, "My colleague tried that and broke printing for a week."

"What did he or she do?" you ask.

"I'm not quite sure, but you'd better not touch it."

In short, printing has become a Pandora's box that no one wants to touch. It is surrounded by more folklore and black magic than any other area in modern computing. This section is an adaptation of a white paper by Damian Ivereigh from Cisco Australia, which describes the general problems with printing in a large corporate environment and the general methods for solving these problems. Ivereigh details how he solved the particular problems at Cisco. Using software almost entirely downloadable from the Internet, he produced a highly visible, mission-critical, fault-tolerant print system used everyday by over 10,000 people worldwide.

NOTE
This whole section on Cisco's use of Linux to resolve and support its printing needs was adapted from a white paper written by Damian Ivereigh, from Cisco in Australia. An edited version of this article can also be found in October's issue of *Linux Journal*. Nothing from this white paper was changed, except to follow the flow of this book. For additional information, contact Damian via e-mail at damian@cisco.com.

In a nutshell, the solution depends on multiple Linux servers, which, by communication with each other, effectively work as a single distributed machine. This approach offers to solve many of the problems inherent not only in print systems but, more generally, for any network resource (such as mail or disk space) in a large corporate network.

A distributed machine may sound very complex, but there is very little magic to it. As you will see, the magic comes from applying the traditional Unix model of combining many little pieces into a whole that becomes significantly greater than its parts.

Printing Strategies

First, there are some general problems that face printing in a corporate environment. Printers are based on mechanical parts that are slower and less reliable than the computers that send jobs to them, thus requiring job queues and frequents status updates.

Although the vendors are trying to create standards (for example, their work in the Printer Working Group, the PWG), the current standardization is very poor, and in the vacuum, printer manufacturers have tried to make their printers talk as many different standards (or emulations) as possible. Few of these emulations work really well or allow good user control of the printer.

Essentially, there are two main strategies for organizing printing:

- Direct client-to-printer
- Via a central print server

Direct Client-to-Printer

The client connects directly to a printer and takes complete control as it sends its print job. Any printer status is sent directly back to the client. Once the printer has finished, the client disconnects and the printer is available for another client. This strategy has advantages and disadvantages.

ADVANTAGES

Simpler in small offices.   Each person's machine is set up in isolation of everyone else's—there's no need to think about any bigger issues.

Problems (usually) only affect single users.   Each person works in almost complete isolation. Provided the printer does not fail, the user can carry on printing, regardless of anyone else's problems.

Users controls their own queue directly.   To cancel a job they just cancel it on their own machine using whatever tools their operating system provides.

DISADVANTAGES

Difficult to perform any global changes.   If, say, the IP address of the printer changes, the engineers have many client machines to track down and reconfigure.

Each client machine has to compete for the printer. If the printer is already busy when a client tries to print, the client has to keep retrying until the printer is free. This is very inefficient.

Difficult to provide an orderly queue. Since all clients get control of the printer in a random order, there is no guarantee when any particular client's job will start printing or that jobs will be printed in any particular order. To make matters worse, it is almost impossible for a client to know that other clients are waiting for the printer.

A client can only print to the printers that support its protocol. For example, an Apple Mac can only talk to the printers that support Appletalk.

Difficult to track down and cancel unknown jobs. For example, if a printer is busy printing a 2000-page document, it can be difficult to find out which client is sending it. Then, to actually stop the print job, the sysadmin has to get the appropriate permissions on that client machine.

A fix to one protocol can break others. Service technicians, who tend to be experts in their own field and no one else's, can easily break things for other protocols. For example, how many times has an engineer reset a printer to fix a Novell printing problem and, in the process, broken the TCP/IP setup (which that technician doesn't understand anyway)?

Some printers cannot switch well between different protocols. For example, some printers, particularly the older ones, have even been known to crash completely (requiring a reboot) switching between TCP/IP and Appletalk.

Central Print Server

With this strategy, the client sends its print job to the central print server and disconnects. The print server takes the job and adds it to the queue for the designated printer. The print server then connects to the printer and sends the job. Any status is sent to the print server, not the client. Again, there are advantages and disadvantages.

ADVANTAGES

Client machine can send and then forget. Since the print server has significant storage capacity, it can receive jobs anytime, regardless of what the printer is doing. The client machine can just send the job whenever it wants and is free to move on to something else.

Orderly queueing.   The jobs go through a central queue that prints them according to the order they are received. Every user should be able (operating system permitting) to see all the jobs that are waiting to print on a printer by looking at this print server queue.

Cancel any job.   A sysadmin may kill any job on the print server, regardless of its source.

Job rerouting.   If a printer fails, it should be easy to reroute all the jobs from the broken printer to a working one.

Central point of maintenance.   Any printer changes can be made on the print server alone, since this is the only thing that talks directly to the printer.

DISADVANTAGES

More complex.   Requires a sysadmin to set up the print server and keep it running.

Can easily produce a single point of failure.   If the print server dies, all printing stops, unless you have a good backup print server that you can easily swap into place.

Loss of user queue control.   Menial tasks such as print job cancellations fall on the shoulders of sysadmins if the users no longer have the permissions (or skills) to do this themselves.

Usual Print System

Most larger companies make a half-hearted attempt at the central server approach. The real problems begin when more than one central server is implemented. The Unix sysadmin sets up a Unix print server, the Windows people set up an NT server, and some of the clients skip the servers completely and go directly to the printer. All jobs meet at the printer, where chaos ensues.

You now have all the problems of the central server approach compounded with all the problems of the client-to-printer approach, plus a few extra thrown in for good measure. Printer changes must be implemented on multiple servers by multiple sysadmins leading to multiple potential errors. Multiple machines (now servers instead of clients) compete for the same printer, there's no orderly queuing, and you still don't know where that damn 2000-page document is coming from!

To make matters worse, each different environment now has a different name for the same printer, which makes tracking down printers even more difficult. When users have problems, they probably don't know which environment they are trying to print from. They'll call the wrong sysadmin, who can't find users' printer names in their environments. The sysadmin then suggests the users call a different group who will pass them on to another group and so on. Five sysadmins later, the users are back to the first sysadmin. Overall, this is a frustrating experience for everyone.

The printing challenges for Ivereigh at Cisco were great. Here is some background information.

Ideal Print System

After a few months of dealing with these problems, Cisco (through Ivereigh) decided there had to be a better way. Ivereigh sat down and detailed what he believed to be the ideal print system. It had to include the advantages of the server approach, yet mitigate some of the disadvantages.

Multiprotocol.   The server needs to be able to speak all the different protocols that clients want to send and that printers want to receive.

Ultra-reliable.   Use redundancy to remove the single point of failure inherent in most central server approaches.

Single point of queuing.   No matter where the job comes from or the route that it takes, all jobs for a particular printer must land in a single queue handled by one machine.

Expandable and flexible.   Cisco is a growing company. Any system has to be able to scale well and allow frequent reorganization.

Centrally, decentrally, and remotely manageable.   Cisco has offices worldwide, some of which have local expertise, some which don't.

Cheap.   The system has to be affordable for the small offices, yet expandable for use at headquarters.

Queue management devolved to the users.   Sysadmins don't have time and users want control. Let the users have what they want.

Avoid duplication.   Any information duplicated by hand is prone to error. Even entering the IP address into both the printer and the print server should be considered a duplication.

Simple to manage.   No matter how many servers are added for redundancy or capacity, the management of these must remain simple.

What follows is a history of how Ivereigh brought Cisco toward producing this ideal print system using Linux.

Initial Cisco Configuration

When Ivereigh began the project, Cisco's printing was not where it was supposed to be, as shown in Figure 5.1. Some of the printing was done with the client-to-printer method, some via two small print servers, which he was detailed to look after. Although these two servers by no means controlled the entire print system, it was widely presumed that he did!

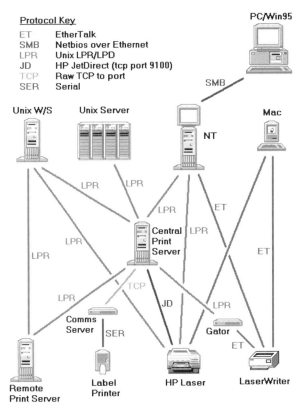

Figure 5.1   Original configuration of the print system at Cisco prior to Linux implementation.

The company's big Unix servers were sometimes printing to one print server, sometimes to the other. The Unix workstations were printing either via the print servers or directly to the printer. The Apple Macs (used extensively on the desktop) always printed direct. Most of the printers only talked Appletalk, so Gatorboxes (from Caiman Systems) were used to translate the Unix print jobs into Appletalk.

Caiman Systems had since gone out of business and the Gatorboxes themselves were intermittently crashing. In the past, the systems administrators had started to enable TCP/IP protocols on some of the Hewlett-Packard (HP) printers such that the Unix print servers could talk to them directly. This required either plugging in an IP address into each printer (via the front panel) or setting up a bootptab entry in each print server so that a printer could find its IP address using the BOOTP protocol.

In theory, one print server was the main one and the other was a backup. However, these two servers were substantially different in the way they were configured. The duplication of the setups was manual (configure the print queue on both machines). Some central Unix servers were queuing to the primary and others to the backup print server. Some printers were set up for printing on some of the central Unix servers and others not. A lot of time was used to track down print problems only to find they usually originated from an incorrect configuration.

Many companies tend to go on with problematic systems settings like this, where systems administrators are asked to do repetitive tasks, which are often boring and unfulfilling. As Ivereigh describes, there is nothing more frustrating than treating the symptom, while ignoring the disease.

One of the main advantages of Ivereigh's approach to improve the systems was that he never decided to throw out the old system entirely; he just slowly improved on it, tackling the biggest problems first.

Removing Duplication in the Client LPR System

Every printer needed to be individually set up on each Unix server (the LPR client). This meant a lot of manual work (which is highly prone to error), either when setting up a new Unix server or when creating a new printer. Ivereigh looked at the client LPR system and realized that it had a very simple job to do: just forward the job to the print server, regardless of the printer name.

Here is a typical /etc/printcap entry for the printer **foo**, which sends the job straight on to the print server **prntsrv**:

```
foo:\
        :mx#0:\
        :sh:\
        :sd=/var/spool/lpd/foo:\
        :lf=/var/spool/lpd/foo/log:\
        :lp=/var/spool/lpd/foo/.null:\
        :rm=prntsrv:\
        :rp=foo:
```

The only thing that is different for a different printer, is the word **foo**. Thus, he took the LPR source and replaced the routines that look for the entry for a particular printer in /etc/printcap with routines that faked the entry. If LPR asked for the printer **bar**, then his routines would return a printcap entry much like the preceding one, but with **bar** in place of **foo**. The only other variable was the name of the print server—this was looked up from a master configuration file that he created for the whole system. There were a few other things to do, such as create a spool directory, but essentially this is all the work the routines did.

The remainder of the LPR code executed as before, not realizing that anything had changed. Since he hadn't touched the remainder of the code, he had very few bugs. But he had removed a large source of information duplication. He could now be sure that all the company's printers were available on all the central Unix servers with the print jobs being sent to the correct print server.

Note that the client will also accept a print job for a nonexistent printer (it doesn't know the difference) and try to send it to the print server. The print server will reject the job, but will not say why (the protocol doesn't allow it). The client keeps retrying for 48 hours before finally rejecting the job and e-mailing the user. This is not an ideal situation, but was acceptable at Cisco.

Removing Duplication in the Print Servers

The next step was to tackle the duplication within each print server. Several files were used to control the printers: /etc/printcap and

/etc/bootptab as well as some setup files used by each printer. Each file contained the same information, just in a different format.

There were three different ways of talking to the various printers as set up in the /etc/printcap file:

- JetDirect for HP printers using their TCP/IP JetDirect interface
- Raw TCP for serial printers attached to TCP/IP-to-serial converters
- LPR protocol for EtherTalk printers (attached to Gatorboxes) or to remote print servers that were not under Ivereigh's control

To eliminate duplication, Ivereigh needed a master configuration file, from which he could generate the various configuration files required for JetDirect, raw TCP, and LPR protocols. The master configuration file contained all the information that might be required by any protocol, such as the name, IP address, Ethernet hardware address, the remote server, and remote printer name. He created a script **mkprint**, which generated all the other configuration files, created the spool directories, and so on.

Not only was this method simpler than editing the individual files manually—it was much less prone to error. For example, since the IP address supplied to the LPR system was the same one supplied to the BOOTP system, they had to match. He could not get them wrong.

NetAtalk

As mentioned earlier, the Gatorboxes were causing many problems. Often an individual print queue on the Gatorbox would stop receiving print jobs and require someone to log on to the Gatorbox and restart it. They seemed to have significant memory leak problems which would cause the whole Gatorbox to run out of memory and crash, requiring someone to physically go to the box and press the reset button.

Researching first the Columbia AppleTalk Protocol (CAP) and then NetAtalk as possible ways of getting the print servers to talk EtherTalk directly was a smart alternative. Both seemed to work pretty well, but it appeared that NetAtalk was being more actively developed and required less load on the machine through the use of kernel-level drivers.

Ivereigh modified the **mkprint** system to allow for this new type of printer. Now he could get the Gatorboxes out of the loop. No longer did he have to set up a printer on the Gatorboxes as well as the print servers. Another duplication was removed.

PCs and the Web

Cisco started introducing PCs into the desktop. Ivereigh did not realize it at the time, but this was the beginning of a major push to change from Macs to PCs. The Desktop Technology Group, who managed the PCs, introduced an NT server as the PC print server and Ivereigh started getting calls to kill print jobs that did not exist on his servers.

Ivereigh forged some links with the Desktop Technology Group and suggested that they redirect the print jobs from their NT server through his print server rather than going direct to the printers. He could now see (and cancel) all the print jobs. However, the NT server did a poor implementation of the LPR protocol. For one thing, once it had sent the print job, it considered that job printed and the users could not see, from their PCs, either their own job or what was in the total print queue.

To mitigate this loss of visual feedback, he created a simple Web page which would ask for a printer name and then display the print queue simply using the output of the **lpq** command. All the other information for the page was generated by extending **mkprint** again.

Now Ivereigh had a much tidier print system with all the jobs following a well-defined path from the client to the printer. The ideal print system had taken shape, as shown in Figure 5.2.

Location Codes

Cisco decided to expand the facility it had in Research Triangle Park (RTP), North Carolina, to include a full data processing center. It seemed sensible to place a print server there to reduce print traffic going back and forth across the WAN link.

Ivereigh created a complete duplicate of one of the print servers he had in San Jose for this RTP print server. Recognizing the impending manageability problems with multiple servers and the requirement for quick failover, he decided to organize printers into more manageable groups based on physical location. He called these groups *location codes* or *loccodes*. He assigned each loccode group of printers to a single

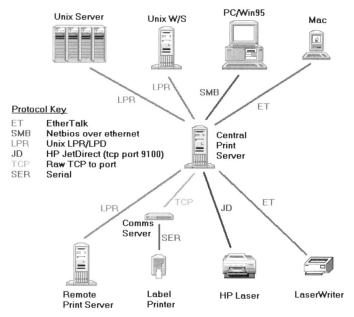

Figure 5.2   New print system takes shape at Cisco.

server, which actually sends jobs to those printers. Any other servers receiving jobs for those printers would simply forward the jobs to that designated server. The advantage of this system was that, in case of a server failure, he could now move these loccodes (and their associated printers) quickly to another operational server, providing failover capability.

To actually accomplish this behavior was quite straightforward: He first copied the master configuration files over to each print server (using **rep**). He then modified **mkprint** such that it took notice of the loccode and which server it was running on as it created the /etc/printcap entries. For each printer, it would extract its loccode and figure out which server was assigned that loccode. If that server was the one that **mkprint** was running on, it would proceed to create a printcap entry as before; otherwise, it would create an entry that simply forwarded the print job to that server.

For example, suppose the printer **foo** had a loccode of SJK2 (San Jose, Building K, 2d floor) and the loccode was listed as being assigned to server print-sj. The printcap entry for this printer on the server print-sj would be as before:

```
foo:\
        :mx#0:\
        :sh:\
        :sd=/var/spool/lpd/foo:\
        :lf=/var/spool/lpd/foo/log:\
        :lp=/var/spool/lpd/foo/.null:\
        :if=/usr/local/atalk/ifpap:\
        :of=/usr/local/atalk/ofpap:
```

However, the entry on any other print server would be as follows:

```
foo:\
        :mx#0:\
        :sh:\
        :sd=/var/spool/lpd/foo:\
        :lf=/var/spool/lpd/foo/log:\
        :lp=/var/spool/lpd/foo/.null:\
        :rm=print-sj:\
        :rp=foo:\
```

The last two lines are what tell the lpd program to forward the job to the print-sj print server.

Thus, it did not matter which print server a job landed on, it would automatically be forwarded to the correct print server. Using this scheme, there was no way that a printer could receive jobs from more than one print server. This immediately provided the *single point of queueing* mentioned previously as part of the ideal print system.

Ivereigh wrote a simple script called **allmkprint** which would do the copying of the master configuration files and run a **mkprint** using **rsh** on all the print servers. He extended the Web interface so it, too, would realize if it were being asked for a printer that resided on a different print server and forward the user's browser to that print server.

He now even had a rudimentary failover procedure in place: If a server died, just move all the loccodes across to another print server and run **allmkprint**.

Samba

Every time a new printer was installed, not only did Ivereigh have to create a queue on his Unix print servers, the Desktop Technology Group had to create a separate queue on their NT servers. This was becoming a pain. To make matters worse, the drivers on the PC had to be carefully matched with the drivers used under NT. Could he take the NT servers out of the loop?

He decided to investigate Samba and was extremely impressed with its ability to provide the same services to PCs using the same protocols that NT used. Essentially, you could make a Unix machine pretend to be an NT server. Samba is also extremely configurable—so much so that you could easily be confused by the enormous array of choices it gives.

Expecting rejection based on a religious argument of NT versus Unix, Ivereigh approached the Desktop Technology Group with the idea of taking over PC printing. Their response was, "Really? You mean you'll take over setting up and managing these pain in the *@! printers for us? Hey, it's all yours!"

The Samba protocol (SMB), however, has a severe limitation: The browsing (that allows the user to get a list of available printers) is done using a single UDP packet and you are therefore limited to about 8K worth of printer names and descriptions. In Cisco's environment, this translated to about 50 printer names per server.

However, he found that Samba had the ability to use different configuration files according to the name that the PC thinks the server is called. For example, suppose that for one physical server, he registers the two pseudoserver names **pserver1** and **pserver2** in Microsoft's version of DNS, WINS. The PC will see two servers: **pserver1** and **pserver2**, both referring to the same physical Samba server. The Samba server will pick a different configuration file and serve a different set of printers according to which pseudoserver the PC thinks it is talking to. This allows you to effectively break the 8K barrier by breaking the printers up into smaller groups.

The printing itself is simple. The Samba configuration files specify a program or script to run when a print job is received. Usually this is a simple lpr command. The PC queue display is done by converting the output of the lpq command.

The print servers could, of course, talk all the different printer protocols. Add to this the Samba capability of receiving jobs from any PC, and now any PC can send a job to any printer—even an AppleTalk printer.

Service Groups

Ivereigh could have just associated the pseudoserver names with the loccodes. However, he found this lacked the flexibility that he needed.

Since the PC printer path (in the form of \\pseudo-server\printer-name) was fixed in people's PCs, he found that if he moved a printer from one loccode to another, people would have to reinstall the printer on their PCs. This caused a problem when he was making administrative changes such as splitting a loccode up or joining two together—in this case he wanted to be able to make these changes without involving the user.

This is best explained with the example shown in Figure 5.3. Take two offices in Texas: Houston and Dallas. A print server (called legolas) is installed in Houston, which also serves the Dallas office. Ivereigh creates a loccode TEXAS, assigned to legolas, which contains all the printers in the two offices. People print to these printers using the pseudoserver print-texas. The two Texas offices then grow so big that he had to install a new server, gollum. Since he cannot split a loccode between two servers, he has no choice but to replace the TEXAS loccode with two new loccodes: DALLAS and HOUSTON (with pseudoserver names print-dallas and print-houston). However, since

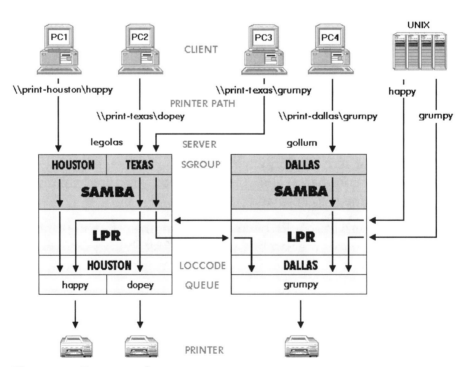

Figure 5.3 Texas example.

people still have the name print-texas in their PCs, he wants this old pseudoserver name to work as well.

The only way to do this is to not associate the pseudoserver name directly with the loccode, but to another grouping: the *service group* or *sgroup.* Ivereigh could associate a loccode to one or more of these sgroups. Conversely, each sgroup could have multiple loccodes associated with it. To use database parlance, loccodes and sgroups have a many-to-many relationship. The sgroup concept allows you to split, join, or move loccodes without changing the client PCs.

To return to the Texas example now using sgroups, Ivereigh would start with a loccode called TEXAS, associated with an sgroup called TEXAS, with the psuedoname print-texas. After installing the new server, he assigns the two new loccodes DALLAS and HOUSTON to gollum and legolas, respectively. He associates the loccode HOUSTON with a new sgroup HOUSTON (pseudoserver print-houston) and the loccode DALLAS with a new sgroup DALLAS (pseudoserver print-dallas). He keeps the sgroup TEXAS and associates both the loccodes HOUSTON and DALLAS with it. Now, even if users used the old print-texas pseudoserver (sgroup TEXAS), they would have access to any of the printers in both the HOUSTON and DALLAS loccodes.

Enter Linux

Samba, and all these various sgroups, were beginning to put a sizable load on the print servers. Ivereigh's group had upgraded the print servers at Cisco headquarters in San Jose to two Sun Sparc 20s; however, the growth in PC usage was soon outstripping even this. To make matters worse, Windows 95 has a very short time-out when asking for a listing of the printer queue (less than 3 seconds). If it times out, the printer is marked on the PC as offline, which requires the user to go into the settings and put the printer back on online. This was generating too many calls.

Ivereigh decided to bite the bullet and introduce a couple of Red Hat Linux machines as Samba print servers. The servers were HP XM4s: 120-MHz Pentiums, 32M RAM, and 1GB hard disk. These were the same PCs that were used as the standard desktop machines at Cisco.

Ivereigh had not ported the entire printing system from SunOS to Linux, so he could not use them as final print servers; that was still left to one of the two Sparc 20s. This was possible because of the sgroup and loccode system previously explained.

Simple Distributed DataBase

Due to the growth in Cisco and the sheer amount of day-to-day print administration, Ivereigh had allowed the engineers access to edit the master configuration file itself. However, this was creating a problem: Since the file was simply edited with **vi**, there was no locking and he was beginning to have problems with people overwriting each other's changes. In addition, the file itself was getting so big that the **mkprint** program was taking a significant amount of time to run. He needed to put this configuration data into some sort of database.

He wrote what he thought would be a simple distributed database (SDDB). He soon discovered that the first two words are a contradiction in terms. It is actually more like a network directory than a database—it performs a similar function to Sun's NIS (Yellow Pages).

NIS maintains separate domains, each of which has a master server and multiple copy servers. While each NIS server can store the data for multiple domains, the data never merge. A client has to *bind*, or attach, to a particular domain on a particular server and can only query data in that domain.

SDDB also maintains separate domains, each with its own master server and copy servers. Each master server receives record updates for its own domain and propagates these changes to all the other servers across all domains. The data from each domain is merged on each server into a single contiguous database—the original domain being stored on each record. Thus, when a client queries the data, it does so across all the domains.

The records themselves are held as a field=value list of variable length. Only the values defined are stored in the record and these can be added to at any time.

Indexes are held in memory using a red-black tree algorithm; all creation and comparing is done using user-supplied functions, so the indexes themselves are very flexible. SDDB allows for multiple indexes and can detect and reject duplicate entries, unlike NIS which only allows one index on each file (or table).

The SDDB servers themselves are completely stateless (that is, they do not store any information between client requests) and use a fast UDP protocol to perform all the transactions. A modification sequence number (which is analogous to a modification time) is held on each record so that a master server can decide what records have been updated and should therefore be propagated to the other servers. Since only the modified data is transferred, the propagation delay can be made very short—it is currently about 30 seconds.

SDDB has an API (interface) for both C and shell scripts. Thus, you can use either to inquire, update, or delete records in the database. The database itself is not tied to the print system—it could be used to store any sort of record-orientated data.

Effect of Simple Distributed Database

Ivereigh installed SDDB onto every print server and converted all the master configuration data into SDDB records. SDDB could now provide the configuration data for **mkprint**, which produced the configuration files (/etc/printcap and others). He rewrote **mkprint** in C (it was originally written in shell and awk script), which enormously improved its speed. It now did not have to perform any rcps since the data was already present on the local server. He rewrote the Web (CGI) programs so that they no longer relied on the output of **mkprint** and received their information directly from SDDB.

He wrote a front end on SDDB that was designed for the print system, called **pradmin**. It used a simple command-line interface, not dissimilar to the Cisco router interface. Now, multiple people could update the database simultaneously without fear of clashing.

As more and more programs came to rely on SDDB and the data it contained, SDDB became the glue that tied all the print servers together. A single update would affect many servers, which would all act in unison. Every print server knew about every printer at Cisco and acted accordingly. The distributed machine started to take shape.

Linux Goes into the Field

Cisco had started a spree of buying up small companies, particularly in the San Francisco Bay area. It was time to start installing more print servers. It made sense to use Linux machines, since they were cheap. A Linux print server cost less than $2000, less than a third of its commercial rival, Sun's Sparc 5.

Ivereigh ported and rewrote the remainder of the programs that, until then, had only worked on SunOS. Now the Linux machines could perform the full cfunction of a print server.

A print server was installed miles down the road in Scotts Valley. Aside from a few teething problems, it worked. Then one was shipped to Sydney, Australia. The system was preconfigured with an IP address so that all that the sysadmin in Sydney had to do was hook up the power and the network and power it on. It worked flawlessly. The SDDB server came up, copied its data down, Ivereigh ran a **mkprint** and off it went.

Rdist

Rdist is a tool that allows the mirroring of directories between servers. Either this can be done by doing an exact mirror (including the deletion of files) or just adding to and replacing what is already there.

Using the tool, Ivereigh could now put together a directory structure on a master distribution server and have it mirrored throughout all the other servers automatically. This was yet another massive time-saver as the number of servers managed increased. He even included the /etc/passwd and /etc/group files among those files which are updated using **rdist**.

Setting up a new server became very straightforward: Install a vanilla Red Hat release, then **rdist** the print system on top of this.

New Web Stuff

Ivereigh also had to do another rework of the Web pages, as he had to add the ability to stop and start print queues as well as delete a print job and send a test page.

He discovered that using SNMP he could display an HP printer's front panel display, which greatly aided in fixing the run-of-the-mill problems, such as "Toner Out."

The Web interface became the preferred tool for diagnosing printer problems and was made available to everyone. It allowed users to fix many of their own printer problems and to not call Ivereigh.

Failover

As mentioned earlier, loccodes provided a rudimentary failover procedure. However, it would have been an arduous task to update all those loccode and sgroup records to denote a new server in the case of a failure.

Ivereigh added a backup server field to the loccode and sgroup records and created a new SDDB table called **pserver**. In it was detailed, among other things, the state of the server (up or down). He changed **mkprint** such that when it created the configuration files, it would check the state of the primary server (as designated on each loccode and sgroup record). If a server was marked as down, **mkprint** would direct LPR to use the backup server instead.

Now failover was simply a matter of marking the dead server as down in SDDB and rerunning **mkprint** on all the servers.

Back-Ending of LPR

The only problem with the **mkprint** system was that any updates to the SDDB records were not instantly reflected in the print servers. Could the various programs be made to bypass their configuration files and read SDDB directly?

Ivereigh pulled open the LPR code and again replaced the routines that read the /etc/printcap file. This time, however, they read an SDDB record and created an in-memory printcap entry accordingly, using the same algorithms that **mkprint** used.

He then did the same thing with BOOTP. It no longer needed to read /etc/bootptab, but rather read its information straight from SDDB. Now, whenever changes were made in SDDB, the print queues were created instantly and the BOOTP server was immediately available to service the BOOTP request.

Now failover didn't even require a **mkprint** to be run. Samba was now the only program left that didn't read its information directly from SDDB.

Linux Takes Over

After an extreme power outage at the San Jose headquarters data center and general lack of performance due to capacity problems, the visibility of the print system was raised. Suddenly, the managers realized that without the print system, nothing was printed and production lines stopped. The order came down to "double the capacity of the print system immediately." Ivereigh was assigned another person, Ben Woodard (bwoodard@cisco.com), to provide a much-needed extra pair of hands. Although originally employed by Cisco as a Microsoft Windows support-line technician, within a few months Ivereigh had converted him into a die-hard Linux fan.

They installed ten new Linux servers in the San Jose headquarters data center. They now had Linux print servers spread around the world:

- 13 servers at San Jose Headquarters
- 3 servers around Silicon Valley
- 4 servers spread around Europe
- 2 servers in RTP, North Carolina
- 2 servers in Tokyo, Japan
- 1 server in Sydney, Australia

On August 1, 1997, Ivereigh and his team retired the Sparc 20s and the other Axil machines. They are now completely reliant on Linux servers. It is noteworthy that there is not a single line of commercial code anywhere. They have (or at least have access to) the source code for every single program that they have running.

The Future

Ivereigh and his team have recently started replacing the print function in the Cisco branch offices. Up until now, they have used local NT servers (with all their associated problems) to manage their printers. Although the branch offices only have 5 percent of their printers, they account for about 50 percent of their support calls. They had, as of spring of 1998, deployed 30 servers in these branch offices, with many more on the way—there are about 200 branch offices in all.

There is still plenty of work to do as Cisco expands the system to meet the needs of its printing clients. It is considering the following:

Improve SNMP features: Enable traps, so that the printers notify when they have a problem.

Create print queues using Java: The creation of print queues still requires someone who is happy to log on to the system and run **pradmin,** the printer queue administration program. Why not allow anyone with a browser and the right authorization to create queues?

Replace the LPR program with LPRng or even an implementation of the Internet Printing Protocol (IPP): LPR is showing its age; there are many facilities that LPR does not provide (sending printing options such as duplex, for example).

Extract page counts from the printers using SNMP: You should be able to schedule regular maintenance visits by engineers in much the same way as you do with a car.

Implement a DHCP server: Many printers now support DHCP as well as BOOTP. A DHCP server would allow you to avoid allocating IP addresses to printers.

Work on SDDB in order to make it usable as a general purpose network directory service: It also needs a new name.

Conclusion

Using regular Unix tools and SDDB, Ivereigh has created a distributed machine, with multiple facets in the form of physically separate servers spread around the world. There really has been no magic in this—it has simply been accomplished by fixing problems in a general way, with an eye toward the future. Linux has proved itself quite capable of holding its own in this large, mission-critical environment.

Fluke Corporation

Fluke manufactures portable electronic test equipment. The company uses Linux for the following functions:

X-Windows:

- X-Windows server (runs applications, possibly exports display)
- Network file server
- Samba server for a network of PCs
- NFS server for other PCs and Unix systems

Print server

- Print spooler using lpd (Unix, NFS clients)
- Print spooler using Samba (PC clients)

Office productivity software

- Document preparation with ApplixWare
- Document preparation with TROFF, NROFF, GROFF, or derivatives
- Document preparation with FrameMaker
- Other document management
- Internet client software—WWW
- NCSA Mosaic
- Lynx
- Other browsers
- Internet client software—mail
- Pine
- Mail

Electronic mail server

- POP3 server
- IMAP server
- SMTP server (sendmail, others)
- SMTP mail router

Network services provided to local users

- HTTP (World Wide Web) server or cache
- Accepts Telnet connections
- Accepts secure-shell (ssh) connections
- Other services

Software development tools

- C and/or C++
- Perl
- tcl/tk
- Bourne, Korn, C, or another shell; using **sed**, **awk**, **grep**, and similar tools

NOTE For additional information about Fluke's use of Linux, contact Mark Hinds via e-mail at zoro@fluke.com

Triton ETD

A manufacturer of TWTs, TWTAs, klystrons, thyratrons, and glass power tubes, Triton ETD uses Linux for the following functions:

X-Windows

- X-Windows terminal (display, keyboard, mouse—applications run elsewhere)
- X-Windows server (runs applications, possibly exports display)

Network file server

- Samba server for a network of PCs
- Office productivity software
- Document preparation with LyX
- Spreadsheets created with NeXS
- Internet client software—WWW
- NCSA Mosaic
- Other browsers
- Internet client software—mail
- Other mail clients

Network management

- Internet or WAN router
- Network services provided to local users
- HTTP (World Wide Web) server or cache
- Accepts Telnet connections

Software development tools

- C and/or C++
- Bourne, Korn, C, or another shell; using **sed**, **awk**, **grep**, and similar tools

NOTE

For additional information on Triton ETD's use of Linux, contact Danny Holstein via e-mail at danny@holstein.tritonetd.com.

U.S. Navy

The U.S. Navy uses Linux to provide pay and personnel services to the southern San Diego, Colorado, and New Mexico areas. The administration uses Linux for the following functions:

X-Windows

- X-Windows terminal (display, keyboard, mouse—applications run elsewhere)
- X-Windows server (runs applications, possibly exports display)

Network file server

- Samba server for a network of PCs

Print server

- Print spooler using Samba (PC clients)

Modem communications

- Server answers the phone, provides PPP, SLIP, or term logins
- Internet client software—mail
- Pine
- Other mail clients

Electronic mail server

- POP3 server
- IMAP server
- SMTP server (sendmail, others)
- SMTP mail router

Network services provided to local users

- HTTP (World Wide Web) server or cache
- Accepts secure-shell (ssh) connections
- Runs one or more database servers
- Other services

Network services provided to remote users over dial-up or the Internet

- HTTP (World Wide Web) serv_remoteer or cache
- Accepts secure-shell (ssh) connections
- Runs one or more database serv_remoteers

Software development tools

- C and/or C++
- Java
- Perl

U.S. Army

The U.S. Army uses Linux in the processing of orders and distributing information relating to U.S. Army publications. The administration uses Linux for the following functions:

X-Windows

- X-Windows terminal (display, keyboard, mouse—applications run elsewhere)
- X-Windows server (runs applications, possibly exports display)
- Internet client software—WWW
- NCSA Mosaic
- Lynx
- Internet client software—mail
- Pine

Network services provided to local users

- HTTP (World Wide Web) server or cache
- Other services

Software development tools

- C and/or C++
- Perl
- Bourne, Korn, C, or another shell; using **sed, awk, grep,** and similar tools
- Others

References

Young, Robert, interview at TechWeb, by John Borland, September 30, 1998.

Seruntine, Cliff, USENET.

Ivereigh, Damian, *Linux Journal*, June, 1998, p. 31.

CHAPTER 6

Integrating Linux Solutions with Business

L inux not only is proving itself as a great server operating system (OS), but it's turning out to be a reliable desktop OS as well. It is certainly more crash-proof than Microsoft Windows 98 and much cheaper, too, as you can download Linux for free from many sites on the Internet (which is actually one of the main reasons for the fast proliferation of Linux in the past year and a half).

People tend to think that Linux competes with Windows 98. Every so often you find Linux users promoting it as the solution for the Windows 95/98 shortcomings. It seems, though, that Windows 95/98 have their own space and do not directly compete with Linux. It might be true that Linux threatens Windows 98 market share, especially in light of the battles between Microsoft and Sun over the Java code present in Windows 98 (during late November 1998). After all, Linux outsold Windows 98 a couple months after Microsoft released it.

Linux has its merits, but it also has its shortcomings, especially when targeted for the business application world. What you need to focus on is not what Linux can do for your business today, but on where you want to go tomorrow and the fact that Linux is the most likely OS to take you there.

What this chapter tries to elucidate is that Linux does not run neck and neck with Microsoft's products, nor does it with the whole Unix family of products. The proposition of being open source, available to anyone, makes it unique in its approach to business strategies. Although it's tempting to see Linux as David, ready to throw a stone right at Goliath's forehead (Microsoft), this is nothing but romanticism. Most know all too well that Windows 98 and its applications are not as stable as users would like them to be, that technical support is very poor but expensive, that it is inflexible and insecure, and all the other perils that plague these systems. People in charge of supporting them are familiar with such error messages as: "Consult an Expert" and "Reinstall Windows 95."

But you must recognize that, aside from these annoying problems you have, Windows 98 is an extraordinary operating system. Windows 98 is very easy to use, install, and configure. For the features it provides, it is also very inexpensive and has impressive international support. In addition, it has excellent development tools, supports nearly every major hardware manufacturer, and you find a large variety of high-quality software available in almost every category for the platform. These characteristics are not yet shared by Linux.

However, Linux has a different set of advantages. It is rock-solid, has excellent support, is extremely flexible and secure, is free, and it is graciously open. From a technical point of view, it is incomparably superior to Windows 98.

Furthermore, companies have invested billions of dollars in software and training for the Windows platform. It will take some time until Linux becomes a great contender and runs PowerPoint, for example. MS Word files are already interchangeable with Applix's Applixware suite, as well as most of the Microsoft Office Suite, but performance is still an issue.

Nonetheless, most end users will not take advantage of the extra flexibility and security offered by Linux. It is not that they have no use for it, it is just that they are so used to working with what they have (Microsoft) and so wary of changes, that they don't really care about the advantages they may get.

Even though Linux provides an unmatched flexibility and power for the user, including powerful command-line tools, permissions, and stability, users are more comfortable using Windows 98 than taking the time to climb the Linux learning curve. It is unlikely this trend will change in the near future and this is one of the main advantages Windows has over Linux. Windows 98 is much more user-friendly than Linux, especially when considering the amount of third-party products already developed for it.

But, as mentioned earlier, Linux does not compete directly with Windows. Actually, it is at its best exactly where Windows falters. It is strong in support for different software platforms. It is designed to be sturdy and take heavy workloads day in, day out. It has very powerful tools for the Internet. In addition, it picks up the security buck where Windows passes it—nobody wants to operate a Web server or, for that matter, any server without having 100 percent confidence in it. Linux provides it!

For these reasons, when looking at Linux at work, you should not look at it as a replacement for Microsoft's Windows 98, rather, try it as a server and manager for Windows, complementing Windows' weaknesses and guaranteeing a high level of service to the corporation. It's generally a good idea to keep end users from knowing that it's Linux that is offering the advanced services they're using. This will decrease your users' resistance curve. Later, you can announce that the improved performance of the network for all aspects, such as printing, accessing the Internet, and providing file service, is due to your Linux implementation of a few months ago.

If you look back in time, when Microsoft first introduced Windows NT, the approach was the same. It was not meant to replace Unix or Novell, but to coexist with them, easing the administrators' management tasks, in particular, the ones related to cross-platform and multi-protocol environments. The natural competitors to Linux are, in reality, Windows NT (and Windows 2000) and the other version of Unix found out there. In a server role, Linux really shines.

Linux as an Alternative

In every step of the initial cost equation, you will be saving money with Linux. To begin with, it is free, or almost free, if you want to take into account the cost of distribution. Then, it requires far less computer resources than its competitors. It is portable to several platforms. So, instead of supporting NT, Solaris, Ultrix, and AIX, each with its own expenses for training, documentation, and so on, you only have to support Linux. That aspect alone can save an organization thousands of dollars every month.

As for applications, not only does Linux have all kinds of applications available for free or very inexpensively, but also bugs are usually corrected and new features added constantly—not on the next release! In addition, since most of the applications come with the source code, you can always add new features to it. Linux itself is often updated very quickly, too. Security holes and bugs are quickly tracked and fixed, frequently in a matter of hours. This fact alone can save a corporation thousands of dollars in the case of a mission-critical server crash or vulnerability.

Another advantage of Linux is the amount of documentation and superior technical support it has. Linux vendors such as Red Hat don't put you on hold for half an hour and then charge you big bucks for online support. To begin with, there is outstanding online support for Linux available. The support you receive when calling a Linux vendor is superior to any other OS vendors, mostly due to the nature of the professionals providing technical support. Most of them use Linux at home. How many people do you know who use Ultrix or even NT at home?

If your business is connected to the Internet, you will get an infinite knowledge base, always willing to help, generally for free. Antagonists will say: "Other OSs have their own mailing lists and Usenet groups, too." But the fact is, no other Internet support group is even closely as effective as Linux's. Linux is unique in that it offers many more tools to fix your problems. There is a positive attitude among Linux users with regards to support: Many people learned a lot of what they know through the Linux Internet support channels. Now they feel in many ways obliged to help lots of other people, who will learn a lot of what they know through these channels.

Administrative costs are much lower in Linux, and administration is much easier for Linux than for any other OS. An argument many people use in favor of NT is that it is so easy to administrate. A lot of Unix people were at first fearful of losing their jobs when NT came out. Now, most NT sites have a dedicated administrator. The fallacy of Microsoft's argument is that administrative costs are not affected by creating new users in a GUI instead of using a shell script, or even editing a file. They are not affected by day-to-day operations when things go right, and they are not affected by performing ordinary maintenance. What really skyrockets your administrative costs is when things go wrong. And anyone supporting networks knows that they do, with any system. When it happens, you need clear error messages. You need trace and debug capabilities. And you need documentation.

Another factor that increases your administrative costs is when you have to do anything that is out of the ordinary. When that happens, you want flexibility. And while NT may be acceptable for cooking pasta, finer dishes will require tools and flexibility you can only get from Unix. Because Linux is so flexible, you can frequently eliminate routers, bridges, and other equipment, which not only add to additional hardware cost, but also contribute to making your network more complex, introduce new environments to be learned, and become yet more failure points. With Linux, cost involved in the maintenance of such equipment can often be eliminated and, other times, greatly reduced.

Integrating Linux and Windows 98

Using Linux with Windows 98 is not a very complicated task. Most of the work is handled by the Samba suite, a host of programs designed to work with the SMB protocol, capable of most services you expect from a network server: handling logins, sharing hard drives, printers, and so on. Samba is especially useful when you have a mixed Unix/Windows 98 environment.

Samba fools Windows 98 into thinking that it is talking to an NT server. You can have network profiles, unified registries for all your machines, login scripts, and, generally, have most of the bells and whistles available with NT. The only problem you may have is that logins take a little longer to complete when compared to NT. As far as performance, Linux with Samba is generally a little slower than NT, but tolerable, and the issues that make it slower are already being worked out. The configuration files have a format similar to the Windows .ini files, which makes it easy to share printers, hard disks, CD-ROMs, and so on.

Linux e-mail comes mostly configured. Sendmail is usually configured correctly and POP server already comes installed. When integrating

Linux with Windows 98, all you really need to do is to install a browser.

Integrating Linux with Existing Platforms

Linux can be integrated with a variety of platforms. Linux has turned beta testing into an art form, allowing users to add features freely and interoperate, but its creator keeps control of the kernel.

NOTE

This section is based on a contribution by Vince Arkmen, largely based upon an earlier HOWTO by J. David Bryan, from MIT (jdbryan@alum.mit.edu). Vince added information on Linux and changed the organization somewhat, but has left Bryan's text more or less intact wherever it still applies. I thank Arkmen, Bryan, and also Arthur D. Jerijian from UCLA for additional information about the Unix **dd** command.

TIP

You can find a full version of this document at www.windows-nt.com/multiboot/directboot.html. Make sure to check that site for the latest version of this document, as updates are made every so often, when necessary.

For instance, you can have a system directly multibooting Linux into Windows NT, Windows 95, and DOS from the Windows NT boot loader. It is possible to boot directly into each of these operating systems using the Windows NT 3.51 boot loader (note that this procedure will not work with NT versions prior to 3.51). Specifically, you can boot directly into DOS, without going through Windows 95, from the NT multiboot menu. Actually, you can have IBM's OS/2 and other operating systems added to this procedure, given an understanding of the way the particular boot sequence works for the operating system. The two required conditions for bootup are as follows:

- The correct system files must be present with the required names.
- The correct boot sector must be executed.

To illustrate this level of integration of Linux with other business platforms, take a look at a case scenario presented by Arkmen. The information contained in this section was derived from a number of sources, including several articles from the Microsoft Knowledge Base, public domain knowledge from Usenet postings, and the 95WRK.HLP file supplied on the Windows 95 final beta CD-ROM (the relevant page is entitled "Installing Windows 95 for Dual Booting with Windows NT").

The System

When Arkmen first set up his machine, he set it up with Windows NT 3.51 Workstation, Windows 95, DOS 6.22 (with WFW 3.11, though this does not matter), and Slackware Linux (kernel 1.2.13). Subsequently, he upgraded it to Windows NT 4.0 and Linux kernel 2.0.29 with no difficulties. This case study describes how he did it.

CAUTION

If you are planning to implement such a mix of OSs into your own system or are planning to reproduce the results achieved by Arkmen, he recommends you install DOS first, then Windows 95, then Windows NT, and then Linux. Otherwise, inserting another operating system in arbitrary order can leave your system in a pretty unsatisfactory state.

Requirements

Here are the absolute bare minimum requirements for reproducing what is described in this case study:

The NT boot loader. This won't work without Windows NT (3.51 or later) and its boot loader.

A FAT-filesystem boot partition. Make sure that your first primary partition is formatted FAT, as this is where the boot files for the various operating systems will go, and it is the one filesystem that all these operating systems can read. If you have some other partition scheme and want to duplicate the system described here, you are on your own.

A good partition scheme. Use DOS on this first FAT partition, as DOS tends not to boot from other locations reliably. Moreover, though DOS and Windows 95 can go on the same partition, do not put them on the same partition if you want to also maintain a copy of Windows 3.1x, as it can become extremely tricky to sort out which files belong to Windows 95 and which files belong to Windows 3.1x.

Finally, these instructions assume that Windows NT gets its own partition and that Linux gets its own partition.

Drive C: therefore contains all of the start-up files for all operating systems. A listing of all files (including hidden files) should contain at least the following NT system start-up files:

- BOOTSECT.DOS
- BOOT.INI
- NTDETECT.COM
- NTLDR

If you have Windows 95 installed, then you should also have the following files if DOS was booted more recently than Windows 95:

- IO.SYS
- MSDOS.SYS
- MSDOS.W40
- WINBOOT.SYS

or the following files, if Windows 95 was booted more recently than DOS:

- IO.DOS
- IO.SYS
- MSDOS.DOS
- MSDOS.SYS

If you have not installed Windows 95 yet, then you should have just the following DOS files:

- IO.SYS
- MSDOS.SYS

Finally, you should have a Linux bootsector file that points to the volume on which you have installed Linux (with **LILO**):

- BOOTSECT.LNX

Arkmen describes how to create this little gem later on in this section.

The End Result

When you are done, and you reboot, you will get the NT boot loader menu (it starts out at the top of the screen with "OS Loader V3.51") with (at least) these choices:

- Windows NT 3.51

- Windows 95

- DOS 6.22

- Linux

and when you select a choice, you will then see one of the following messages on the screen (depending on which system you select):

- "NTDETECT V1.0 Checking Hardware"

- "Starting Windows 95 . . ."

- "Starting MS-DOS . . ."

- "LILO . . ."

Before You Start

Before you start this installation, do the following:

1. Make backups of the files BOOT.INI and BOOTSECT.DOS in the root of C: (BOOT.INI is hidden; BOOTSECT.DOS may be) if you already have NT installed.

2. It's not a bad idea to have a backup of your Linux lilo.conf file (usually /etc/lilo.conf) if you already have Linux installed.

3. Be sure you have BOOTABLE Windows NT Setup Diskettes (three diskettes). If not, run winnt32 /o from the installation CD-ROM to make them.

4. If you intend to install DOS, be sure you have a BOOTABLE DOS diskette that contains (at a minimum) **edit, fdisk, attrib, sys,** and **format.**

5. If you intend to install Windows 95, be sure you have the Windows 95 installation disks and/or CD-ROM handy.

6. If you intend to install Linux, be sure you have your Linux boot/root disk(s) handy.

7. If you have not installed Windows 95 before but intend to, be sure that you can boot into Windows NT (and into DOS if you have it installed) correctly before you do so.

8. If you have installed DOS, Windows 95, and Windows NT and just want to make DOS a bootup option from the NT boot loader, then be sure you can boot into Windows NT, Windows 95, and DOS (via Windows 95). If you can't reach DOS from Windows 95, you may need to add the line "BootMulti=1" to the [Options] section of your Windows

95 MSDOS.SYS (do this from within Windows 95, to be sure you edit the right file).

9. If you have installed Linux, be sure you can start Linux (with **LILO** or via boot/root disks). Typically, the only way to set this up initially is to have **LILO** write its boot information into that master boot record. (This means that it will come up before NT's boot loader. This is okay, because the procedure herein will unify things.)

10. It will help (but is not necessary) to have a hex dump program available (or you can use the NT **DEBUG** command) so you can look at the contents of the BOOTSECT files and verify their correctness.

What You Will Need To Do

The steps needed to implement directly booting to an arbitrary operating system are as follows:

1. Create a boot sector file for that operating system (such as Windows 95, DOS, or Linux).

2. Edit your BOOT.INI file to add bootup choices for the particular operating system (such as Windows 95, DOS, Linux, and any other operating systems that you use).

Create the DOS Bootsector File

What NT's boot loader uses to load any given operating system is a tiny bootstrap file that points it at the rest of the operating system's boot code. These files are pretty easy to create and maintain, given the right tools (and a fair amount of patience). For creating boot sector files, there are a couple of methods.

1. **On a machine with Windows 95 and Windows NT.** If you already have Windows 95 and Windows NT working, then the BOOTSECT .DOS file in the bootup directory (the root directory of the C: drive, usually) is the Windows 95 bootsector file. (This is not the same as the DOS bootsector file.) If you have this file, back it up as BOOTSECT .W40 or BOOTSECT.W95, or some other name that you will remember as being the Windows 95 bootsector.

   Now, in order to add DOS to the mix, you need a BOOTSECT.DOS that contains a DOS bootsector. The good news is that NT will make one for you. The bad news is that you have to go a fair way through the setup program for it to generate the BOOTSECT.DOS (which takes about 1 second). To do this, use your NT installation and setup disks/CD-ROM to repair your NT boot files. This process will create a new BOOTSECT.DOS file.

This file is your DOS bootsector file. *Save this file!* You will want to copy this file to BOOTSECT.622 or some other file name that you'll remember as being the actual DOS bootsector file. Otherwise, Windows NT setup will overwrite this file the next time you install, upgrade, or repair it, as BOOTSECT.DOS is the default file name for the bootsector file.

2. **On a machine with DOS and Windows NT but without Windows 95.** Alternately, if you're setting up a machine from scratch or you just haven't installed Windows 95 yet, and if you installed NT over DOS, then the BOOTSECT.DOS file in the bootup directory *is* the DOS bootsector file.

Save this file! You will want to copy the actual DOS BOOTSECT .DOS file to a new file with a different name because Windows NT will overwrite this bootsector file if you install or reinstall it, as BOOTSECT.DOS is the default file name. So, you can just copy this file to BOOTSECT.622 or some other name that you'll remember as being the DOS bootsector file.

Create the Windows 95 Bootsector File

If you don't yet have a Windows 95 bootsector file (by having backed one up in the preceding process), then there are a couple of ways to create one. First, if you have DOS and Windows NT installed, but have not installed Windows 95 yet, back up your DOS bootsector file (as previously described) and run Windows 95 setup from DOS. Once this process completes, you'll probably need to repair your NT installation. When Windows NT setup finishes fixing your bootup files, copy the resulting BOOTSECT.DOS file to BOOTSECT.W40 or BOOTSECT.W95 or some other file name that you'll remember as being the Windows 95 bootsector file.

If you already have Windows 95 and Windows NT installed and you want to make a bootsector file specifically for Windows 95, then you can use Windows 95 SYS.COM to rewrite Windows 95's system files onto the hard disk. Then you will need to install or reinstall Windows NT, and once it finishes installing, the resulting BOOTSECT.DOS file will be the Windows 95 bootsector file. Save it to BOOTSECT.W40 or BOOTSECT.W95 or some other file name that you will remember as being the Windows 95 bootsector.

Create the Linux Bootsector File

So far so good? If you've installed DOS, Windows 95, and Windows NT, then right about now your machine should load DOS (directly, if you've installed the DOS bootsector file into your BOOT.INI file, or indirectly, through Windows 95 otherwise), Windows 95, and Windows NT. (And, if somehow all of this didn't kill off **LILO,** then it will probably run **LILO,** and then run the NT loader. This is okay, too, for now). Of course, if you haven't created such a schizophrenic system, your bootup process may be significantly less contorted.

If you had **LILO** installed, but setting up DOS and/or Windows 95 has totally wiped **LILO** from the picture at bootup, don't panic. Just boot Linux from your boot/root floppies with the boot option mount root=/dev/hd? (where /dev/hd? is the *volume* of your Linux installation—that is, the first partition of the first IDE volume would be /dev/hdal, or the third partition of the second SCSI volume would be /dev/sdb3, and so forth). This should get you back into Linux with minimal hassle (all of Linux should still be there—it's just that **LILO** temporarily isn't around to boot it up!).

Once DOS, Windows 95, and Windows NT boot okay, it's time to create a Linux bootsector file and to remove **LILO** from the master boot record. The major trick here is to install Linux's boot information onto the superblock of the volume on which Linux resides (usually **LILO** wants to write its information to the master boot record, and this won't work for your purposes, because this is where NT puts its boot loader).

If **LILO** is currently set up in the master boot record (MBR), you can go ahead and create a bootsector file directly from the MBR with the following command in Linux:

```
dd if=/dev/hda of=/mnt/c-drive/bootsect.lns bs=512 count=1
```

where /mnt/c-drive is where your bootup FAT partition is mounted in Linux.

Now, assuming that your **LILO** installation currently expects to be in the master boot record, this needs to be changed. The pertinent **LILO** information is in the lilo.conf file (again, usually in the /etc directory). So, with your favorite editor, edit your lilo.conf file as follows: Replace the boot=/dev/hd? line that is currently there (probably boot=/dev/hda) with a line referring to the superblock of the Linux volume (again, this would be /dev/hdb1 for the first partition of the second IDE volume, or /dev/sdb2 for the second partition of the second SCSI volume, and so forth).

At this point, since you're expecting **LILO** just to have to boot Linux, you might also want to comment out whatever menu options are for booting DOS. Once you have made the appropriate changes, save the file and rerun **LILO** (usually /sbin/lilo) to update the boot information. Then remove **LILO** from the MBR. This should teach **LILO** to behave properly when next you launch it.

Following is a sample lilo.conf you can look at to see this information in context. If you did not create a Linux bootsector file previously (if, for instance, you have been booting Linux from a floppy or with LOADLIN and didn't already have **LILO** installed in the MBR), then you need to go ahead and create such a file from the superblock of your Linux partition—the new home of **LILO.** You can use BOOT-PART from Windows or **dd** from Linux.

NOTE

If you get tired of always having to manually update your Linux bootsector file each time you run **LILO,** you can have **LILO** build it for you. Once you have the initial bootsector file built (by the previously described means), you can point **LILO** to it by setting the boot=line in your lilo.conf as follows:

```
boot = /mnt/c-drive/bootsect.lnx # This puts LILO in the bootsector
```

where /mnt/c-drive is where you have your primary boot partition mounted in Linux (usually /dosc or something similar). Now each time you rerun **LILO** (assuming you have the DOS partition mounted read-write), **LILO** will rebuild the file for you, eliminating the need to rebuild it manually.

With BOOTPART, once Linux is correctly installed in the superblock, it can only boot if the boot loader in the MBR passes control to it. The way to make this exchange take place is to create a bootsector file for it that NT's boot loader can use to start **LILO** and to tell the NT loader where to find the file. You should use the shareware utility BOOT-PART (found on the CD-ROM that accompanies this book), as it is designed exactly for this purpose. Running BOOTPART with no parameters should display all partitions on the machine and with which filesystem they are formatted. Then, running BOOTPART with a partition number and a bootsector file name should create a new bootsector file (and possibly add it to your BOOT.INI file, but that's jumping ahead a bit). For this process, follow the instructions for BOOTPART, as the exact incantation may change somewhat from version to version. And, when you do create the file, it is recommended that you use the file name BOOTSECT.LNX, but again, use whatever file name you will remember as being the bootsector for Linux.

NOTE

For more information on BOOTPART, take a look at www.winimage.com/bootpart.htm.

Now, beware that if you have BOOTPART install the bootsector file into your BOOT.INI file directly, it may put in a line like this:

```
bootsect.lnx="Linux"
```

But this line frequently isn't enough. You will want to specify the full path to the bootsector file, particularly if you have more than one drive, as follows:

```
c:\bootsect.lnx="Linux"
```

or whatever the correct path to the file really is, using **dd**.

Alternately, if you want to make the BOOTSECT.LNX file from within Linux, you can do it with the **dd** command. If **LILO** is installed in the master boot record (MBR), then do the following:

```
dd if=/dev/hda of=/mnt/c-drive/bootsect.lnx bs=512 count=1
```

Otherwise, if **LILO** is installed in the superblock of the Linux partition, then do the following:

```
dd if=/dev/hda? of=/mnt/c-drive/bootsect.lnx bs=512 count=1
```

where hda? is your boot partition in Linux and /mnt/c-drive is where your C: drive is mounted. If you like, you can even have **LILO** boot from this bootsector file by setting the boot= parameter in /etc/lilo.conf:

```
boot = /mnt/c-drive/bootsect.lnx
```

Remove LILO from the Master Boot Record

The only complication to all of this is removing **LILO** from the master boot record (MBR). To do this, you have to rewrite the MBR with the command

```
fdisk /mbr
```

from Windows 95 or DOS or with the command

```
/sbin/lilo -u /dev/hda
```

From Linux, which will uninstall **LILO** and restore the MBR to its pre-**LILO** state. *Note:* The first option will and the second option might wipe out your master boot record. If this is the case, you will have to use your NT installation disks/CD-ROM to repair NT's master boot record files.

Add DOS to the BOOT.INI File

Once you have all these bootsector files floating around, it's time to plug them into the NT loader. (*Note:* The following procedure can be used from any of the available systems; Arkmen used DOS. Be aware, though, that until NT is set up, there is no BOOT.INI file, so you must have set up Windows NT by this point.) Also, the addition of items to the BOOT.INI file can be done in whatever order you want, but, of course, if a menu selection refers to a not-yet-created or invalid boot-sector file, then your results will be less than favorable (probably the blue screen of death and a nasty message).

To get the correct system files (with the correct names), edit the BOOT.INI file (hidden and read-only) present in the bootup directory (probably the root of C:).

You should have lines something like the following:

```
[boot loader]
timeout=10
default=multi(0)disk(0)rdisk(1)partition(1)\WINNT
[operating systems]
multi(0)disk(0)rdisk(1)partition(1)\WINNT="Windows NT Version
3.51"
 c:\bootsect.dos="Windows 95"
```

Edit the c:\bootsect.dos line and add a new line following it, as depicted in Table 6.1.

Table 6.1 Editing the c:\bootsect.dos Line and Adding a New Line Following It

BEFORE EDITING	AFTER EDITING
c:\bootsect.dos="Windows 95"	c:\bootsect.w40="Windows 95" /WIN95
New line	c:\bootsect.622="MS-DOS 6.22" /WIN95DOS

The /WIN95 and /WIN95DOS switches cause NTLDR to rename the DOS and Windows 95 system files back and forth so that the correct names are used with the operating system selected. (If you have not noticed before, look at the hidden files in the root of C: when running DOS and Windows 95. Under Windows 95, the DOS files are renamed IO.DOS and MSDOS.DOS; under DOS, the Windows 95 files are renamed WINBOOT.SYS and MSDOS.W40; IO.SYS and MSDOS.SYS belong to the current operating system.)

NOTE
The /WIN95 and /WIN95DOS switches are only recognized by NTLDR version 3.51. The NTLDR from versions 3.5 and earlier won't recognize these switches, so the renaming won't take place.

You have also requested that Windows 95 be booted using the boot-sector in the file BOOTSECT.W40, while DOS is booted using BOOT-SECT.DOS, which is what all of this furious creation of bootsectors was about.

Add Linux to the BOOT.INI File

Again, be aware that there is no BOOT.INI file until after you install NT, so make sure that NT is running before you attempt this section.

Adding the Linux bootsector file (BOOTSECT.LNX or whatever name you called it) should be trivial. To install your new bootsector file into the BOOT.INI bootup menu, just add the line

```
c:\bootsect.lnx="Slackware Linux"
```

If you use BOOTPART to create your bootsector files, it has an option to go ahead and insert the newly created file into the BOOT.INI list. If you do this, be aware that you may need to edit the BOOT.INI file by hand, to correct for what may be considered a bug in BOOTPART. Also, you might want to edit the line to set the exact name which comes up in the bootup menu. In any case, adding Linux's bootsector file to your BOOT.INI should bring Linux into the picture. Then, when you select your new Linux option, it should fire up **LILO**, which in turn boots Linux.

Add Other Operating Systems to the BOOT.INI File

As mentioned at the top of this explanation, this procedure should work for OS/2 or FreeBSD or whatever other operating system you want to insert, given that it can be made to boot the given operating system without trashing the master boot record. BOOTPART is ideal for this; in fact, it may even describe the steps necessary to add OS/2 Boot Manager partitions. Still, you have to experiment at your own risk. If you have sections to add to this HOWTO, please mail them to Arkmen.

Reducing Training Time

Linux can provide technical managers with cost-effective, reliable training tools. Training on new applications is not always a budget item in many corporations. Usually, businesses are looking for cost-effective solutions, and finding training tools that are both cost-effective and reliable is not easy. This is especially true in a technical environment. To teach Unix and Web-based technology, Linux can provide technical managers with solutions to this dilemma.

NOTE
The following section is an adaptation of Charles Kitsuki's recommendations for training on Linux. A full version of his article can be found at www.ssc.com/lj/issue53/2615.html, or you can contact him via e-mail at kitsukic@pixi.com.

One alternative is to try to set up a Linux system for training. This section provides you with an example, implemented by Kitsuki, to establish a training system on a token-ring network.

Setting Up a Linux Training Environment on a Network

Convincing others of the benefit of using Linux as a training tool may not be a problem. After all, it's assumed you already convinced your corporation to use Linux already, didn't you? Nonetheless, this can be a problem if you are presenting your proposal to adopt or convert your system to Linux, as training represents another line item in the budget. Usually, corporations, especially small-medium businesses, are concerned about the system's maintenance and material costs. They are looking for a system that won't add substantial costs or bring additional work to other groups. Well, Linux meets both criteria.

For this example, consider the computer candidate for the Linux system as being a Compaq Pentium 166-MHz machine with 64MB of RAM. Add to it a 1.2GB drive and a 4x ATAPI Sony CD-ROM. Not a major investment at all! At the time of this writing, a similar computer may be purchased for less than $500.

Now, as a training system, multiple users will need access to this machine, so a LAN connection is required. The network here is token ring (but it could be anything, actually Ethernet–TCP/IP will probably be cheaper). You will need network cables and a spare IBM token ring PCI card for the connection.

After the hardware installation, the system is ready for software installation. Red Hat's Linux distribution is one of the best distributions today, which you can find on the CD-ROM that accompanies this book. Another distribution, the Slackware version of Linux 2.0, is very good. It provides many of the Unix features that systems administrators already use in its core systems. The first step of software installation involves creating boot and root diskettes. Slackware provides several different installation options, depending on the hardware. The bare.i and color.gz files on the Slackware installation CD-ROM are the optimal choice for your setup. Once these files are copied to a hard drive on another computer, the **rawrite** command included on the CD-ROM is used to create the boot and root diskettes.

The boot diskette initiates the target system, which begins loading a subset of the Linux operating system into memory. Next, the root diskette is loaded. This is enough to start the installation of the system.

The next step involves creating a native Linux partition on the hard drive, then loading the operating system. Slackware provides an easy way to do this with its setup process. This process is menu-driven, and it allows you to install a mixture of utilities. The setup in this environment includes the basic Linux system and X utilities.

After installing the software, configuring the system's start-up should be next. The start-up routine is set to load the kernel from the hard drive. At the time, no network configuration should take place, because Slackware requires you to recompile the kernel if you have a token-ring card.

At this point, the initial system should be tested by running some of the nonnetwork commands. After checking the system, the kernel is rebuilt for a token-ring network. Rebuilding the kernel so it recognizes an IBM token-ring card with a Tropic chip set is rather painless. This does require superuser access rights, however.

First, from the /usr/src/Linux directory, the **make config** command is run, starting a shell script that prompts the end user with questions to configure the operating system. The prompts usually default to the system's last kernel configuration. Following is the kernel modification for the token-ring card:

```
<<Token Ring driver support (CONFIG_TR) [N/y/?]-Y
  IBM Tropic chip set based adapter support
  (CONFIG_IBMTR) [N/y/m/?]-Y>>
```

No other commands need to be changed. Following the kernel configuration, the next four **make** commands must run for the system to recognize the changes:

```
make dep: make clean; make zImage; lilo
```

Briefly, these commands create the necessary dependencies, remove object files, create the kernel image, and allow the Linux loader to recognize the kernel. Creating the kernel image takes the most time. Depending on the machine, it could take as long as a couple of hours.

After the kernel is rebuilt, the file /etc/rc.d/rc.inet1 needs to be changed. This file loads all of the network addresses for the system. The Ethernet network setup is then modified to a token ring by changing eth0 in the **ifconfig** command to tr0:

```
/sbin/ifconfig eth0 ${IPADDR} broadcast\
${BROADCAST} netmask ${NETMASK}
```

The rc.inet file is set with the appropriate IP addresses. The host file /etc/hosts should be modified to provide an alias to some common systems. The entire system should be tested using the **ping** command and by running a few Telnet sessions.

Although the system includes many of the X utilities, you don't need to set it up to run the X-Window System. These utilities are accessible from Windows NT workstations with X emulators, such as PCXware. Most users usually run these utilities, since they are accessing this system using Telnet and browser sessions from their workstations when running Windows NT 4.0.

The next step involves configuring an Apache Web server for the Linux machine. You can obtain the server in a compressed format from the CD-ROM with this book. You can use the **uncompress** command to unpack the files in a directory called /usr/local/httpd. In the setup, end users are supposed to create and view their home pages.

For example, end users should be able to access the company's home page, called index.html. This requires a modification to the srm.conf file, which locates home pages and sets special parameters that affect servicing of end users. This file is located in the /var/lib/httpd/conf directory. You will change the value of UserDir from local_dir to the directory of the company's Web page.

In addition, the port number in the main server configuration file /var/lib/httpd/conf/httpd.conf needs to be changed from 80 to 82. The reason it needs to be changed is that another process uses port 80. Once the changes to the configuration files are done, the following command is activated in the /etc/rc.d/rc_httpd file:

```
/usr/sbin/httpd -f
```

This starts the Apache httpd server whenever the system is booted. Overall, the entire installation of the server should be straightforward and should not require much effort.

The final step of the installation involves creating processes that would make the system maintenance-free. The **cron** command provides the Linux user with this capability. The **cron** command runs backup and file-cleanup processes at specific times of the day. For the backup process, it runs a script that compresses and transfers essential files to another machine. Another process run by the **cron** command purges old log and trash files periodically. The two processes are somewhat maintenance-free. In order to create these scheduled jobs, the administrator must run the **crontab -e** routine from the root login, which provides a vi editor environment. Using this editor, the administrator can create a list of jobs for the **cron** command to run at specific times. For example, the administrator could create an entry to tell users to log off the system every day at 6:00 P.M. in order to do backups at this time.

For training purposes, you should load the system with C++ and Perl. Programmers can safely run C++ and Perl code without affecting the larger systems. The Linux system can host a group home page that links to users' Web sites. You can include tutorials on how to create Web pages and even have a link in the main page to an experimental Structured Query Language (SQL) database. It demonstrates to the user how to use HTML commands to connect and extract data from a SQL database.

CHAPTER 7

Subverting the Push
for New Technology

I t's all over the headlines! Linux is finding an ever increasing space in corporate networks everywhere. Already gaining the fame of being a very solid operating system, Linux is challenging the notion of *new technology* as the solution to run an entire IT department, with the paradox of using an inexpensive, powerful, easy to install system with nearly 30 years of API tuning, instead. In addition, this technically old operating system provides features that not only enable IT groups to run a huge range of obsolete hardware, but also serve as the solutions for business challenges of tomorrow, starting with its full Y2K compliance.

This chapter takes a look at what many call the Linux revolution on corporate networks. For many, Linux is hype; for many others, it is a Robin Hood solution, with all the passion of the gurus and devoted Linux users, who restlessly steal features from expensive systems and provide them free to everyone that needs or wants to use them. Linux is more than a subversion to the push for new technology, it is a romantic odyssey of IT groups moving from the cathedral model to the bazaar one.

Linux Is Quietly Replacing Servers

Linux is actually a powerful version of Unix, only that it's free, has modern features, a large range of programming and development tools, and runs seamlessly on obsolete hardware (and happily on new), with enough power to handle jobs such as Web and print server functions.

How many people are using Linux in at least some area of their organization? "If you go by the statistics the magazines are keeping, the range seems to run between 10 and 30 percent of the respondents," says Robert Young, president of Red Hat Software, a Linux company based in Research Triangle Park, North Carolina. Young says that the high number, about 34 percent, came from a survey of Linux users by a German magazine. He also noted that Linux use is growing. The surveys consistently show an increasing percentage of the respondents using Linux in some form. "The low numbers tend to be from earlier surveys," Young says.

Linux is especially popular in Eastern Europe and the republics of the former Soviet Union. It is also quite popular in Asia and other developing countries. From being a firewall to a Web server, Linux is, by some estimates, the second most common operating system on the net. Part of the standard Linux distribution package is the Apache Web server, one of the most popular servers available. Other Linux applications range from print servers to ftp servers to data collection. Linux has flown on the space shuttle and has logged data in Antarctica, among other jobs. As a desktop operating system, it is quite functional, especially to users already familiar with Unix.

Linux Everywhere?

Free Linux may be too revolutionary or amateur for the business mindset. This sort of slogan, more than an argument, does attract students, Unix hackers, and universities trying to keep a close watch on research budgets. But in the business world, when it comes to software, especially operating systems, *free* can represent a lot of money. Linux is a combination of power, stability, and features. This is the catch that attracts the enterprises.

Technically, Linux isn't Unix. It works like it, but it isn't. As discussed earlier, Linux is currently distributed under the GNU (which stands for Gnu's Not Unix) General Public License (GPL), which means, among other things, that the source must accompany software. A network of hundreds of volunteers around the world handles development and maintenance.

Among the items included in a typical full Linux distribution (Slackware, in this case) are the operating system; the X Free86 X-Windows package; NTeX; TeX; the GNU compilers for C, C++, Objective C, FORTRAN 77, Tcl, TclX, make, byacc, GNU Bison, flex, C libraries, GNU common LISP, TCP/IP networking, SLIP/PPP, IP accounting, firewalls, Java kernel support, BSD sendmail, cnews, nn, tin, trn, inn, fvwm95, GNU chess, and the Apache HTTP server; and the Arena and Lynx Web browsers.

Linux is designed for the low end of the Unix world. It runs, and runs well, in 4MB of memory on an Intel 386 processor—something not even Windows 3.1 could manage. A complete single-user installation with X-Windows and the software development tools really needs a 486 and takes more space, but it still fits nicely in 8 to 12MB of RAM and 40MB of disk space.

Within its limits, Linux is powerful. A Linux server can easily support between 100 and 300 users. There is also a fair amount of Linux software available. Although Linux tends to be weak in desktop productivity applications, it comes with a full set of development tools, mostly from the GNU project, and there are a fair number of programs available for servers, networks, and specialized functions such as statistical and scientific computing.

The combination of power, ease of installation, and free distribution makes Linux ideal for small jobs in a Unix shop. A knowledgeable Unix user can decide to set up a Web server in the morning and have it running that afternoon, without worrying about licensing or authorization for software purchase or anything else remotely bureaucratic.

Although Linux is free, it is recommended that you do as most people and pay for one vendor-backed distribution, such as Red Hat's, which is bundled with this book. In return, you get a complete package, usually on CD-ROM, easier installation, and some level of support. The cost of a Linux CD-ROM usually runs between $20 and $100, depending on the distribution. Typically, the buyer gets a month or two of telephone support, with more available at additional cost. Figure 7.1 is a screenshot of Red Hat's Web site.

Red Hat has established a system of support through third parties. Support providers sign on with Red Hat as Linux supporters and offer their services to the Linux public. What the support providers can't handle they can refer back to Red Hat.

The Linux development model produces a paradoxical situation. While formal support for Linux is nonexistent unless you buy it from a vendor, actual support for the OS tends to be quite strong. Linux has a large, active community of supporters, many of whom write drivers and other updates and make them freely available. This means that drivers for new hardware are likely to be available for Linux even before they are available for other versions of Unix, such as Solaris.

The same principle applies to security fixes. Linux's large network of volunteers tends to be very quick in producing patches. For example, when the Pentium II bug was discovered, Linux was one of the first operating systems to offer a solution to the problem.

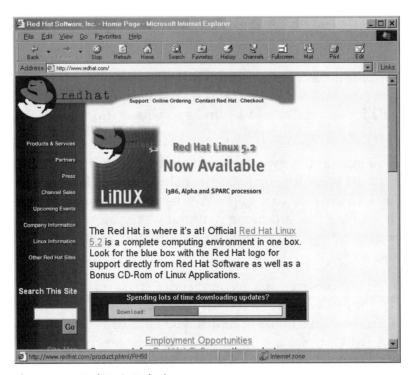

Figure 7.1   Red Hat's Web site.

Of course, this also means that support for Linux applications depends primarily on the interest and energy of the people who wrote them. If the application is popular, users through the Linux newsgroups will better support it.

There are a number of Usenet newsgroups to which Linux users go for help. The response time on the typical question there compares favorably with the e-mail support from a lot of vendors. Of course, this isn't as good as calling up a knowledgeable support person directly, but that kind of immediate support is hard to find anyway.

Overall, in support, Linux fares about as well, and about as badly, as most other Unix versions. Although Linux is easier to install and set up than, say, Solaris, it is not significantly easier to administer. Support comes mostly through the user community, via the Usenet newsgroups. There is an extensive collection of FAQs on such things as Linux installation, configuration, and troubleshooting. Much of this material has been published in book form by such publishers as Walnut Creek.

NOTE

Red Hat Linux is available by unrestricted FTP from Red Hat's site and many mirror sites on the Internet; however, companies and developers may charge money for Linux as long as the source code remains available. Red Hat Linux is available on CD-ROM for $49.95 in a boxed set that includes additional items that make up this price. The items included are installation documentation, installation support from Red Hat, Netscape Navigator, and hundreds of application packages.

Linux versus Other Operating Systems

There are tens of thousands of users of Red Hat's Linux operating system throughout the world. The current feature list of Linux is impressive. For example, it runs on a wider range of PC equipment than any other non-Microsoft OS. When you consider that Linux also runs on Digital Alpha computers, Sun Sparc, and now Apple PowerMac hardware, Linux has even Microsoft's OSs beat. In addition, it offers a reliable and stable multitasking/multithreading environment on all these platforms, with support for SMP (symmetric multiprocessing), along with hardware drivers for virtually all popular hardware. However, the factors that will ensure the long-term success of Linux have little to do with the current list of features, and much more with how it is licensed.

This solves problems such as occurred in the original Unix project. AT&T held the copyright to Unix and many groups including the University of California at Berkeley helped AT&T build it. When finished, AT&T was able to exercise its copyright to restrict everyone's use of the technology that had been cooperatively built.

Under the GPL, Linux's Linus Torvalds and others may hold copyrights but they have no more right to restrict the use of it than you or Red Hat does. This small burden of lack of restrictive control ensures that Linux and its related technologies will continue to evolve to the equal benefit of all of its users.

There is a lot of money being invested in Linux development. Commercial Linux companies such as Red Hat Software invest directly in Linux both via code that they write and contribute back under the GPL. Red Hat Software's role in Linux development relates to Linux developers being largely uninterested in ease-of-use features. If you have the skills to help write operating system code, you also have the skills to install and manage an OS without pull-down menus, dialog boxes, and configuration tools. Features that most people who might benefit from using an advanced operating system require using them productively.

By contributing valuable ease-of-use features to the Linux OS under the GPL, Red Hat makes the Linux OS useful for a greater number of computer users, thereby expanding the Linux community. In turn, Red Hat is able to make a living selling Linux CD-ROMs, books, and applications to this rapidly expanding Linux marketplace. But contributions from companies like Red Hat Software represent only a small part of the funds going into Linux development.

From supercomputing projects at NASA to software, the users fund the work in development at Empress Software for their own benefit. The fact that this work also benefits the larger Linux-using community is simply serendipitous in the true sense of that word.

The story of the Iomega Zip driver in Linux is another good example. Grant Guenther, the head developer at database-maker Empress Software, was encouraging the use of Linux as a development OS at Empress. It gave his development teammates access to low-cost workstations at work and at home.

When Empress chose Zip drives as a company standard for transferring data, Guenther found that they were not supported under Linux.

So, he had a choice. Abandon Linux and purchase significant numbers of licenses of expensive commercial alternatives that come without compilers or source code—both of which are valuable features of Linux to software developers—or spend some time researching and writing his own Zip driver for Linux. So he did. Guenther, as head of development for a commercial database company, had both the skills and training to do this work well. Having built it, he then posted it on the Internet asking for help in testing and improving. It quickly became part of the Linux OS for use by anyone who had an Iomega Zip drive.

Empress Software would have charged several thousand dollars for Guenther's services had it been approached professionally to write such a driver. Under the Linux/GNU model, the incentive was not direct cash but the indirect benefit he and Empress continues to receive from their use of Linux. Now, consider that Empress and Red Hat are only two of several thousand organizations that include literally all the major government research institutions. Add to it most universities and a majority of commercial research and software development teams, and you begin to get an idea that the remarkable breadth and quality of the Linux OS is no accident.

The huge amount of development effort behind Linux will result in this technology staying at or ahead of any commercial OS project you can name. An illustrative example is security. Because of the wide-open nature of Linux and its available sources, security issues are identified, debated, and repaired in real time. The problem is discussed openly, the patches are tested widely, and the problem is worked on until it's resolved to everyone's satisfaction. While this open discussion of security issues in Linux has occasionally confused users of traditional OS into thinking that Linux has security problems, the reverse is true: All OSs have security problems, Linux simply identifies and solves them faster.

If you try to figure out how companies such as Red Hat can succeed in competing with corporate giants such as Microsoft and IBM in the operating system business, you might think of people like Grant Guenther, developers from the University of Helsinki, the National Aeronautics and Space Administration (NASA), and all the college and commercial research teams around the world working on Linux. Suddenly the question becomes, "How is Microsoft going to compete with Linux?"

Linux in Business

Linux provides the ideal basis for a quick and dirty Unix solution to a specific problem. The cost is minimal, especially if you have an old Intel or Sparc box kicking around. There are enough development tools and utilities out there to let you do useful things with them.

Ironically, one of the most popular uses for Linux on Sparc is to update older Sun boxes that originally ran SunOS. The Sparc version of Linux will run on most early Sun workstations, including the IPX, 1+, Classic, and Sparcstation 5 and 10 boxes. For users who can't upgrade to Solaris, or for whom the upgrade is too expensive, Linux provides a good way to squeeze additional use out of older systems.

One of the reasons for Linux's success has been Sun's perceived lack of support for Solaris x86. In these days of Java-based computing, the product is no longer key to Sun's strategy for the desktop, and users have been complaining for years about Sun's apparent lack of interest in them.

One of the biggest drawbacks to Linux in business is old-fashioned FUD—fear, uncertainty, and doubt generated by the Linux freely distributable model. To a lot of people *freely distributable* equates with *unsupported* and *hobby quality.* In fact, Linux is neither. Using it does, however, require adapting to a different way of managing software. Getting the most out of Linux requires staying in touch with the Linux community to find out about such things as upgrades and patches and using the Internet newsgroups as a major support tool. Long-time Unix users tend to be more comfortable with this model than management, so it usually takes a major selling job to get Linux accepted as an important part of the enterprise.

Software Supporting Linux

Linux has GCC, Emacs, X-Windows, all the standard Unix utilities, TCP/IP (including SLIP and PPP), and all the hundreds of programs that people have compiled or ported for it.

You can download a DOS emulator from tsx-11.mit.edu/pub/linux/ALPHA/dosemu, which will enable you to run DOS itself and some, not all, DOS applications. Be sure to look at the README file to determine which version of dosemu you should get. Also, you might find it worth it to check the DOSEMU-HOWTO, which is located at sunsite.unc.edu/pub/Linux/docs/HOWTO.

Work has been progressing on an emulator for Microsoft Windows binaries, known as WINE. iBCS2 (Intel Binary Compatibility Standard) emulator code for SVR4 ELF and SVR3.2 COFF binaries can be included in the kernel as a compile-time option. Some companies have commercial software available, including Motif.

Furthermore, you can get Linux materials by FTP as well. There are three main archive sites for Linux:

- ftp.funet.fi(Finland, 128.214.6.100) : /pub/OS/Linux
- sunsite.unc.edu(US, 152.2.22.81) : /pub/Linux
- tsx-11.mit.edu(US, 18.172.1.2) : /pub/linux

The best place to get the Linux kernel is ftp.cs.helsinki.fi/pub/Linux_ Kernel. Linus Torvalds uploads the most recent kernel versions to this site. The Debian distribution is available at ftp.debian.org/pub/debian, and the Red Hat distribution at ftp.redhat.com.

The contents of these sites are mirrored (copied, usually approximately daily) by a number of other sites. Using a site closer to you will enhance the speed of file transfers:

- ftp.sun.ac.za/pub/linux/sunsite/ (South Africa)
- ftp.is.co.za/linux/sunsite/ (South Africa)
- ftp.cs.cuhk.hk/pub/Linux/ (Hong Kong)
- ftp.cs.cuhk.hk/pub/Linux/ (Hong Kong)
- ftp.spin.ad.jp/pub/linux/sunsite.unc.edu/ (Japan)
- ftp.nuri.net/pub/Linux/ (Korea)
- ftp.jaring.my/pub/Linux/ (Malaysia)
- ftp.nus.sg/pub/unix/Linux/ (Singapore)
- ftp.nectec.or.th/pub/mirrors/linux/ (Thailand)
- ftp.dstc.edu.au/pub/linux/ (Australia)
- sunsite.anu.edu.au/pub/linux/ (Australia)
- ftp.monash.edu.au/pub/linux/ (Australia)
- ftp.sydutech.usyd.edu.au/pub/linux/ (Australia)
- ftp.univie.ac.at/systems/linux/sunsite/ (Austria)
- ftp.fi.muni.cz/pub/UNIX/linux/ (Czech Republic)
- ftp.funet.fi/pub/Linux/sunsite/ (Finland)

- ftp.univ-angers.fr/pub/Linux/ (France)
- ftp.iut-bm.univ-fcomte.fr (France)
- ftp.ibp.fr/pub/linux/sunsite/ (France)
- ftp.loria.fr/pub/linux/sunsite/ (France)
- ftp.dfv.rwth-aachen.de/pub/linux/sunsite/ (Germany)
- ftp.germany.eu.net/pub/os/Linux/Mirror.SunSITE/ (Germany)
- ftp.tu-dresden.de/pub/Linux/sunsite/ (Germany)
- ftp.uni-erlangen.de/pub/Linux/MIRROR.sunsite/ (Germany)
- ftp.gwdg.de/pub/linux/mirrors/sunsite/ (Germany)
- ftp.rz.uni-karlsruhe.de/pub/linux/mirror.sunsite/ (Germany)
- ftp.ba-mannheim.de/pub/linux/mirror.sunsite/ (Germany)
- ftp.uni-paderborn.de/pub/Mirrors/sunsite.unc.edu/ (Germany)
- ftp.uni-rostock.de/Linux/sunsite/ (Germany)
- tp.rus.uni-stuttgart.de/pub/unix/systems/linux/MIRROR .sunsite/ (Germany)
- ftp.uni-tuebingen.de/pub/linux/Mirror.sunsite/ (Germany)
- ftp.rz.uni-ulm.de/pub/mirrors/linux/sunsite/ (Germany)
- ftp.kfki.hu/pub/linux/ (Hungary)
- linux.italnet.it/pub/Linux/ (Italy)
- ftp.unina.it/pub/linux/sunsite/ (Italy)
- giotto.unipd.it/pub/unix/Linux/ (Italy)
- cnuce-arch.cnr.it/pub/Linux/ (Italy)
- ftp.flashnet.it/mirror2/sunsite.unc.edu/ (Italy)
- ftp.nijenrode.nl/pub/linux/sunsite.unc-mirror/ (Netherlands)
- ftp.LeidenUniv.nl/pub/linux/sunsite/ (Netherlands)
- ftp.nvg.unit.no/pub/linux/sunsite/ (Norway)
- ftp://sunsite.icm.edu.pl/pub/Linux/sunsite.unc.edu/ (Poland)
- ftp.rediris.es/software/os/linux/sunsite/ (Spain)
- sunsite.rediris.es/software/linux/ (Spain)
- ftp.cs.us.es/pub/Linux/sunsite-mirror/ (Spain)
- ftp.etse.urv.es/pub/mirror/linux/ (Spain)
- ftp.etsimo.uniovi.es/pub/linux/ (Spain)

- ftp.luna.gui.es/pub/linux.new/ (Spain)

- ftp.switch.ch/mirror/linux/ (Switzerland)

- ftp.metu.edu.tr/pub/linux/sunsite/ (Turkey)

- unix.hensa.ac.uk/mirrors/sunsite/pub/Linux/ (United Kingdom)

- ftp.maths.warwick.ac.uk/mirrors/linux/sunsite.unc-mirror/ (United Kingdom)

- ftp.idiscover.co.uk/pub/Linux/sunsite.unc-mirror/ (United Kingdom)

- sunsite.doc.ic.ac.uk/packages/linux/sunsite.unc-mirror/ (United Kingdom)

- ftp.dungeon.com/pub/linux/sunsite-mirror/ (United Kingdom)

- ftp.io.org/pub/mirrors/linux/sunsite/ (Canada)

- ftp.cc.gatech.edu/pub/linux/ (United States)

- ftp.cdrom.com/pub/linux/sunsite/ (United States)

- ftp.siriuscc.com/pub/Linux/Sunsite/ (United States)

- ftp.engr.uark.edu/pub/linux/sunsite/ (United States)

- ftp.infomagic.com/pub/mirrors/linux/sunsite/ (United States)

- linux.if.usp.br/pub/mirror/sunsite.unc.edu/pub/Linux/ (Brazil)

- farofa.ime.usp.br/pub/linux/ (Brazil)

Hardware Supporting Linux

In order to run Linux for your business you need at least a 386, 486, or 586 (Pentium) Intel boc, with at least 2MB of RAM and a single floppy drive to install Linux. To do anything useful, more RAM (4MB to install most distributions, and 8MB is highly recommended for running X) and a hard disk are required. Linux also supports the VESA local bus and PCI. IBM's microchannel architecture (MCA) proprietary bus and ESDI hard drives are mostly supported.

TIP

Have the HOWTOs and a lot of Linux documentation handy when trying out the product. This is one of Linux's major strengths (documentation), so take advantage of it. Try downloading them via FTP from ftp://ftp.funet.fi/pub/OS/Linux/doc/ HOWTO, ftp://tsx-11.mit.edu/pub/linux/docs/HOWTO, and ftp://sunsite.unc.edu/ pub/Linux/docs/HOWTO.

Essentially, Linux does not take up much disk space. About 10MB for a very minimal installation is suitable for trying it out and not much else. If you want to try a more complete setup, you can squeeze a more complete installation including X-Windows into 80MB. However, installing almost all of Debian 0.93R6 can take up to 500MB, including some space for user files and spool areas.

For additional information on MCA bus and which cards Linux supports, check the Micro Channel Linux Web page, at http://glycerine.itsmm.uni.edu/mca.

Linux also runs on 386 family–based laptops, with X on most of them. There is a relevant Web page at www.cs.utexas.edu/users/kharker/linux-laptop/ that can provide you with a lot of information on using Linux on laptops and notebooks. But Linux will never run fully on an 8086 or '286 because it requires task-switching and memory management facilities not found on these processors.

You can also use Linux for embedded systems by relying on the Embeddable Linux Kernel Subset (ELKS). This is a 16-bit subset of the Linux kernel, which will mainly be used for embedded systems.

For more information on Linux for embedded environments, check www.linux.org .uk/Linux8086.html.

Accessing Other Filesystems

If you don't want to migrate to Linux right away, you can share it with another operating system, such as DOS, OS/2, 386BSDx, Windows 95/98, and Windows NT, on a single hard drive. Linux uses the standard MS-DOS partitioning scheme, so it can share your disk with other operating systems. However, beware that many of these other operating systems are rather fussy.

Accessing DOS

DOS's FDISK.EXE and FORMAT.EXE, for example, can sometimes overwrite data in a Linux partition because they sometimes incorrectly use partition data from the partition's bootsector rather than the partition table. In order to prevent programs like these from doing this, it is a good idea to zero out—under Linux—the start of a partition you created, before you use MS-DOS, or whatever, to format it. Type the following:

```
$ dd if=/dev/zero of=/dev/hdXY bs=512 count=1
```

where hdXY is the relevant partition; for example, use hda1 for the first partition of the first (IDE) disk.

Linux can read and write the files on your DOS and OS/2 FAT partitions and floppies using either the DOS filesystem type built into the kernel or mtools. There is kernel support for the VFAT filesystem used by Windows 95 and Windows NT.

To access files on a DOS partition or floppy, use the DOS filesystem. For example, type the following:

```
$ mkdir /dos
$ mount -t msdos -o conv=text,umask=022,uid=100,gid=100 /dev/hda3
/dos
```

If it's a floppy, don't forget to unmount it before ejecting it. You can use the conv=text/binary/auto, umask=nnn, uid=nnn, and gid=nnn options to control the automatic line-ending conversion, permissions, and ownerships of the files in the DOS filesystem as they appear under Linux. If you mount your DOS filesystem by putting it in your /etc/fstab, you can record the options (comma-separated) there, instead of defaults.

Accessing High Performance File System (HPFS)

Linux access to HPFS partitions is read-only. HPFS filesystem access is available as an option when compiling the kernel or as a module. You can mount HPFS partition, using, for example, the following:

```
$ mkdir /hpfs
$ mount -t hpfs /dev/hda5 /hpfs
```

Accessing Amiga Fast File System

The Linux kernel has support for the Amiga Fast File System (AFFS) version 1.3 and later, both as a compile-time option and as a module. The file Documentation/filesystems/affs.txt in the Linux kernel source distribution has more information. Linux supports AFFS hard-drive partitions only, though: Floppy access is not supported due to incompatibilities between Amiga floppy controllers and PC and workstation controllers. The AFFS driver can also mount disk partitions used by the Un*x Amiga Emulator by Bernd Schmidt.

Accessing Unix File System (UFS)

Recent Linux kernels can also mount (read-only) the UFS filesystem used by System V; Coherent; Xenix; BSD and derivatives such as

SunOS, FreeBSD, NetBSD, and NeXTstep. UFS support is available as a kernel compile-time option and a module.

Accessing SMB and Mac Filesystems

Linux supports read-write access of Word for Windows and Windows NT SMB volumes. There is also a suite of programs called Samba that provide support for Word for Windows networked filesystems (provided they're for TCP/IP). Information is available in the README file at sunsite.unc.edu/pub/Linux/system/network/samba.

For more information about Samba, there is an SMB Web site at samba.canberra.edu.au/pub/samba.

There is a set of user-level programs that read and write the Macintosh Hierarchical File System (HFS). It is available at sunsite.unc.edu/pub/Linux/utils/disk-management.

Running Windows Programs under Linux

There is a project, known as WINE, to build an MS Windows emulator for Linux, but it is still not ready for general distribution. The existing version works, for the most part, but performance is still very poor and it's not bullet-proof yet. If you want to contribute to its development, look for the status reports in the comp.emulators.ms-windows.wine newsgroup.

There is an FAQ about WINE, compiled by P. David Gardner, at sunsite.unc.edu/pub/Linux/docs/faqs/Wine-FAQ/ which is worth checking it out.

If you need to run MS Windows programs, the best alternative is to reboot. **LILO,** the Linux boot loader, can boot one of several operating systems from a menu.

Newsgroups Supporting Linux

There are ten international Usenet newsgroups devoted to Linux:

- comp.os.linux.announce is the moderated announcements group; you should read this if you intend to use Linux. Submissions for that group should be e-mailed to linux-announce@news.ornl.gov.

- comp.os.linux.answers contains all the FAQs, HOWTOs, and other important documentation. You should subscribe to this, too.

Also worth reading are the other groups in the comp.os.linux.* hierarchy—you may find that many common problems are too recent to find in this FAQ but are answered in the newsgroups. These groups are as follows:

- comp.os.linux.setup
- comp.os.linux.hardware
- comp.os.linux.networking
- comp.os.linux.x
- comp.os.linux.development.apps
- comp.os.linux.development.system
- comp.os.linux.advocacy
- comp.os.linux.misc

Remember that since Linux is a Unix clone, most all of the material in comp.unix.* and comp.windows.x.* groups will be relevant. Apart from hardware considerations, and some obscure or very technical low-level issues, you'll find that these groups are the right place to start.

Why Linux Is Not Ready for Prime Time

Linux has a couple important drawbacks in the corporate world. The first is that it is not an enterprisewide operating system. For example, it doesn't have good support for multiprocessing (although this is being worked on and may be available soon). Further, Linux is optimized for the low end of the Unix spectrum—x86s, older Sparcs, and the like. This isn't so much a policy decision as it is the result of the way Linux is designed and maintained. The people who work on Linux generally don't have much interest in, or access to, enterprise server hardware.

Similarly, while there are some system management tools available for Linux to do such jobs as remote management, the selection and functionality of these tools is limited compared to, say, Solaris. Linux has a good selection of systems administration tools, but that's not the same thing.

At the very low end, the desktop, Linux has some problems as well. Although easy to install, Linux is not intended for complete novices. The entire structure of Linux, from the distribution to the documentation, assumes some knowledge of computers in general and Unix in particular. An experienced user will probably find a Linux desktop a powerful tool but a novice is likely to be baffled without a resident expert.

Software is another consideration. Although there is a fair amount of it, not much falls in the desktop productivity category. There are programming tools galore and a lot of sophisticated applications for scientific, statistical, and engineering use. But such things as word processors and spreadsheets are thin on the ground.

Linux isn't Solaris, and it won't scale across the entire enterprise. But it is a good, cost-effective implementation of Unix. The combination of very low price and the ability to run on less-advanced platforms gives commercial Linux an important and growing niche in the Unix market—even in Sun shops.

CHAPTER 8

Linux versus Windows NT

This chapter discusses Linux in comparison to NT 4.0. It's aimed at NT professionals who question considering Linux as an alternative if, for the most part, Linux meets their needs. Actually, it seems that both operating systems have their own niches and clientele. Linux does not compete with Windows NT. Thus, in the near future, NT and Linux (instead of just Linux) may run side-by-side in corporate networks, each fulfilling their own roles and missions. But, this is another story, worth another book!

Before reviewing NT and Linux portability to each other, look under the hood of these two operating systems. This chapter attempts to do this from the Linux point of view and relates the concepts of NT to corresponding ones found in Linux. Certainly, your business environment needs OSs with both NT and Linux characteristics, and the way you apply and use these systems will definitely define how successful your business will be in this new information age.

Linux and NT: Aside from the Halloween Document

Microsoft's Windows NT is still relatively new. However, it has roots that go back almost as far as those of Linux and Unix. Windows NT is an operating system that, as do many other operating systems, owes a lot to Unix.

Nonetheless, although NT and Linux address the same world, they do so with very different points of view. Thus, if you are one of those that think Linux provides a direct, feature-for-feature replacement for Windows NT, this chapter is for you. They seem to complete each other (not that one complements the other or vice-versa). How? Look at some of their characteristics.

A Little Bit of History on Windows NT

Not so long ago, talking about general-purpose minicomputer operating systems, undoubtedly Digital Equipment Corporation (Digital) would definitely come to mind. Back in 1988, Dave Scott joined Microsoft to lead the development effort for the new high-end operating system in the Microsoft Windows family, Windows NT. Two primary forces shaped this project:

1. **Market requirements.** As market requirements, NT would have to provide the following:
   - Transparent support for single-processor and multiprocessor computers
   - Support for distributed computing
   - Standards compliance, such as POSIX
2. **Sound design.** The design goals came from leading-edge thinking in operating system theory and design.

What Is in the Name: NT versus Linux

The following is a brief overview of the main components of both NT and Linux and how they measure up to each other. As you will realize, both have different strengths and approaches when supporting information technology (IT) needs.

Operating System Fundamentals

From the start, there is a major difference between these two operating systems. NT was designed for client/server computing, as opposed to Linux, which was designed for host-based terminal computing. Thus, NT should not be literally classified as a multiuser operating system, although it can become one by adding third-party products.

With NT, you do not have users with limited-function dumb terminals, dumb terminal emulators, or X-terminals connecting to an NT-based host. Instead, NT enables you to have users on single-user, general-purpose workstations connecting to multiuser, general-purpose servers with the processing load shared between both. Although you may not find this difference so distinct, it is very important for you to understand it so you can really understand how NT works.

The Kernel and User Mode

In modern operating systems, applications are kept separate from the operating system itself. The operating system code runs in a privileged processor mode known as *kernel mode* and has access to system data and hardware. Applications run in a nonprivileged processor mode known as *user mode* and have limited access to system data and hardware through a set of tightly controlled application programming interfaces (APIs).

NT is an OS based on a microkernel, sharing similarities to Mach, a microkernel-based operating system developed at Carnegie Mellon University. One of the primary design goals of NT was to keep the base operating system as small and as tight as possible. Thus, the protected subsystems provide the traditional operating system support to applications through a feature-rich set of APIs.

This design makes NT a very stable operating system. In addition, NT's design was influenced by many other models, which provide a framework for understanding the inner workings of NT. The most important ones are as follows:

The client/server model.   You probably agree that NT is excellent for the world of client/server computing. In NT, all the applications that a user runs are clients that request services from the protected subsystems, which are servers. The client/server approach results in a modular operating system. The servers are small and self-contained, each running in its own protected, user-mode process, which enables a server to fail without taking down the rest of the operating system with it. Further, this self-contained nature of the operating system components also makes it possible to distribute them across multiple processors on a single computer (symmetric multiprocessing) or even multiple computers on a network (distributed computing).

The object-oriented model.   NT is not exactly an object-oriented system but it does use objects to represent internal system resources. The client requests and the server responds, and oftentimes in the course of conversation the client and server roles alternate between objects.

One of Linux's powerful tools is the file metaphor. NT takes advantage on this metaphor and expands it by using an object metaphor that is pervasive throughout the architecture of the system. NT not only sees all of the components in the Linux file metaphor as objects, but it also sees processes and threads, shared memory segments, and access rights as well.

The symmetric multiprocessing model.   Multiprocessing operating systems such as NT can be either asymmetric or symmetric. The remainder of the processors runs user applications. SMP systems provide better load balancing and fault tolerance. SMP systems, such as NT and many flavors of Linux, are inherently more complex than ASMP ones.

Open Systems and Industry Standard

NT's executive is the kernel-mode portion of NT and, except for a user interface, is a complete operating system unto itself. It differs dramatically in architecture from the Linux kernel, especially since unlike the Linux kernel, the NT executive is never modified and recompiled by the systems administrator.

NT's Process Manager

A *process* is the dynamic invocation of a program along with the system resources needed for the program to run. NT's process differs from Linux's in that it is not an executable entity. NT's process usually contains one or more executable entities known as *threads,* and it is these threads and not the process that the kernel schedules for execution.

The process model for NT works in conjunction with the security model and the Virtual Memory Manager to provide interprocess protection. The Process Manager is the NT-based component that manages the creation and deletion of processes. For example, the parent/child relationship that exists between Linux processes is implemented in the POSIX protected–subsystem of NT.

Virtual Memory Manager

Linux and NT implement 32-bit linear memory addressing and demand-paged virtual memory management. The Virtual Memory Manager maps virtual addresses in the address space of the process to physical pages in the computer's memory. NT and many Linux systems share a common page size of 4K. NT Virtual Memory Manager uses a paging policy known as local first in, first out (FIFO) replacement. When physical memory runs low, the Virtual Memory Manager uses a technique called *automatic working-set trimming* to increase the amount of free memory in the system.

Security Reference Monitor

The Security Reference Monitor, in conjunction with the logon process protected–subsystem and the security protected–subsystem, forms the security model for NT. For a system to be secure, applications must have proper authorization before being allowed to access any system resources. NT's security-model components enforce this policy. These security components provide run-time services to both kernel-mode and user-mode components for validating access to objects, checking for user privileges, and generating audit messages. As with other components in the NT executive, the Security Reference runs exclusively in kernel-mode.

Protected Environment Subsystem

The protected subsystems are user-mode servers that are started when NT is booted. NT 4.0 ships with three environment subsystems:

The Win32 subsystem.   This is the native-mode subsystem of NT, being also the most critical of subsystems. Win32 provides the graphical user interface (GUI) and controls all user input and application output. Win32 is also responsible for determining when the user runs an application that is foreign to the subsystem, defining the application type and either calling another subsystem to run the application or creating an environment for DOS or 16-bit Windows in which to run the application.

The POSIX subsystem.   The Portable Operating System Interface for Linux (POSIX) is a clear, consistent, and unambiguous set of standards developed by the IEEE. Don't underestimate POSIX, as it is not limited to the Linux environment, extending to other platforms such as NT, VMS, MPE/iX, and CTOS.

The OS/2 subsystem. This subsystem supports 16-bit graphical and character-based applications. It provides these applications with an execution environment that looks and acts like a native OS/2 system. Internally, the OS/2 subsystem calls the NT executive to do most of the work, as the Windows NT executive services provide general-purpose mechanisms for doing most operating system tasks.

Domains and Trust Relationships

NT domain should not be confused with a Linux (Unix) domain. In Linux, a *domain* refers to how a particular computer is named on a TCP/IP internetwork, but with NT, a *domain* is a group of servers running NT Server that share common security policy and user account databases. NT has on a domain its basic unit of security and centralized administration.

User Interface and Environment

NT uses a graphical user interface, enhanced in NT 4.0, that closely models a traditional office. The transition from the NT graphical user interface to Linux's command line does require some adjustment for an NT user.

Similarly, with Linux, if you wanted to be a successful systems administrator, you had to know which flat file to edit for any given configuration change. But with NT, configuration information is centrally stored in the registry. Thus, unlike in Linux, with NT you have to know which tool to run. This feature makes the process much easier than searching the entire filesystem for an obscure configuration file with equally obscure configuration entries.

Providing Multiuser Support

Unlike Linux, NT is not exactly a multiuser operating system. With NT, users are capable of connecting to other users' computers, and those to servers and vice versa: It's a peer-to-peer setting. Thus, the relationship between users and clients is one to one; the relationship between clients and servers is many to many. So, in a way, a server is multiuser, it is just that the users are client computers, not people.

Linux Tools for NT

There are several Linux and Unix tools for NT available both commercially and through the public domain that enables NT and Linux (or Unix) to coexist. Following are a few examples:

MKS Toolkit for NT.   The MKS Toolkit from Mortice Kern Systems provides a complete Linux-like user environment, including **ksh**, **vi**, **awk**, and 190 additional utilities and programming tools.

Hamilton C shell for NT.   There are two additional packages with Linux-like environment features. This product from Pearl Software Corporation is an example of a single Linux utility that has been ported to Windows.

Public Domain

- **Linux GUI.**   Examples are Motif and OpenLook, which run on top of X.
- **X servers.**   This can be either dedicated devices, as in the case of X-terminals, or general-purpose workstations running X server software, such as Network File Systems (NFS), which was originally developed by Sun Microsystems. But there are two other common ones: the Andrew File System (AFS) and Remote File Sharing (RFS).

Windows NT to Linux Conversion Tools

NTCRACKER from DataFocus is an example of such a tool, which provides a comprehensive Linux development environment on top of NT. It enables X-based Linux applications to be ported to NT.

NTCRACKER makes NT look like a normal Linux development environment. Existing Linux application source code can be recompiled and run, often without modification. New Linux applications can also be developed using standard Linux tools such as **vi, cc,** and **make**. Additionally, it remains structured exactly like native Linux and can be thought of as real Linux running on NT.

The Need for Porting Windows-Based Applications to Linux

If you are on Linux and need a word processor, typically you either buy a spare PC with a word processor or pay big bucks for a Linux-version one. Worse, your investment on this Linux-based application is restricted to that particular Linux system. You cannot change over to another Linux system.

Unfortunately, most software vendors for Windows-based applications do not readily port their applications to Linux systems because of the huge differences between Windows and the other systems.

The Solution: Writing to Windows APIs

The Windows Interface Source Environment (WISE) is a licensing program from Microsoft to enable customers to integrate Windows-based solutions with Linux/Unix (and Macintosh) systems. Insignia Solutions, for example, using WISE, provides a product that enables shrink-wrapped Windows-based applications to run not only on Macintoshes, but also on non-Intel-based Linux systems. Another company, Locus, provides a product that enables shrink-wrapped Windows-based applications to run on Intel-based Linux systems.

The WISE software development kits (SDKs) enable developers to write to Windows APIs and use the resulting applications on various Linux systems. To get a Windows-based application running on a Linux system using a WISE SDK, the application *source code* must be recompiled on those systems.

Also, you have what are called WISE *emulators,* which enable users to run shrink-wrapped Windows-based applications unmodified on Linux (and Macintosh) systems. WISE emulators make over ten thousand off-the-shelf Windows-based applications available to users on Linux and Macintosh systems and can increase the users' productivity. WISE emulators run *binaries* of Windows-based applications on Linux systems and therefore do not require the source code of applications to be recompiled.

Benefiting from WISE

If you have a fair amount of Unix-based users, you can use WISE to ease the coexistence of Windows NT and Unix (WINE does the same for Linux) and efficiently manage the systems in your organization.

By taking advantage of the emulation capabilities of products based on WISE technology, you can provide maximum compatibility with the many thousands of shrink-wrapped Windows-based applications on the market right at your Unix environment. WISE emulators create a PC-like environment atop Unix systems, on a variety of microprocessor architectures. Your users, who need to utilize existing Unix solutions, can now concurrently use company-standard, Windows-based applications to simplify their jobs. For example, these users can extract data from a back-end Linux system accounting package and analyze the data with familiar Windows productivity tools. Since the Windows APIs are universally available and consistent, you will be able to spend much less money on training, development, testing, and support of applications.

Microsoft has committed to providing WISE licensees with future versions of Windows-family source code, thereby continuing to maximize application compatibility and performance for today's and tomorrow's applications. An open system must facilitate *compatibility* among the products of several vendors. Software systems compatible at the source level permit applications to be recompiled and run natively on a variety of platforms. Software systems compatible at a binary level can run out-of-the-box applications on other hardware platforms, reducing client/server migration costs.

NT versus Linux: A Matter of Security

When discussing NT and Linux, it is important to take into consideration their security systems over TCP/IP networked environments. Obviously, this section does not discuss all the security implications of both OSs. However, it does cover at least the aspects of client/server logon and network resource security. Unfortunately, due to extensibility, the security concerns of Inter-Process Communications (IPC) mechanisms such as Remote Procedure Calls (RPCs), Mailslot File System (MSFS), Named Pipe File System (NPFS), and Network Dynamic Data Exchange (NetDDE), which are also very important to consider, but out of the scope of this book, are not discussed.

Controlling the network security of a computer system is similar to controlling physical access to a building. When auditing a computer system for security, each service must be viewed as an open door, each using a different security mechanism. The administrator must *know what services are present* on a system. Both the Linux and the NT operating systems are insecure as shipped; it takes an investment of time and energy to understand and secure these operating systems. Metaphorically, an operating system can be built like a fort, but delivered with unlocked and hidden basement windows.

Auditing Network Services

No matter how integrated your user security is, both NT and Linux included, it only will be effective as long as it remains in the internal realm. It's like discussing the C2 credentials of NT: Once networked, you lose it! As soon as networking services are involved in your scope of work, you now have session identifications to worry about, which are typically mapped by server services to internal user IDs. When this happens, you must control what network services are running in your system.

Watch Network Services

If you are responsible for the security of a Unix system, your goal is to keep track of two files and a utility:

- The file *inetd.conf*, which controls available network services and applications
- The file *services*, which lists the network port numbers that these services use
- The utility *netstat -a*, which lists all running network services on system

If you are able to know all the security strengths and weaknesses of each of the services listed, as well as the port numbers from which these services can be accessed, and the given access to the control files, you are in a very good position of gaining control over the network security of your Linux system.

With NT, the requirements are a bit different, as you don't have a single location where all the network ports served are listed. Network services, which in NT are known as *objects*, are located throughout the registry, which is stored as four types of system data:

- The system
- The hardware
- The software
- The security

You will find these hives stored as files in the machine's local drive, under the \winnt\system32\control directory.

NT's Filesystem Security: Relying on SMB

You need to secure the filesystem to prevent unauthorized access to information residing in your system. Unfortunately, the filesystem security mechanism implemented by NT is not so secure.

As discussed earlier in this book, NT uses access control lists (ACL) to protect files internally, using plaintext user identifications (UIDs) during transmission, which are associated with the internal access token. The Server Message Block (SMB) file-sharing protocol security mechanism is used to protect network file access. The username and domain information are transmitted using plaintext SMB requests to the server, and the password is encrypted through weak SMB 8-bit encryption. The authentication is accomplished via user-level security, which differs from older share-level ones in that each user is required to have a password, versus one password for that share.

Tokens and encrypted session data are not passed across the network, instead user UIDs are passed via SMB requests/responses. The security objects used for accessing network resources are as follows:

- Security Reference Monitor
- SMB requests
- Server service

Therefore, when a user attempts to connect to a network service via *net use* command, File Manager, or Explorer, the following take place:

- An open resource connection request is passed to the Network Redirector.
- The Redirector uses the Security Reference Monitor and LsaLogin-User to resolve the user's access token to user credentials (username, password, domain).
- The Redirector then creates a SessionSetup SMB request to pass the user's credentials to the user-specified server.
- The server service passes the user credentials to LsaLoginUser and requests a token.

- The LsaLoginUser process encrypts the user/password/domain into LAN Manager and NT OWF password formats.

- LsaLoginUser authenticates the user by calling MSV1_0.

MSV1_0 calls the SAM database, gets the user account name and SID, compares the OWF password to the stored OWF password, and gets all global SIDs of that user. LsaLoginUser then searches its local policy database for user rights associated with all account, group, and local SIDs. LsaLoginUser then creates an access token containing the user rights mask and all SIDs. This access token is then passed to the server service.

The server service saves the token in its user session list and saves a reference to the share name. NT provides a network security system using previously attached network services. This network security mechanism is less secure than the network service attachment process. Whereas username/password/domain information is required during the attachment process, only a UID is required to browse files on an existing share. The server uses this UID to find the correct user token. An NT network security connecting to a new share on a previously attached server enables a client Redirector to note there is a user session with a UID already established to the server.

Linux's Filesystem Security: Relying on NFS

For the same reasons as with NT, you want to secure your filesystem to prevent unauthorized access to information on your network with Linux.

The Linux Network File System (NFS) currently uses AUTH_DES authentication. AUTH_Linux server authentication implicitly trusts the UIDs and GIDs presented by a client system; the client can emulate any user except UID 0, which is root. A superuser on a client has no special NFS access rights on a server. However, only files owned by root on the NFS server are protected. Thus, for a user to login, the following must occur:

- The login program on the client gets the user's NIS record from the public key database.

- The client resolves the NIS record (netname, user's public key, user's secret key) and uses the user's login password to decrypt the secret key, which is stored in memory by the keyserver process.

- The client uses the user's secret key and server's public key to generate a session key.

- The server uses the user's public key and the server's private key to generate a session key.

- The client then creates a random 56-bit conversation key, encrypted with the session key, and sends that to the server.

PART THREE

References and Resources for Linux

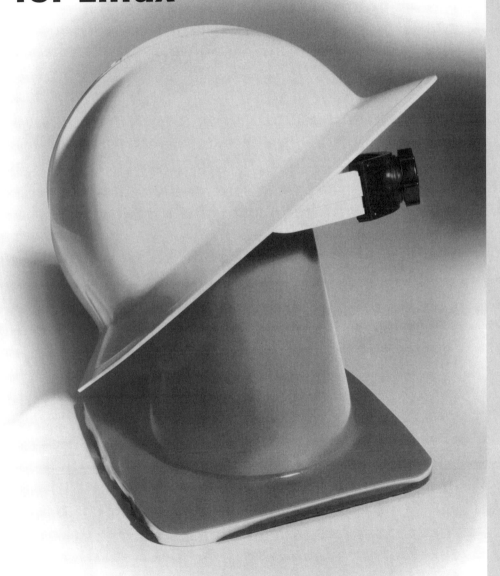

CHAPTER 9

Why Does Microsoft Need Linux?

From his Linux manifesto, Linux Torvalds says, "If Microsoft wanted to, they could take Linux tomorrow, start development on it, and do it completely on their own. There's nothing to stop anybody from doing that. However, they are required to make all the changes available to everybody else. This 'no ownership' idea means that the only entity that can really succeed in developing Linux is the entity that is trusted to do the right thing." You can find Linux Torvalds's Linux manifesto at www.bootnet.com/youaskedforit/lip_linux_manifesto.html.

NOTE
This section is based on an article written by Brett Lamb and Ken Creten from PSW Technologies in the Pacific Northwest. You can e-mail Brett Lamb at Brettandken@ hotmail.com.

Linux has grown into a viable operating system through a level of scientificlike cooperation previously unknown to the software industry. This cooperation is the main benefit of a movement called open source software. The development power of the open source movement parallels the growth in popularity of the Internet, while traditional models for software development are dependent on financial resources.

Even as the largest software vendor, Microsoft does not have the resources to create software that competes effectively with many open source products. The biggest potential threat to Microsoft from an open source project is unquestionably Linux. Microsoft's efforts at dominating the enterprise arena with Windows NT have met with resistance from dissatisfied IT managers who find solutions with Linux. This increased competition from Linux requires a dramatic shift in Microsoft's enterprise strategy to maintain market share. Since Windows NT cannot currently compete with Linux on technological grounds, and Microsoft cannot hope to out-develop this open source project with traditional methods, Microsoft has no choice but to recognize Linux as a serious threat unless it finds a way to harness the power of the open source development cycle.

The General Public License (GPL), under which Linux is published, allows for anyone, including Microsoft, to make changes to the software and redistribute it, as long as that person makes the source code freely available. This is precisely what has allowed Linux and other open source projects to achieve their high quality. So, although some Linux proponents may view Microsoft, especially Windows NT, as a competitor, there is no reason why Microsoft must continue to have a competitive stance toward Linux. Microsoft could benefit greatly from embracing Linux and it could be its best hope of continued growth in the enterprise market.

Microsoft has said little, officially, about its position and strategies regarding Linux, but recently Steve Ballmer, Microsoft's president, said at Comdex, "If customers want more source code, we're going to think about that and how to address that issue. If there's something people would get out of source code availability in NT, we need to think of how to give them that."

TIP
For the full article including Microsoft's statements, check ComputerWorld's Web site at www.computerworld.com/home/news.nsf/all/981117ballmer.

Clearly, this indicates an official awareness by Microsoft of the open source community's influence on its customers' desires, but does not state a clear intention of any specific strategy, nor does it recognize any specific threat from Linux.

The so-called Halloween documents, which can be found at www .opensource.org/halloween.html, though unofficial, may provide greater clues to Microsoft's intentions. Many in the software industry, especially in the open source community, were shocked at the apparent ruthlessness with which Microsoft seemed willing to act in defense of its market dominance.

Microsoft's response, as indicated in its editor's letter found at Microsoft's site (check www.microsoft.com/ntserver/highlights/editorletter .asp), that the leaked memos do not represent an official position or strategy, does little to relieve the anger generated in the open source community.

There are two main suggested lines of defense against Linux in the Halloween documents: legal action against possible patent infringements and the de-commoditization of protocols. While some open source projects may be vulnerable to patent lawsuits, Linux is not because it is based on technology on which the patents have expired, as you can confirm at www.linuxworld.com/linuxworld/lw-1998-11/lw-11-thesource.html. Additionally, any legal action would only increase the animosity the development community already feels toward Microsoft. The goal of de-commoditization of protocols is ostensibly to shut open source projects out of the industry, but as they lose market dominance to Linux, attempts to control open standards will more likely shut Microsoft out instead.

NOTE
▬▬▬ Analyst Robin Bloor of Bloor Research points out, "Any company which ignores standards will not survive" (www.zdnet.co.uk/news/1998/44/ns-5959.html).

Windows NT is floundering in the enterprise market and Microsoft has no hope of extending its hegemony to this sphere. There is a growing doubt among IT professionals that Windows NT is capable of handling mission-critical situations, which explains why it is far behind Unix in market share and is losing ground.

"According to market researcher Dataquest, Unix growth is accelerating and outpacing that of NT. Unix server usage grew 12.7 percent in the past two years, from a 36 percent market share in 1996 to 42.7 percent in the second quarter of this year. NT, by contrast, grew 6.5 percent, half the rate of Unix, from 9.7 percent in 1996 to 16.2 percent in 1998." (*New York Times*, 10/29/98).

TIP
▬▬▬ For additional information about NT versus Unix market share, check the *New York Times* at www.nytimes.com/techweb/TW_Unix_Growth_Still_Outpaces_Win_NT.html.

If Microsoft continues its present focus on Windows NT, its presence in the corporate IT marketplace will be marginalized. This will negatively affect sales of other Microsoft products, which are Windows-dependent. It may be able to maintain a large market share of consumer products, but its overall importance in the software industry will be diminished.

Even the consumer market, which Microsoft now owns, could be threatened by current efforts in the open source community to develop GUI solutions for Linux that will rival Windows in usability and ease of use. Where NT has gained a reputation as an easy-to-use, but relatively inefficient and unstable platform, Linux is known for stability and reliability, is growing in market share, and is widely respected in the industry. As Linux continues to outpace it, Microsoft will be gradually passed up if it continues to rely on Windows NT. The IT world has awakened to this fact and companies such as Intel, IBM, Netscape, and Oracle are making investments in the future of Linux. Conspicuously absent from this list of industry leaders is Microsoft.

In Linux, Microsoft has a ready-made opportunity to enter, and successfully compete, in the enterprise for several reasons.

1. A move to support open source to this degree would help to heal Microsoft's injured public image among developers, network engineers, and, especially, open source advocates.
2. Microsoft will have the advantage of brand recognition and current market dominance over other implementations of Linux.
3. Linux offers new markets for ports of other Microsoft products. The open source community will also benefit from Microsoft's significant mindshare and financial resources if brought to bear on the development of Linux.

It's important that Microsoft observe open source ideals, rather than attempt to subvert the cooperative process, or it will ultimately lose the connection to the community of developers. Without this connection, Microsoft will not have the advantage of mining the development power of open source and will once again find itself competing against, rather than benefiting from, a superior development model. Anything less than a good-faith effort at fair participation in the community and delivery of its best efforts will only further antagonize developers and open source advocates.

Embracing Linux will require a reorientation of Microsoft's economic model and a deliberate shift to a new paradigm. The projected revenue loss could keep Microsoft from considering giving away a free operating system, but it will face lost revenue anyway because, for enterprise solutions, Linux will outsell Windows NT in any case. Open source is quickly outpacing the quality and speed of traditional companies' development abilities and forcing overall software prices down, no matter what Microsoft does.

There could also be some cultural pains experienced in both Microsoft and the open source community. Individuals in each group will perceive cooperation between groups to be consorting with the enemy. Many people in the open source community hate Microsoft, and Microsoft hates to lose. Differences of this type can only be supported by the larger communities at the expense of the mutual benefits. There is no reason Microsoft would have to totally abandon present plans for Windows NT. Although Linux is directly in the way of NT for enterprise applications, Windows NT still dominates the desktop and consumer markets.

Microsoft is left with a difficult choice for which the road ahead is not what it used to be. Windows NT growth in the market has stalled, while Linux is quickly accelerating. Now Microsoft and the world watch as this era enters a critical phase in the growth of the informationscape. Linux and other open source software projects are modeled to take maximum advantage of the free flow of information and processing power that the Internet brings.

While it is not yet understood generally, closed source companies are not prepared to face the challenge created by the open source model. This is new territory. The fundamental rules by which complex software is created are changing. Several major information technology companies are beginning to recognize this. Microsoft, however, has not. All closed source companies will suffer financially in the coming open source paradigm, but the ones who jump on board the open source train the quickest will suffer the least. Microsoft needs a ticket on that train. Microsoft needs Linux.

References

"Unix is Back," *New York Times*, 10/29/98, p. 8.

CHAPTER 10

Using Linux Business Products and Tools

There are several business applications already developed for Linux. These applications vary from desktop applications, and range in function from business suites to very specific symbolic math programs and emulators.

This chapter discusses some of them. Some of them are bundled in the CD-ROM that accompanies this book; for more details, check Appendix C.

Business Applications Overview

Linux is already popular among Internet service providers. About 70 percent of server boxes performing any form of task on the Internet are running Linux (usually Red Hat) with Apache.

In the testing and simulation environment, due to chip design work, a testing machine requires an ultraresilient operating system in order to conduct long simulations, verifications, and synthesis runs. Linux meets muster. Microsoft's Windows NT is a disaster according to more than 95 percent of the respondents to the survey at the Unix versus NT organization. This is hard data.

NOTE

For detailed information about the comparison between Linux and Windows NT discussed in the preceding paragraph, check www.kirch.net/unix-nt.html#compare.

IT managers around the world are being confronted with the decision of whether to continue to build their systems on Microsoft Windows NT Server or switch to Unix operating systems. Now, *Unix* doesn't refer to a single operating system, but to a family of them, which includes AIX, BSDI, Digital UNIX, FreeBSD, HP-UX, IRIX, Linux, NetBSD, OpenBSD, Pyramid, SCO, Solaris and SunOS, just to name the more prominent ones.

It's true that Microsoft's Windows 2000 (formerly Windows NT) is still increasing in popularity, but is it increasing the productivity of MIS operations? The question faced by many doubting IT professionals, including those known to be pioneers in many technologies, is whether profits are being increased as a result of adopting a Windows NT–based solution. It might, at the desktop level, as Windows NT is much more robust than Windows 9x, but for mission-critical applications, how many IT managers do you know that are fully confident in Windows NT 4.0 or the upcoming Windows 2000?

Beginning with acquisition costs, which one is cheaper? Hold on a bit before answering! Here are some line items to be considered in your total cost of ownership (TCO) assessment; consider the following:

- Hardware costs
- Software licenses
- Technical support agreements
- Prices of upgrades/service packs
- Costs of hardware upgrades (more and more memory)
- Profits lost for every hour of downtime
- Personnel costs for recovering/recreating data lost due to product defects in the operating system and/or hardware platform required by your choice of operating systems
- Personnel costs for systems administrators

The preceding list itemizes only some of the factors that contribute to the overall budget resulting from IT's decision to recommend and implement an operating system at a corporate level.

Although money is at the bottom line of the equation, given the complex set of factors just presented, a technically superior combination of server hardware and operating systems could prove to be less expensive in the long run.

It is not news that Unix is a very mature, technically superior group of operating systems with a proven track record for performance, reliability, and security in a server environment. The almost 30 years of continual development, performed often by volunteers who believe in what they're doing, has produced a group of operating systems that not only meets the demands of today's computing needs, but in many cases exceeds them.

Why Windows NT Server 4.0 continues to exist in the enterprise would be a topic appropriate for an investigative report in the field of psychology or marketing, not an article on information technology. Technically, Windows NT Server 4.0 is no match for any Unix operating system or Linux. If this statement is not true, then why does Microsoft use Sun's Solaris instead of Windows NT for Hotmail Web-based e-mail service?

TIP

If you want to find out which operating system a site is running, check www.unix-vs-nt.org/cgi-bin/siteinfo, as shown in Figure 10.1.

Microsoft's Hotmail runs a mixture of Sun Solaris and FreeBSD. Apache 1.2.1 is the Web server software. After Microsoft purchased the company in December 1997, it tried to migrate to Windows NT, but NT was not able to support the demands of 10 million users, which reportedly proved too great for NT, and Solaris was reinstated.

TIP

For the complete story about Microsoft choosing Solaris versus NT check www.unix-vs-nt.org/kirch/hotmail.html.

Figure 10.2 shows the screenshot of Linux Online site, which is a source of lots of useful information on Linux, projects under development, hardware, and applications.

Considering the estimated 7 million Linux users, it is not surprising that there are many applications already developed for it. Linux itself is available in several formats, called *distributions.* Each distribution

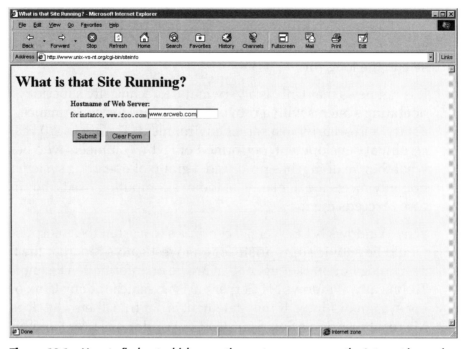

Figure 10.1 How to find out which operating system a server on the Internet is running.

has its own set of features and functionality that makes it unique—some distributions are available for download from the Internet at no charge, others are provided on CD-ROM or floppy disk and have a (usually) nominal charge associated with them. Following is a partial list of applications and tools developed to run under Linux.

Knox Software's Arkeia Network Backup Product

Arkeia utilizes an exclusive multiflow technology to deliver backup speeds that are 200 to 300 percent faster than rival software packages. Its unique transaction engine allows multiple backups and restores to be performed simultaneously with total reliability. This is especially valuable for multiple users backing up or restoring data on their own.

Figure 10.3 is a screenshot of the Knox Software Web site featuring Arkeia Backup software for Linux.

Arkeia's Java interface enables the systems administrator to manage multiple remote backup servers through the Internet as if they were

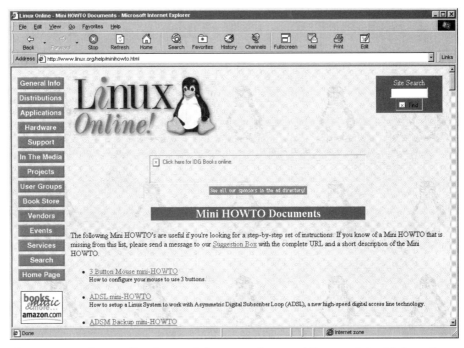

Figure 10.2   Linux Online is one of the many sites providing a variety of information about Linux.

local backups. The product is among the most reliable software you can find. It has a powerful database capable of restoring sites to their original state, in the event of server disasters.

NOTE

For your convenience, an evaluation copy of Arkeia Backup software can be found in the CD-ROM that accompanies this book.

Arkeia integrates with all types of corporate environments and is also available for Unix or Windows NT servers. Also, this is the first software delivered with a Java interface, which effectively neutralizes the problem of heterogeneous computer environments. Operators can use any intranet station to access any remote network. Its universal interface makes it the first software able to backup via the Internet. The product is compatible with a wide range of devices and provides the best plug-and-play solution for effective data security.

Table 10.1 provides a comparison table matrix for you to fill out when comparing the product with other similar ones.

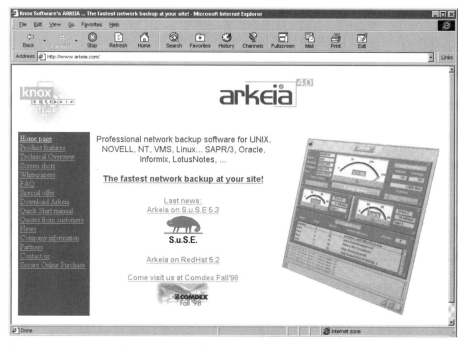

Figure 10.3　Arkeia's home page at the Knox Software Web site.

Using Arkeia for Mission-Critical Application Backup: A Case Study

In this case study, the company in focus has a business based on best-of-breed communication and information technologies. The company has to process huge amounts of data to meet its internal and external decision-making and reporting requirements. This data is vital for the company, since it supports the following:

- Regulatory reporting
- Customer and corporate accounting
- Order entry and customer service systems
- The information system structured around several applications and databases
- SAP: administration, fiscal accounting, human resources, and logistics
- Oracle: customer accounting (200GB), communications traces, and services database (voicemail services and so forth)

Table 10.1   Comparing Arkeia with Other Backup Software Solutions

DESCRIPTION	ARKEIA	OTHER
Centralized network backup	Yes	
Client/server architecture	Yes	
Very high network performances (6 to 60GB/h); ultimate speed is based on many factors and can exceed 60GB/h with current equipment	Yes	
High operational reliability by design	Yes	
NT or Unix backup server	Yes	
NT, Unix, Novell, and VMS clients	Yes	
Centralized administration	Yes	
Remote administration	Yes	
Centralized catalog	Yes	
Optimized catalog size (<½ percent data backed up)	Yes	
GUI administration and user interface	Yes	
GUI control panels	Yes	
GUI warnings with standardized color codes	Yes	
X11 GUI interface–, Motif-, and Openlook-compatible; does not require Motif or Openlook to be loaded	Yes	
Universal Java GUI interface	Yes	
Online help	Yes	
Automatic GUI setup assistants	Yes	
Archive management	Yes	
Authorization and proxy controls	Yes	
Year 2000–compliant	Yes	

- Oracle: inventory, personnel, and rental services
- INFORMIX: identical functions as Oracle, but for another business unit

Arkeia backs up the entire server complex in a centralized manner. While these numbers represent a relatively large production environment, they will increase when several existing servers are attached to the network and other planned servers are acquired to meet anticipated needs.

The backup and restore requirements are directly linked to the company's business needs:

- Computer databases are essential to the company's efficient operation.

- The critical databases and applications must be available and online as close to 24 hours a day, 7 days a week as possible. Backups and restores must be performed when the databases are open, online, and in use.

- Business activity logs must be maintained for two to seven years to support legal inquiries.

Since backups must be done without affecting the production system and applications, the time window for this task must be as short as possible. Additionally, it must be done during off-peak times.

A Complete Backup Solution

A complete backup solution, which includes hardware and software, has been installed at the customer site to fulfill the various requirements. The two main criteria are, in order, data security and backup/restore performance.

Storage Unit

The Emass/Grau ABBA/J Robot storage unit with 20 DLT 4000 drives is being used. It has a storage capacity of 4096 cartridges and can be expanded to 8192.

The robot is driven by two redundant OS/2 PC (AMU), with dynamic failover in case the main OS/2 PC crashes. The OS/2 PC, connected to the two backup servers through a standard Ethernet interface, drives connection and robot sharing. Each DLT drive must be individually managed so that multiple tasks, such as backup, restore, and tape duplication, can occur simultaneously.

Primary Backup Server

The primary backup server is a Sun Enterprise 5000 with the following configuration:

- 4 processors
- 6GB of mirrored hard disks for the Arkeia index
- 512MB RAM
- Differential SCSI connections to the DLT drives

- 2 DLT drives per SCSI interface to enhance reliability, security, and throughput

Secondary Backup Server

The secondary backup server is an HP 9000 with the following configuration:

- 4 processors
- 512MB of RAM

Network Topology

The primary network topology was composed of the following:

- 2 dedicated FDDI rings
- Dual attachment
- 2 Fast-Ethernet 100-Mbit connection

The secondary network topology was composed of the following:

- 10BaseT Ethernet

The Network Backup Software

Arkeia is used to manage the network backup of the 55-server complex. The basic requirements of backup/restore for the site's production data are the following:

- Filesystems of 55 servers, totaling 150GB of data
- Oracle, Informix, and SAP databases, totaling 830GB
- Archive of historic data
- A disaster-recovery plan to restore the backup server in case of a failure.

In order to keep the databases and applications online and available, as well as to meet the short backup window, all backup operations are done in parallel. In addition to performing parallel backups, Arkeia is also required to perform restore requests, at any time, at the production site, without degrading other current operations such as backups.

Arkeia multiplexes data and hosts on the network to perform backups and restores. The multiplexing technique used by Arkeia—similar to the one used to manage telephone calls—is the only one that can offer the required level of performance.

However, this technique alone is not enough to meet the operational requirements for the site based on actual production use patterns. Experience from several preproduction tests conducted by Knox Software shows that there were often three or four backups and one or two restores running at the same time. Arkeia's unique transaction engine performs all backups and restores tasks, in parallel, on the same server. Without the transaction engine, it would be impossible to reliably perform these tasks simultaneously.

Filesystem

The first requirement is to back up the filesystem of the 55 servers on the network. In this scenario, this consists of over 150GB of data spread across 800,000 files when a full backup is done.

During incremental backups, about 30GB of data is written to tape; however, the 800,000 directory entries, plus data and directory entries for new files, must be scanned and processed.

Constraints are as follows:

- Time frame has to be as short as possible—there is a need for speed.

- All servers must be processed during the same period—a massive parallelism of all servers, uses the minimum number of tape drives (thanks to the data multiplexing).

- All hosts are backed up every night with the following strategy: full backup every Sunday night on new tapes and incremental backups every other weekday.

Full Backup Results While in Production

The full backup of 150GB from 55 hosts is simultaneously backed up on 4 DLT4000 in parallel. Total elapsed time must be no more than 6 hours. Note that backed-up hosts are from various manufacturers (DEC, HP, Sun, IBM) and use various operating systems (OSF1, HPUX, Solaris, AIX).

The number of tapes used by a full backup varies according to the compression value of the client machines. Figures obtained in the production configuration show that a DLT4000 cartridge holds about 40GB of filesystem data.

Filesystem data is the most difficult type of data to backup with respect to performance. The performance challenge occurs because of the huge number of small files that do not compress very well.

The average backup speed on 150GB of filesystem data is 25 GB/hour for 6 hours; this translates to 416 MB/min or 7 MB/sec. These performances are the result of numerous small files, which slow the backup speed, and an imperfect balance of the multiplexing. Some of the servers were backed up well before others. However, the preceding results represent the total time to back up all of the servers. The imbalance occurs because of the real-world nature of the information. Some servers contain much more data and files than other servers do and therefore take longer to back up; this increases the overall elapsed time and drags down the average speed.

In a controlled laboratory test, all servers would have been balanced with the same amount of data and the same number of files. This arrangement produces faster filesystem backups because of the balancing. However, it can never be achieved in production: It is impossible to have 55 servers with the exact same amount of data and number of files.

Incremental Backup Results While in Production

Incremental backups take almost exactly the same amount of time as a full backup. The major time consumer, for an incremental backup, is directory scanning. Each file's directory entry must be examined to see if the file has changed since the previous backup. If the file has changed, it is backed up; otherwise, it is not. The actual amount of data being backed up is about 30GB; this is 20 percent of the full backup.

Because of Arkeia's multitasking and multiplexing capabilities and the extremely fast FDDI network, the current bottleneck in filesystem backups is processing directory entries.

Host Data Restoration

The 4GB of filesystem data was restored from a mix of full and incremental backups within 50 minutes. This figure was obtained when a server suffered an unplanned and unexpected disk failure and had to be rebuilt on the fly.

Archiving

Legal archiving, the third requirement, consists of backing up filesystem data twice a week and archiving that data for two to seven years.

The retention period varies depending on the type of data. Once the data has been archived, it is deleted from the client's disk. After the archiving period has expired, the data must be removed from the archive and deleted.

To ensure security, client-side data encryption is performed on sensitive data before it is transmitted over the network.

Arkeia's Backup Index

In the course of backing up all 55 network servers, Arkeia builds a detailed index, which contains a record of all of the files that have been backed up. The index is critical to the correct operation of Arkeia. If the disk that holds the index suffers a failure, then the index must be restored. To ensure that the index is always available or can be quickly recovered, it is backed up as a separate step.

Arkeia's index is completely backed up every day. The backup is done twice onto two different DLT tapes. This redundancy ensures the availability of the index and allows the Arkeia backup server to be completely rebuilt in less than five hours.

The restore information for each file is maintained in Arkeia's online index, for a period of six to eight weeks. The data needs to be retained for this period to cover normal, operational-oriented restores. The index is 1.4GB in size, covers 800,000 file names and 6000GB of database and filesystem data. This means that the index size is about 0.025 percent of the database and filesystem data that was backed up. This astonishingly small value is achieved because of two factors:

- Extremely good index design.
- Stability of file names over time. (Basically, each new file name requires much more index data than the incremental amount of information required to track a modified file.)

Adobe Acrobat Reader

Adobe's Acrobat for Linux allows you to view, navigate, and print PDF files. Adobe Acrobat 3.0 is the fastest way to publish any document on your corporate intranet, on the Web, or on CD-ROM. The free Adobe Acrobat Reader enables you to view, navigate, and browse PDF files seamlessly, either inside a Web browser or in a stand-alone application. Figure 10.4 is a screenshot of Adobe's Acrobat for Linux distribution site.

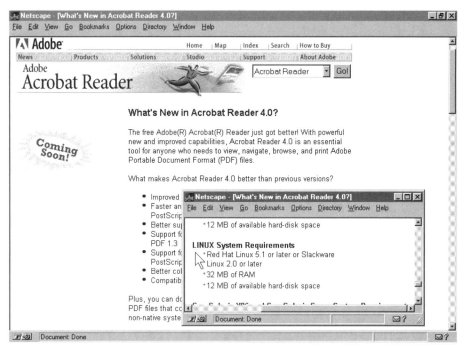

Figure 10.4 Adobe's Acrobat Reader is available for Linux.

Applixware Office Suite

Applixware Office Suite is a fully integrated, cross-platform suite of desktop productivity tools, including word processing and document publishing, spreadsheets, business graphics, graphics editing, data access, and e-mail available from Applix. Figure 10.5 is a screenshot of Applix's Web site at www.applix.com/.

Applix Enterprise: Integrated Customer Interaction Solutions

Designed to streamline an organization's customer service, sales force automation, quality assurance, and help desk activities, Applix Enterprise leverages Web and Java technologies with a unique adaptable architecture to provide superior customer satisfaction.

Applixware: Office and Decision Support Solutions

Applixware is an open suite of integrated desktop tools that enables individual users with time-critical and historical data needs to access, analyze, display, and communicate information from a universal desk-

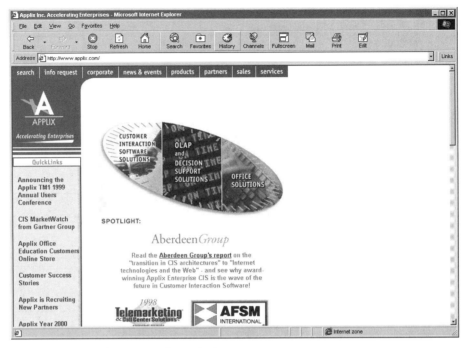

Figure 10.5 Applix Office Suite Web site.

top across heterogeneous client/server environments, including the Web.

Applix Anyware

Anyware is the first commercial applications solution that leverages Java to develop and deploy interactive business applications to networked desktops. Any*ware*. Anytime.

Applix TM1: Real-Time Multidimensional Analysis for Decision Support

Applix TM1 client/server products afford a widely deployable OLAP environment for the real-time enterprise. TM1 enables users throughout the enterprise to share information and collaborate, no matter where they are located. A knowledge worker needs only an understanding of the business, not the structure of the database to use the power of TM1.

BB Stock Pro

BB Stock Pro is a series of powerful tools for stock charting, stock tracking, and analysis from Falkor Technologies. The features include charting, technical analysis, portfolio management, market timing, buy/sell signals, profit testing, custom high/low alert, automatic stock-split detection and management, most-active issues and big price movers, and personalized watch list. Figure 10.6 is a screenshot of the BB Stock Web site.

Credit Card Verification System (CCVS)

The credit card verification process involves several steps.

1. First, a consumer presents credit card information to the merchant.
2. The merchant transmits this data, along with the merchant ID code, to a clearinghouse (also referred to as a *processor* or *acquirer*). This can be done by reading the card and merchant numbers over the phone, by

Figure 10.6   BB Stock is available to a variety of distribution versions of Linux and Unix Solaris.

using a credit card terminal, or by using CCVS or some other piece of software to transmit the information from a computer.

3. The clearinghouse may be the bank that has issued the merchant the credit card account, but it is more likely a firm that has contracted with the merchant's bank to clear charges in exchange for a flat fee and a percentage of every charge processed.

4. The clearinghouse contacts the bank that issued the consumer's credit card and verifies that the charge is acceptable. Upon acceptance, the clearinghouse then sends a confirmation message to the merchant. At the same time, the available credit from the customer's credit card is frozen by the amount of the transaction.

5. At the end of a business day, the merchant (or the merchant's computer or credit card terminal) calls the clearinghouse and verifies all transactions for that day to ensure that the merchant and the clearinghouse agree on what has happened that day. After this upload, the clearinghouse starts the process of transferring the money from the credit card bank to the merchant's bank account.

CCVS from HKS enables your computer and a modem to operate just like a normal credit card terminal but adds even more power and flexibility. Figure 10.7 is a screenshot of HKS's Web site.

Credit Card Verification System uses your computer and modem to simulate a credit card swipe box. CCVS is designed as a stand-alone product with several APIs (application programming interfaces) that allow it to be customized and integrated with third-party software applications or database products.

CCVS is safe, secure, and easy to use. Written in ANSI C and conforming to POSIX standards, CCVS is portable and designed to be easily integrated with modern operating systems, programming languages, and the Internet. It is designed for easy scripting and programming, so users can use CCVS to automate Web commerce and batch processing or to enhance any application that requires credit card processing.

CCVS's powerful features can be accessed in a number of ways. The company offers users the following:

A C library with a documented API, enabling users to integrate CCVS seamlessly with existing applications.

A tcl extension, enabling use of CCVS with server-side tcl such as NeoWebScript.

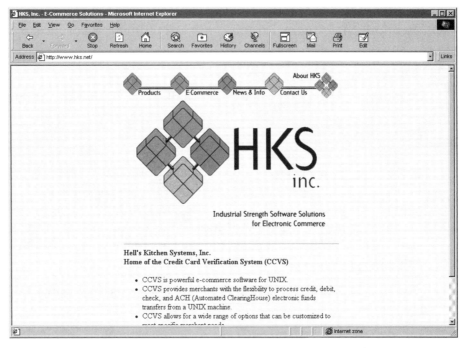

Figure 10.7 HKS's Web site. HKS is the distributor of Credit Card Verification System for Linux.

A Perl 5.0 module, allowing CCVS to work with the most popular cgi programming language in use today.

The ability to quickly construct custom GUIs using tcl/tk. Typical development time is less than a day.

A CLI program with source code, showing how to use the C API for interactive use.

A Curses interface for phone operator use.

Compatibility with Address Verification System (AVS), allow merchants to check for stolen credit cards. Many clearinghouses offer a better rate to merchants who use AVS, even on orders taken over the phone.

Support for multiple merchant accounts, allowing users to open their very own virtual malls with unlimited storefronts.

The ability to conduct multiple transactions in a single session, which approaches leased line performance (two seconds per transaction!) with no extra cost or complexity.

The ability to test and do development programming on the product without charging real credit cards, providing reassurance to merchants.

Year 2000 compliance.

Six months of free telephone and e-mail support with free upgrades.

Ishmail

Ishmail from Hal Software Products is a powerful yet easy to use tool for reading, composing, organizing, and filing electronic mail. Ishmail handles multimedia mail. It supports the MIME, has a graphical user interface, is built using the X-Window System and OSF/Motif, and is compatible with the CDE Desktop. Figure 10.8 is a screenshot of Ishmail's Web site.

Ishmail is available for a variety of Unix systems, including the following:

- SunOS
- Solaris (Sparc and Intel x86)
- IBM AIX
- Hewlett-Packard HP-UX
- DEC Digital Unix
- Linux
- SGI IRIX
- BSDI

Flexible Connections with IMAP, POP, and Local Mail Servers

You can work with mail folders on your system, on systems on your local network, or on remote servers using the popular POP or IMAP protocols. Ishmail lets you organize messages in folders and has various options for sorting the messages and searching through message contents. Folders can be organized in directories. The file format used for the folders is similar to the format used by other Unix mail tools such as mailx, Elm, mh, xmh, exmh, MMDF, and Z-Mail.

Ishmail has powerful tools for automatically filing messages as they arrive or as they are sent to selected folders. You select messages for

Figure 10.8 Ishmail's Web site. Ishmail delivers e-mail power to Linux.

automatic filing using patterns (simple strings or regular expressions) that are compared against message headers, body, or both.

You can define alerts and icons for incoming mail. A handy dialog box allows entry of patterns to search for in incoming mail messages. When a pattern is matched, a command (alert) is run. You can specify both the patterns to be matched and the commands to be run. Icons can be defined the same way. When incoming mail matches a pattern, the Ishmail icon changes to the bitmap design of your choice.

Ishmail has a text editor tool for composing messages. It handles both standard ASCII text and MIME Enriched Text. You can apply formatting changes such as different font styles and sizes, colors, justification, and indentation. Multipart messages with attachments are easily created, and the attachments flow with the text rather than simply adding to the end of the message.

If you prefer to use a different editor tool, such as **vi** or Emacs, you can do so easily. You can also use a tool, such as **ispell**, to check the spelling of your messages.

You can define aliases for other users' names or groups of user names. A dialog box provides an easy way to create or change aliases. The aliases are stored in a format (.mailrc) that is compatible with other mail tools. Ishmail can share alias files with programs such as Z-Mail and Elm.

Maxwell Word Processor

Maxwell is a free Linux word processor that provides all the usual features you would expect. Figure 10.9 shows Maxwell's Web site.

Maxwell was written by Andrew Haisley, Dave Miller, and Tom Newton. It was originally destined to be commercial software, but, for various reasons, this is unlikely to happen. The developers have decided to release the source code to Maxwell under the GNU GPL to ensure continued development on it. Everyone can help with this effort.

If you just want to use Maxwell, download the binary release. If you want to build Maxwell to do some development on it, download the source. Both can be found on the CD-ROM that accompanies this

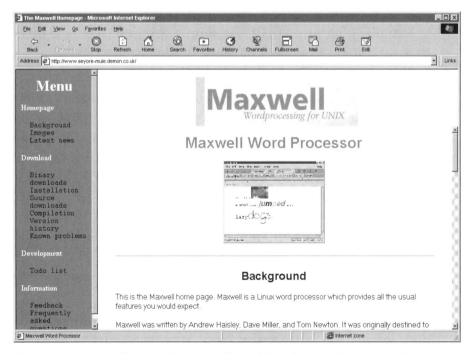

Figure 10.9 Maxwell's Web site. Maxwell provides a free word processor for Linux.

book. Expect problems with building in the first instance since it has not been built on a wide variety of systems. Figures 10.10 and 10.11 show screenshots of Maxwell's main screen and the spelling screen, respectively.

StarOffice

StarOffice 5.0 can boost business productivity as all tasks can be done from a perfectly integrated workplace. It doesn't matter if you are editing texts or spreadsheets, creating presentations, or working in a team. You can also surf the Internet and read and write e-mails or news postings. You will never again have to start various individual programs to manage specific tasks. Figure 10.12 shows Star Division's Web site, which is the home of the developer of StarOffice.

StarOffice 5.0 is the only high-end office software available worldwide that supports all commonly used operating systems: not only the Windows operating systems but also OS/2, Macintosh, and the diverse Unix-based systems such as Sun Solaris and Linux.

Completely new possibilities are open with StarOffice for Java, as it can be loaded onto a network computer (NC).

Figure 10.10   Maxwell's main screen.

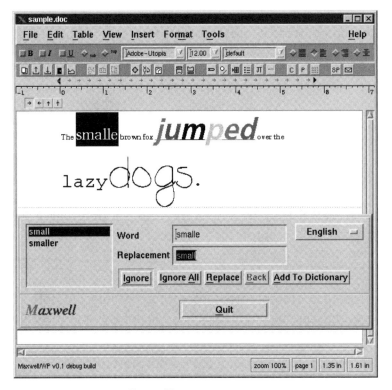

Figure 10.11   Maxwell's spelling screen.

NOTE

For additional information on StarOffice, please send an e-mail to Star Division at us.marketing.feedback@stardivision.com.

StarOffice is one of the most efficient office suites for Linux, preventing Linux users from sacrificing any features of a modern office suite. Star Division confirms its solidarity with the Linux community and, with StarOffice 5.0 for Linux, continues on this successful path.

For all noncommercial users, such as schools and home users, StarOffice can be downloaded free of charge. For companies and all users in the business sector, Star Division offers a commercial version of StarOffice 5.0 for Linux.

Linux for Manufacturing: Considering Real-Time Linux Applications

Microsoft's Windows NT and now Windows CE are typically at the forefront of discussions about real-time operating systems for manu-

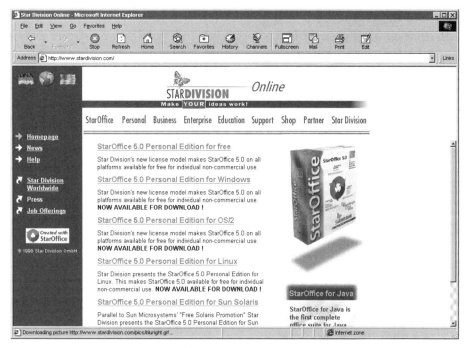

Figure 10.12 Star Division's Web site showcasing its flagship product, StarOffice.

facturing. Much has been said and demonstrated about their application in industrial settings, but many still look at these options with hesitation due to concerns about deterministic operation. Linux is the latest operating system to enter this discussion, particularly given the significant boost it enjoyed when Netscape recently announced its plans to support the OS, but is the industry ready for it? Better yet, is Linux ready for IA?

Unlike NT, Linux was not developed from scratch. It grew out of reused code and ideas from Minix, a more deterministic, Unix-like OS with a small footprint that was developed for 386 machines. Since then, its development has been driven by several thousand developers scattered throughout the world that are connected only by the Internet.

The Linux user base has grown to about 7 million installations, rivaling that of Microsoft's Windows NT. The operating system's major strengths are its multiuser, multitasking capabilities and ability to run on platforms ranging from Intel x86 and Motorola 68k or PowerPCs to Sparc, Mips, and Digital Alpha.

OpenLinux standard 1.1 outperformed Microsoft Windows NT version 4.0 in recent benchmark tests and the OpenLinux server exhibited excellent scalability and predictability with a near linear rise in performance. Implementing a superset of the POSIX standard, Linux can also interoperate with many other OSs, including those from Microsoft, Apple, and Novell.

In addition, Linux supports COM/DCOM as well as OMG's CORBA implementations. It also supports a wide range of interfaces, including X Windows, Emacs, and TCP/IP networking, and it benefits from nearly 30 years of API tuning in the Unix community.

The fact that Linux is free and its source code completely open is a major contributor to its current popularity. Hundreds of thousands of developers from around the world, many of them hardware vendors, have developed a variety of devices drivers without the burden of expensive source code licenses or restrictive nondisclosure agreements. This open sourcing has made it possible for manufacturing implementations that need a real-time operating system to incorporate a real-time kernel, similar to what companies such as VenturCom are doing with NT and CE.

Bare-bones Linux is natively well suited for soft real-time applications. Hard real-time support can be implemented with schedulers such as the New Mexico Institute of Technology's RT-Linux, where a small real-time kernel coexists with the POSIX-like Linux kernel, permitting real-time functions to operate in a predictable and low-latency environment. RT-Linux uses a simple real-time executive to run a non-real-time kernel as its lowest priority task, using a virtual machine layer to make the standard kernel fully preemptable.

The potential for Linux to be adopted for factory floor applications is growing, but it is still early to predict how rapidly Linux will conquer IA. Linux enables IT to develop customized and effective IA solutions at a significantly lower cost relative to other OSs. Most Unix or Linux applications can be recompiled to run on the other system with minimum effort. Technical expertise is widely available, much more than for any other OS, since the source code has been available for anyone to learn and master. With Linux, you also have all the graphics capabilities of Windows, but without the disadvantages of MS-DOS.

The open source model pioneered with Linux developers and now followed by Netscape will soon become an important factor to consider when deciding on a real-time OS. Similar to the past experience with hardware, software is now becoming a commodity that the industry increasingly requires to be open. Thus, open and nonproprietary real-time OS source code will be the catalyst of a new business strategy, empowered by the users, which will promote close partnership between users and suppliers.

Linux may soon emerge as another real-time OS option for manufacturing applications. Features not natively supported by Linux can be readily developed and easily incorporated in the operating system. Linux is Y2K-compliant since it does not store data in a simplistic field-by-field fashion. Instead, it stores it as an incremental count of seconds. The current size of that counter is good until 2038. By then, Linux will be using 64-bit counters, which are good until the next Big Bang.

The Care and Feeding of a Linux Systems Administrator

Linux systems administrators are actually not that hard to find, and if you locate one who is a bit rough around the edges but eager to get to work, you'll have a great experience. There are some ways to attract and retain skilled Linux systems administrators; following is a list.

Training

Linux people tend to enjoy self-development. Most of them are self-taught and will consider resources given to them for education as valuable assets. For example, subscriptions to *Linux Journal*, authority to buy books and information resources, and access to computer-based training are all good hooks.

Creative License

To do great systems administration requires both methodical performance and intuitive creation. If you help the sysadmins internalize corporate goals and don't stifle their efforts to excel by saying, "It's not supposed to be done that way," you will create an environment that allows significant development for your networks.

Technologies

New programs and hardware attract the inquisitive nature of a Linux systems administrator. Although not everything can be turned to profit, a little willingness to experiment can go a long way toward building long-term reliability in your sysadmins. If they can detect a possible advantage, let them pursue it. Even if it doesn't pan out, they know why not and can then filter new ideas through that knowledge.

Entrepreneurial Challenges

If you can distill a business problem so that you understand the outcome desired, you can give this to the systems administrators and free them of any unnecessary constraints. This is similar to a small business challenge—make something happen where it hasn't happened before. Linux people often build mindsets that are tangential to the norm. If you can detail the need clearly, they can often come up with solutions that perform better than conventional answers.

Open Systems Authority

Systems administrators tend to be rather possessive of their network. While maintaining user access and functionality, you can allow the sysadmins to configure the network for performance and security. Allow them their "possession" and it will repay you when you need them to come in at 2:37 A.M. one Sunday morning.

On the Other Hand . . .

There are also some things you need to be more aware of when dealing with systems administrators. Not that there is a lack of understanding or intelligence on their part, nor are your needs and considerations ignored by them; however, the personality and mindset needed to do technical work often does not come in the same brain as the skills and personality of a successful businessperson. The more you can understand them, the better off all of you will be.

Leadership

Probably the biggest struggle between systems administrators and upper management comes from neither side understanding the other. When you can come to terms with this mutual need, you can start to build the environment for a truly successful operation. For example, most sysadmins dislike meetings and feel they are wasted time. Many managers need those meetings to help them share ideas and needs and to be updated on what's happening. If you can have the systems administrator prepare a brief report and distribute it before the meeting, most questions can be answered. And those questions that remain can be resolved and answered through e-mail.

Guidelines

Systems administrators tend to enjoy technology, and sometimes you will have to refocus them on providing the business solutions you need. Let them know the budget constraints, time-line issues, and other considerations that are actually needed.

Mission Orientation

Closely related to guidelines is the focus on what your business is actually doing. It would not hurt a sysadmin to be funded for the entire time of research. However, that would not do well for your bottom line. You will need to keep the mission a top priority, while still allowing room to create.

Social Skills

Many technical questions have simple answers, and often a technician cannot understand why others can't figure them out. This is even more frequent when your business isn't technically oriented yet you have to have significant resources available. There will be times when you will need to filter the interactions between sysadmins and end users to keep things on a professional level.

List of Internet/Web-Based Linux Resources

There are several Internet sites that discuss Linux and its resources. The following is a partial list of various Linux resources you can easily find:

- Linux consultants worldwide: consult.cyrius.com/
- Samba: samba.anu.edu.au/samba
- Linux for EDA: www.linuxeda.com
- Independent analysis: www.kirch.net/unix-nt.html#compare
- Best Technical Support Award: www.infoworld.com/cgi-bin/displayTC.pl?/97poy.supp.htm
- Real-time Linux: luz.cs.nmt.edu/~rtlinux/
- The best historical view of Linux: www.wired.com/wired/5.08/linux.html
- Fired for choosing Linux?: www1.zdnet.com/anchordesk/story/story_1774.html
- The LinuxOS Web page: www.linuxos.org/
- Linux Online: www.linux.org/
- *Linux Journal:* www.ssc.com/lj/index.html

- Links to Linux groups worldwide: www.cosmoseng.com/LUG.htm
- Red Hat: www.redhat.com
- Debian: www.debian.org
- Caldera: www.caldera.com
- Infomagic: www.infomagic.com
- Slackware: www.cdrom.com

What's on the CD-ROM

The following is a list of the software (evaluation copy or free distribution) included on the CD-ROM that accompanies this book. You must abide by all copyright license agreements that accompany each piece of software.

BB Stock Pro V3.3

- RedHat 5.X glibc version, with LessTif shared library
- SGI IRIX 6.X version, with Motif shared library
- Update historic data via Internet, either direct connection or behind firewall via proxy server
- getquote utility, can be run as cronjob for scheduled quote update
- Year 2000–compliant

Installation

FOR SOLARIS

- download bb_solaris.tar, stkdata.tar.gz
- For Linux: download bb_linux.tar, stkdata.tar.gz
- For IRIX: download bb_irix.tar, stkdata.tar.gz

FOR LINUX

- tar xf bb_linux.tar—for Linux, to extract install.sh
- ./install.sh

You can run BB Stock Pro after the installation is completed.

RedHat Linux

BB for RedHat Linux is based on LessTif's Motif. For those who do not have LessTif, libXm.so.2.0 at $BB_HOME/libXm.so.2.0 has been included. To set up libXm.so.2.0 in /usr/X11R6/lib, become the superuser.

```
mv libXm.so.2.0 /usr/X11R6/lib
cd /usr/X11R6/lib
ln -s libXm.so.2.0 libXm.so
ldconfig -v
```

In case you want to download the entire LessTif, it is available at www.lesstif.org.

For some RedHat users who do not have /usr/lib/libstdc++.so.2.8, download libstdc++ from www.falkor.com/dldir/redhat/libstdc++ .so.2.8.0 and install it as the superuser.

```
mv libstdc++.so.2.8.0 /usr/lib
ln -s libstdc++.so.2.8.0 libstdc++.so
ldconfig -v
```

Setup Environment

BB Stock Pro needs an environment variable BB_HOME, which is the root directory of BB.

o sh/ksh users

```
Put the following into $HOME/.profile
BB_HOME=$HOME/bb3.3; export BB_HOME
PATH=$PATH:$BB_HOME/bin
```

o csh users

```
Put the following into ~/.login or ~/.cshrc
setenv BB_HOME $HOME/bb3.3
path = ( $path $BB_HOME/bin )
```

Ready To Run

To run BB Stock Pro, just type

```
startbb
```

You'll need an authorization code to generate a 30-day evaluation license. Enter it with copy/paste to avoid typos.

PBQ3FXAVKJ4R0MPE

- You can click either of the two leftmost buttons in the toolbar to load a stock.
- You can also try the auto-run feature by clicking the Run button in the toolbar. This loads each stock in your watch list automatically.

Error

You can check the FAQ Web page at www.falkor.com/faq.html for the following problems and solutions:

- You get the error "BadDrawable" due to a lack of colormap cells and the program quits
- On Linux, you get a segmentation fault when starting Linux. (It could be because your libc is incompatible). You may need to download a different version of BB; currently, two versions of BB are available:

  RedHat 5.X glibc (libc.so.6)

  Linux97 (libc.so.5.4.x)

Update Daily Quote

BB Stock Pro V3.3 has a convenient feature to allow you to update your historic data via Internet. You can click Update Historic Data via Net from the Update menu to connect to the Web site and update your historic database. The daily data is available at 6 P.M. Pacific time. If you don't have an Internet connection to make use of this feature, you can continue to receive daily quotes via e-mail and update the database by clicking Update Historic Data via File from the Update menu.

BB Stock Pro just announced the getquote utility, which is a command to download the daily quote from the Web site with either a direct

Internet connection or through a proxy server and also to update your historic database. You can set up getquote as a cronjob to do daily quote maintenance automatically. See the man page getquote.man for details on how to set up a cronjob.

Historic Data

When you register your BB Stock Tool, you can get 50 additional historic data (any U.S. stocks) for free to start tracking your own portfolio. You will also be eligible for free future upgrades of the software. If you have questions or suggestions, please let Falkor Technology know.

Support

For help or support, visit Falkor's Web site at www.falkor.com/. Please specify the platform and describe your problem as fully as possible.

IMPORTANT

Falkor Technology Inc. ("Falkor") is willing to license this software, and related materials (the "Software") only on the condition that you agree to all the terms of this agreement. Please read these terms carefully. After reading the terms, if you agree to them and download the Software, your use of the Software will be governed by this Agreement. If you do not agree to these terms, do not download the Software.

License and Certain Restrictions
If the software you download is for a trial period, you agree to use the software only for a 30-day period. If you wish to continue to use the software after the 30-day trial period, you must purchase the software license (for a fee) with Falkor to obtain the registered license for the product. There is no refund once the registered license has been issued.

You may copy the Software provided that you reproduce all copyright and other proprietary notices that are on the original copy of the Software. You may transfer the Software and all rights under this Agreement to another party together with a copy of this Agreement if the other party agrees to accept the terms of this Agreement.

The Software contains trade secrets, and in order to protect them you may not decompile, reverse engineer, disassemble, or otherwise reduce the Software to human-perceivable form. You may not modify, adapt, translate, rent, sublicense, assign, lease, loan, resell for proof, distribute, or network the Software, or related materials or create derivative works based upon the software or any part thereof. Title, ownership rights, and intellectual property rights in and to the Software belong to Falkor and its licensors. The Software is protected by the copyright laws of the United

States and international copyright treaties. Title, ownership rights and intellectual property rights in and to the content accessed through the Software are the property of Falkor, and where applicable, to the licensor content owners and may be protected by applicable copyright or other law. This Agreement gives you no rights to such content.

Limitation of Liability

Under no circumstances, and under no legal theory, contract or otherwise, will Falkor or its licensors, be liable to you for any damages, including any lost profits, lost data or other indirect, special, incidental or consequential damages, arising out of the use the Software or any data supplied.

Certain Limitations

This Software does not recommend or endorse any specific investment, investment strategy, or guarantee the performance of any investment. Although the Software may provide some general financial guides, Falkor and its licensors do not endorse, recommend or give any investment or financial advice regarding the nature, potential value, or merits to any investment, transaction or strategy or financial condition. Falkor and its licensors will have no responsibility of any kind to you, or to any other party, on account of any inaccuracies in or untimeliness of the data, or for any delay in such data contained in the Software.

Falkor and its licensors cannot warrant that the operation of the Software will be uninterrupted or error free, that the software will meet your requirements. Falkor, its licensors, distributors or dealers are not responsible for any financial losses due to the direct or indirect use of this software.

Maxwell Word Processing

Installation

Download the binary distribution. Unarchive the file into /usr/local as the root user. Then run /usr/local/maxwell/bin/maxwell. If you do not want to put maxwell into /usr/local, you can put it elsewhere and set the MAXHOME environment variable to point to it. For example, if you want it to go under the /home/myuser directory under csh, type the following:

```
cd /home/myuser
tar -xzvf maxwell-0.5.3.tar.gz
setenv MAXHOME /home/myuser/maxwell
$MAXHOME/bin/maxwell
```

Or under bash:

```
cd /home/myuser
tar -xzvf maxwell-0.5.3.tar.gz
export MAXHOME=/home/myuser/maxwell
$MAXHOME/bin/maxwell
```

General User Assistance and Information

The software accompanying this book is being provided as is without warranty or support of any kind. Should you require basic installation assistance or if your media is defective, please call our product support number at (212) 850-6194 weekdays between 9 A.M. and 4 P.M. Eastern Standard Time. Or, we can be reached via e-mail at wprtusw@wiley.com.

To place additional orders or to request information about other Wiley products, please call (800) 879-4539.

Partial List of Linux Consultants

This appendix contains a listing of companies providing commercial Linux-related support in the United States. You will find the complete worldwide listing on the CD-ROM. If you want to find a Linux consultant or consulting firm in your area, this listing will probably be of help to you.*

TIP

The Linux Consultants HOWTO is supported by Red Hat Software. This cooperation between the Consultants HOWTO and Red Hat guarantees that all Support Partners of Red Hat's Commercial Support Program are listed in the Consultants HOWTO.

Martin Michlmayr is the hero responsible for maintaining this list and can be contacted via e-mail at tbm@cyrius.com. This list is being constantly updated by Martin. What appears in this appendix is a partial list of his v9.40, last updated on November 8, 1998. For the most updated list, please check ftp://tsx-11.mit.edu/pub/linux/docs/HOWTO/Consultants-HOWTO.

This listing is known as the Linux Consultants HOWTO. It is a listing of companies providing commercial Linux-related support. If you con-

---

*The author wishes to thank Martin Michlmayr for his willingness to share this comprehensive list and for allowing it to be published.

tact any companies listed in this document, please mention the Linux Consultants HOWTO.

The Linux Consultants HOWTO is supported by Red Hat Software. This cooperation between the Consultants HOWTO and Red Hat guarantees that all Support Partners of Red Hat's Commercial Support Program are listed in the Consultants HOWTO.

If you are part of any company providing Linux support, please fill out the following form and contact Tim Bynum at tbm@cyrius.com. Please note that he accepts 8-bit characters (for instance, German umlauts).

Name:

Address:
(If you are located in Germany, please specify your Bundesland)

Phone:

Fax:

E-mail:

URL:

Contact:
(name of contact person)

Type of support:
(e.g., phone, E-mail, remote network administration, in-house, on-site)

Special expertise:
(e.g., installation, programming services, systems administration, Internet and intranet connectivity, firewall installation, troubleshooting, training)

Following is a list of consultants providing Linux support in the United States.

Collective Technologies AnswerDesk
9433 Bee Caves Road, Building 3, Suite 100, Austin, TX 78733
Phone:
(888) 2PSAPSA
E-mail:
answerdesk@colltech.com
URL:
www.colltech.com/answerdesk

Contact:
Mike Carpenter
Type of support:
Phone and e-mail.
Special expertise:
AnswerDesk is an open systems phone support desk specifically designed to provide a backstop with difficult senior administration issues. We support administrators working with all Unix platforms, including Linux. Our client list includes a wide variety of Fortune 500 companies utilizing open systems, many with mission-critical support requirements. Our technical database is supported by hundreds of the best systems administrators in the business. For the individual Linux user, we offer per-incident support of all postinstallation issues. We are a Red Hat Commercial Support partner and are able to provide all support after installation for Red Hat Linux. For the corporate Linux administrator, we offer the same service, as well as a contract option, to buy yearly, 24-hour-a-day, 7-day-a-week support.
Sample prices:
Upon request.
Last modified:
May 21, 1998.

DCA Online (Dutch Computer Association)
26 Tobacco Road Weston, CT 06883-1612 U.S.A.; Binnendams 75 NL-3373 AC Hardinxveld-Giessendam, The Netherlands
Phone:
(203) 222-8267
Fax:
(203) 226-7037
E-mail:
linux@dcaonline.com
URL:
www.dcaonline.com
Contact:
Peter Leonard Krebs
Type of support:
Phone, e-mail, remote network administration, off-site, or on-site to any continent. Willing to move globally, given short notice and transport.

Special expertise:
Administration, installation, configuration of single or multiple Unix machines. Intranet and Internet connectivity, including design and implementation of network routing, masquerading, filters, firewalls, and security. Large-scale Web site design (1000 pages or more), especially for corporate (Fortune 100, 500) or global commerce applications, including Dynamic HTML generation, scripting, SSL, and back-end hosting or connectivity for those sites.
Sample prices:
Upon request.
Last modified:
November 8, 1998.

Free Electron Labs
428-B Moseley Drive, Charlottesville, VA 22903
Phone:
(804) 295-1905 (do not call in the morning!)
Fax:
(804) 295-1975
E-mail:
whitis@freelabs.com
URL:
www.freelabs.com
Contact:
Mark Whitis
Type of support:
Visit my Web site before trying to contact me via phone, fax, or e-mail. I have been paid to travel as far as Chile and Hawaii to do a job; I generally keep the trips short and do the actual development at my own offices.
Special expertise:
I do software development and consulting. I do not do help desk or end-user support. Scientific applications, commerce and financial transactions, computer security, networking, system administration, WWW, ISPs, and device drivers.
Sample prices:
US$100–$200/hour plus expenses with substantial minimum.
Last modified:
September 19, 1997.

InfoMagic, Inc.
11950 N. Highway 89, Flagstaff, AZ 86004
Phone:
(900) 786-5555
Fax:
(520) 526-9573
E-mail:
support@infomagic.com
URL:
www.infomagic.com/support/linux
Contact:
Henry M. Pierce
Type of support:
Individuals who purchase InfoMagic Linux Developer's Resource get
free e-mail and fax-back support. Support via phone for our Linux
Developer's Resource or any Linux vendor's Linux CD is US$2.00/
minute in the United States. Everyone is welcome to look at our sup-
port Web pages. International customers needing phone support
should contact us via e-mail first.
Special expertise:
Everything related to InfoMagic Linux Developer's Resource.
Sample prices:
Fixed service contracts, including remote maintenance are available
starting at US$50/engineering hour. Please contact us by e-mail for
additional information.
Last modified:
February 19, 1997.

NDA
800 West Cummings Park, Suite 2050, Woburn, MA 01801; 1818
Gilbreth Road, Suite 234, Burlingame, CA 94030; 1137 Pearl Street #207,
Boulder, CO 80302
Phone:
(617) 937-3338
Fax:
(617) 937-3775
E-mail:
info@nda.com
URL:
www.nda.com

Contact:
Peter Richards
Type of support:
Phone, e-mail, remote network administration, and on-site, 24-by-7 emergency response service.
Special expertise:
Unix.
Sample prices:
US$60–$150 based on task.
Last modified:
June 23, 1997.

REALM Information Technologies
5555 Oakbrook Parkway, Suite 605, Norcross, GA 30093
Phone:
(770) 446-1332
Fax:
(770) 446-9164
E-mail:
linux@realminfo.com
URL:
www.realminfo.com
Contact:
Michael D. Ivey
Type of Support:
Phone, e-mail, remote network administration, in-house, and on-site.
Special expertise:
System administration, Internet and intranet connectivity, firewall, network-attached storage, training.
Sample prices:
Upon request.
Last modified:
September 26, 1998.

Starshine Technical Services
903 Harriet Avenue, Campbell, CA, 95008-5119
Phone:
(800) 938-4078

E-mail:
consulting@starshine.org
URL:
www.starshine.org
Contact:
Jim Dennis
Type of support:
Phone, e-mail, remote network administration, and on-site.
Special expertise:
System administration, installation, configuration, troubleshooting, upgrades, custom scripting, and training. Custom firewall (proxy, masquerade, and packet filter) configuration and installation. Internet and intranet server design, configuration, and integration (including commerce sites with automated transaction processing and secure Web servers). Technical writing and editing.
Sample prices:
US$95–$125/hour. Quarterly and annual rates for support contracts are available. Special rates available for technical editing.
Last modified:
August 7, 1997.

Triangle Software Corporation
2375 Riverglenn Circle, Atlanta, GA 30338-5940
Phone:
(800) 625-7787, (770) 455-9089
Fax:
Available to clients.
E-mail:
triangle@cottongraphics.com
Contact:
Ben Cooper
Type of support:
In-house.
Special expertise:
On-site Java and ANSI C++ training. Java labs use the Linux JDK; C++ labs use GNU g++. Classes are very well reviewed by students.
Sample prices:
Upon request.
Last modified:
October 14, 1998.

DataCrest, Inc.
272 Snow Drive, Suite 103, Birmingham, AL 35209
Phone:
(888) 941-3282, (205) 941-3282
Fax:
(205) 941-1843
E-mail:
wh@datacrest.com
URL:
www.datacrest.com
Contact:
Walker Haddock
Type of support:
Phone, e-mail, remote network administration, in-house, and on-site.
Special expertise:
Database (SQL), routers, network computers, systems administration, mail and messaging, installation, programming services, Internet and intranet connectivity, firewall installation, troubleshooting, training.
Sample prices:
US$85–$150/hour.
Last modified:
February 28, 1998.

73.2. The Net Effect, LLC
P.O. Box 885, Mobile, AL 36601
Phone:
(334) 433-0196
Fax:
(334) 433-5371
E-mail:
grs@theneteffect.com
URL:
www.theneteffect.com
Contact:
Glenda Snodgrass, Managing Partner
Type of support:
On-site support in Greater Gulf Coast area. Phone, e-mail support to other locations. Remote administration, diagnostics, troubleshooting, etc.

Special expertise:
Internet connectivity, intranet development, database design and management, Web site development, Web, mail, FTP server installation and maintenance, electronic security evaluation, firewall installation and maintenance, Linux system administration for LAN and WAN.
Sample prices:
Upon request.
Last modified:
January 9, 1998.

Arizona Network Engineering Services
843 South Longmore Drive, Suite 1097, Mesa, AZ 85202
Phone:
(602) 926-0914
Fax:
(602) 926-8602
E-mail:
kevin@aznes.com
URL:
www.aznes.com
Contact:
Kevin Carpenter
Type of support:
Phone, e-mail, remote network administration, and on-site.
Special expertise:
Installation, administration, ISP, SQL database servers using Linux and native Windows clients, Internet and intranet connectivity, maintenance.
Sample prices:
Standard US$50/hour, client pays expenses, contracts available upon request.
Last modified:
January 16, 1998.

M. Cooper
P.O. Box 237, St. David, AZ 85630
Phone:
(520) 720-9431
E-mail:
thegrendel@theriver.com
URL:
personal.riverusers.com/~thegrendel

Contact:
Leo M. Cooper
Type of support:
Phone and e-mail.
Special expertise:
We offer setup, programming, and training.
Sample prices:
US$20–$50/hour, negotiable.
Last modified:
June 22, 1997.

LOD Communications
1231 East Artesian Way, Gilbert, AZ 85234
Phone:
(602) 632-0613
E-mail:
support@lod.com
URL:
www.lod.com/cns.html
Contact:
Todd Lawrence <lawrence@lod.com>
Type of support:
Phone, remote network administration, and on-site.
Special expertise:
We provide training in all forms of Unix system administration and
networking. We can generally provide our own transportation any-
where in the continental United States for on-site consultation.
Sample prices:
US$30 for phone support; US$50/hour with fixed/flat rate estimates
for remote (Telnet/rlogin) consulting; US$75/hour with fixed/flat rate
estimates for on-site Unix consultation
Last modified:
November 3, 1997.

Mechanix Computer Consulting
1515 S. Extension, Mesa, AZ 85210
Phone:
(602) 668-6325
Fax:
(602) 668-6325

E-mail:
shindle@toocool.com, shindle@goodnet.com
Contact:
Stephen Hindle
Type of support:
Phone, e-mail, remote network administration, and on-site.
Special expertise:
Fifteen years programming, experience with Linux kernels from 0.99 to 2.1.x. Installation, programming services, Perl, and connectivity.
Sample prices:
US$40/hour for programmer analyst; US$35/hour for programmer; hourly rates vary with length and nature of contract; fixed-price contracts are also available.
Last modified:
May 3, 1998.

M&S Group, Inc.
1038 E. Brentrup Drive, Tempe, AZ 85283
Phone:
(602) 491-7599
Fax:
(602) 491-7599
E-mail:
nikitin@asu.edu
URL:
www.m-and-s.com
Contact:
Sergey Nikitin
Type of support:
Phone, e-mail, in-house, and on-site.
Special expertise:
Training, workstation design and manufacturing.
Sample prices:
Upon request.
Last modified:
November 3, 1997.

Jay Ts
P.O. Box 410, Sedona, AZ 86339
Phone:
(520) 282-0549

E-mail:
jayts@bigfoot.com
URL:
www.kachina.net/~jay
Contact:
Jay Ts
Type of support:
Phone, e-mail, remote network administration, in-house, and on-site.
Special expertise:
Seventeen years of experience with Unix, C programming, Linux. Specialties: installation, configuration, programming, systems administration, troubleshooting, system analysis and upgrades, setting up and programming of Web servers, optimization of hardware reliability and data integrity.
Sample prices:
Rates vary based on a large number of factors. For on-site systems administration and troubleshooting, rates are typically from US$100–$300/hour. Hourly rates decrease as the total number of hours increase. For on-site visits, travel expenses are added.
Last modified:
March 27, 1998.

Corprotech, Inc.
3065 N. College #118, Fayetteville, AR 72703
Phone:
(501) 973-9500
Fax:
(501) 973-9503
E-mail:
info@corprotech.com
URL:
www.corprotech.com
Contact:
Don Faulkner <dfaulkne@corprotech.com>
Type of support:
Phone, e-mail, fax, remote network administration, in-house, and on-site.
Special expertise:
Our Linux team specializes in network design, security, and strategic planning. We are well prepared to assist in systems administration and troubleshooting.

Sample prices:
Our average hourly rate is US$100. Service contracts are available.
Please feel free to call for more details.
Last modified:
March 22, 1998.

A. C. Technologies
1844 Fell Street, San Francisco, CA 94117
Phone:
(415) 831-6689
Fax:
(415) 831-6687
E-mail:
info@ac-technologies.com
URL:
www.ac-technologies.com
Contact:
Rick Henry
Type of support:
Phone, e-mail, remote network administration, and on-site.
Special expertise:
Turnkey intranet solutions. PC-based Unix workstations and servers.
Database programming.
Sample prices:
Upon request.
Last modified:
November 8, 1998.

BayLinks Communications
555 Fulton Street, Suite 207, San Francisco, CA 94102
Phone:
(415) 553-8550
Fax:
(415) 487-9755
E-mail:
sales@baylinks.com
URL:
www.baylinks.com
Contact:
Sashi Shrestha <sshrestha@baylinks.com>
Type of support:
Phone, e-mail, remote network administration, in-house, and on-site.

Special expertise:
Internet and intranet connectivity, programming services, systems administration, firewall installation, troubleshooting, training.
Sample prices:
US$110/hour for on-site; US$60/hour remote administration.
Last modified:
December 9, 1997.

Carumba Inc.
35 West 20th Avenue, Suite #308, San Mateo, CA 94402
Phone:
(650) 572-2644
Fax:
(650) 572-2644
E-mail:
jauderho@carumba.com
Contact:
Jauder Ho
Type of support:
Phone, e-mail, and on-site.
Special expertise:
Installation, programming services, systems administration, Internet and intranet connectivity, firewall installation, troubleshooting, training; LDAP, Netscape directory server, calendar server.
Sample prices:
US$65–$120/hour depending on job and requirements.
Last modified:
September 13, 1997.

Casey-Dakota
3915 Wilshire Avenue, San Mateo, CA 94086
Phone:
(888) KCD-WEBB
Fax:
(415) 638-1363
E-mail:
hib@kcd.com
URL:
http://kcd.com
Contact:
Hib Engler

Type of support:
E-mail and remote network administration.
Special expertise:
Oracle on Linux, Internet, Web applications.
Sample prices:
Upon request.
Last modified:
November 5, 1998.

CustomLogic
11292 Coloma Road, Suite C, Gold River, CA 95670
Phone:
(916) 853-4920
Fax:
(916) 853-4924
E-mail:
info@customlogic.com
URL:
www.customlogic.com
Contact:
Tom Henderson, Brian Reid
Type of support:
Phone, e-mail, remote network administration, in-house, and on-site.
Special expertise:
Server sales and setup, networking setup. Web servers, intranets, and mail. Administration and custom software development.
Sample prices:
Upon request.
Last modified:
May 8, 1998.

CyberNautix, Inc.
4369 North Wislon Avenue, Fresno, CA, 93704
Phone:
(800) 7 NAUTIX; (800) 762-8849; (209) 222-9781
Fax:
Available to clients.
E-mail:
info@cybernaut.com
URL:
www.cybernaut.com

Contact:
Brian Haney
Type of support:
Phone and remote network administration.
Special expertise:
Installation, configuration, systems administration, Internet and intranet connectivity, Internet and intranet application development.
Sample prices:
US$75/hour, special fixed-price projects, or maintenance subscription.
Last modified:
June 6, 1997.

CyberShell Engineering
440 N. Winchester Boulevard, Suite 32, Santa Clara, CA 95050
Phone:
(408) 260-9541
Fax:
(408) 260-9541
E-mail:
medi@CyberShell.com
URL:
www.CyberShell.com
Contact:
Medi Montaseri
Type of support:
Phone, e-mail, remote network administration, on-site, and in-house.
Special expertise:
Web application development, database programming and administration, tools development and automation, test automation, regression, load, performance testing, project management, Unix and Linux administration, capacity planning, network management automation and training (Perl, C, CGI, Unix administration, computer networks, Unix).
Sample prices:
Upon request.
Last modified:
September 25, 1998.

DEC Consulting
929 20th Street, #28, Sacramento, CA 95814

Phone:
(916) 443-9051
E-mail:
info@dec.net
URL:
www.dec.net
Contact:
David Goldsmith <dhg@dec.net>
Type of support:
Phone, e-mail, remote network administration, and on-site.
Special expertise:
Unix and Internet security, secure Internet commerce, software development, CGIs, systems administration, and firewalls.
Sample prices:
Upon request.
Last modified:
January 23, 1998.

Paul C. Eastham's Linux Consulting
Santa Clara, CA U.S.A.
Phone:
(408) 241-3831
E-mail:
paul@monarchcom.net
URL:
www.monarchcom.net/~paul/linux.html
Contact:
Paul Eastham
Type of support:
Remote network administration and on-site.
Special expertise:
Network and network services configuration, ISP specific tasks (modem pools, dial-up networking config, virtual hosts), Web server config, scripting, CGI and Web scripts, automated fault monitoring and notification.
Sample prices:
Upon request.
Last modified:
March 21, 1998.

Evolve Computer Solutions
1556 Rambla Brisa, San Marcos, CA 92069
Phone:
(760) 746-2757
Fax:
(760) 751-0612
E-mail:
info@evolveinc.net
URL:
www.evolveinc.net
Contact:
Sean P. Kane
Type of support:
Phone, e-mail, in-house, and on-site.
Special expertise:
System design (complete hardware and software solutions), installa-
tion (distributions, X11, applications), etc.
Sample prices:
US$40–$75/hour.
Last modified:
June 22, 1997.

David Fetter
888 O'Farrell Street, Suite E1205, San Francisco, CA 94109
Phone:
(415) 567-2690
E-mail:
dfetter@best.com
URL:
www.best.com/~dfetter
Contact:
David Fetter
Type of support:
Phone, e-mail, remote network administration, and on-site.
Special expertise:
Installation, systems integration, systems administration, Internet and
intranet connectivity, troubleshooting.
Sample prices:
US$100/hour plus travel expenses. Negotiable for noncommercial
entities.

Last modified:
November 28, 1997.

Herlein Engineering
2034 Filbert Street, San Francisco, CA 94123
Phone:
(415) 519-3650
Fax:
(415) 440-9015
E-mail:
gherlein@slip.net
URL:
www.herlein.com
Contact:
Greg Herlein
Type of support:
Phone, e-mail, and remote network administration.
Special expertise:
System setup, administration, Web services, custom software develop-
ment, Internet connectivity, security and firewall solutions, training.
Sample prices:
Upon request.
Last modified:
March 21, 1998.

Hiverworld Consulting
2342 Shattuck Avenue, #321, Berkeley, CA 94704
Phone:
(510) 848-0740
E-mail:
sales@hiverworld.com
URL:
www.hiverworld.com
Contact:
John S. Flowers
Type of support:
Phone, e-mail, remote network administration, and on-site.
Special expertise:
Familiar with all aspects of Linux installation, development, and sup-
port, including firewalls and Internet security, C++ development, and
large-scale system integration.

Sample prices:
Upon request.
Last modified:
May 3, 1998.

Integration Engineering
2140 Redwood Highway H22, Greenbrae, CA 94904
Phone:
(415) 505-6135
Fax:
(415) 831-9763
E-mail:
Aftyde@tyde.net
URL:
www.tyde.net
Contact:
Arthur F. Tyde
Type of support:
Phone, e-mail, remote network administration, and on-site.
Special expertise:
Fifteen years industry experience, project management, disaster recovery, and systems engineering in the enterprise. Designed and implemented automated workstation distribution, software distribution, and enterprise systems management solutions. Experience on laptop, desktop, mini, and mainframe hardware. Founder and president of the (San Francisco) Bay Area Linux Users Group.
Sample prices:
Upon request.
Last modified:
September 27, 1998.

Inter@ctivate Consulting Group
2244b Carmel Valley Road, Del Mar, CA 92014
Phone:
(619) 793-4060
Fax:
(619) 793-4069
E-mail:
sean@interactivate.com
URL:
www.interactivate.com/

Contact:
Sean Dreilinger
Type of support:
Phone, e-mail, remote network administration, and on-site.
Special expertise:
Research, training, and marketing of networked information services, with an eye toward PD and GPL solutions, i.e., Linux!
Sample prices:
Free consultation. Per project and hourly rates negotiable.
Last modified:
August 7, 1997.

Internet Infrastructure Consulting, Inc.
457 College Avenue, Palo Alto, CA 94396-1525
Phone:
(650) 523-1759
Fax:
(650) 321-8855
E-mail:
info@iicons.com
URL:
www.iicons.com
Contact:
Paul Caloca
Type of support:
Phone, remote network administration, and on-site.
Special expertise:
Red Hat Commercial Support Partner, installation, systems administration, Internet and intranet connectivity, firewall installation, troubleshooting.
Sample prices:
Upon request.
Last modified:
June 26, 1998.

Linux-Consulting
RING, Inc.
P.O. Box 70958, Sunnyvale, CA 94086
Phone:
(408) 245-8400

Fax:
(408) 245-6448
E-mail:
alvin@planet.fef.com, alvin@Linux-Consulting.com
URL:
planet.fef.com, http://www.linux-consulting.com
Contact:
Alvin Oga
Type of support:
E-mail, remote network administration, and HOWTO-miniSearchEngine.
Special expertise:
We install, set up, test, and maintain your Linux machines, provide
custom Internet access and connectivity and custom Internet
servers.
Sample prices:
Upon request.
Last modified:
June 22, 1997.

Linux Services
849 Almar #C266, Santa Cruz, CA 95060
Phone:
(408) 781-0111
Fax:
(408) 426-5796
E-mail:
webmaster@linux-tech.com
URL:
www.linux-tech.com
Contact:
David Correa
Type of support:
Phone, e-mail, remote network administration, and on-site.
Special expertise:
Linux software installation and support, systems administration,
Internet connectivity, firewalls, Web site design and adminis-
tration.
Sample prices:
Upon request.

Last modified:
October 1, 1998.

The Los Angeles Research Coalition
425 S. Clementine Street #220, Anaheim, CA 92805
Phone:
(714) 533-4600
E-mail:
larc@lahackers.org
URL:
www.lahackers.org/linux
Contact:
Chris Sullivan
Type of support:
Phone, e-mail, remote network administration, in-house, and on-site.
Special expertise:
Security, Internet connectivity, training, firewall installation, turnkey
systems.
Sample prices:
Upon request.
Last modified:
March 21, 1998.

Dialog Group
92 Corporate Park Suite C-702, Irvine, CA 92606
Phone:
(714) 967-0625
E-mail:
roger@maplesoftware.com
Contact:
Roger McCarty
Type of support:
In-house and on-site.
Special expertise:
Install and configure hardware and software for Internet and intranet
systems: Web servers, gateways, firewalls, CGI programming. Custom
software development and database design.
Sample prices:
Upon request.
Last modified:
June 14, 1998.

Oration, LLC
7 West 41st Avenue, Suite 78, San Mateo, CA 94403
Phone:
(888) 672-8320
Fax:
Available to clients.
E-mail:
sales@oration.com
URL:
www.oration.com
Contact:
John Pramod
Type of support:
E-mail, remote network administration, and on-site.
Special expertise:
Network design, security assessments, installation (Intel and Digital Alpha), systems administration, Internet and intranet connectivity (Web, mail, and file servers), firewall installation.
Sample prices:
Upon request.
Last modified:
February 14, 1998.

Predictive Science
2008 Conquista Avenue, Long Beach, CA 90815
Phone:
(562) 592-6884
Fax:
(562) 592-6884
E-mail:
lganders@gte.net
URL:
www.predictivescience.com
Contact:
Leonard G. Anderson
Type of support:
Phone, fax, e-mail, remote network administration, and on-site (LA area only).
Special expertise:
Installation, configuration, systems administration and troubleshooting for Linux servers, workstations and networks. Specializing in

Small Office Home Office (SOHO) connectivity to the Internet and corporate intranet. Integration of Windows 95 and NT workstations with Linux servers for maximum productivity. Web programming services including CGI (using C or Perl).
Sample prices:
Upon request.
Last modified:
November 8, 1998.

QuickStart Group—Linux Installation Help and Hotline Support
2096 Walsh Avenue, Suite B, Santa Clara, CA 95050
Phone:
(408) 815-5425
Fax:
(408) 249-3979
E-mail:
linuxsupport@schieck.com
URL:
www.dnai.com/~clifs/linuxsupport
Contact:
Clif Schieck
Type of support:
Phone, e-mail, and on-site.
Special expertise:
Linux installation, setup, troubleshooting, and contract hotline support for Red Hat Software and Caldera. Network setup and Internet connectivity for small business and home network installation (5+ systems). Wireless network products for small businesses and home (Proxim). X-Windows setup support. Shell scripting (Perl, csh). Linux training courses.
Sample prices:
Upon request.
Last modified:
October 14, 1998.

RCT Design
Santa Barbara, CA 93117
Phone:
(805) 683-9717
Fax:
(805) 683-0717

E-mail:
bob@zooid.com
URL:
www.zooid.com
Contact:
Bob Tellefson
Type of support:
Phone, e-mail, and remote network administration.
Special expertise:
Turnkey Linux systems with support, Internet and intranet servers, remote access, gateways, firewalls, Web site design, database access, and CGI programming.
Sample prices:
US$45/hour.
Last modified:
June 22, 1997.

RG Consulting
1751 East Roseville Parkway #1828, Roseville, CA 95661
Phone:
(916) 786-7945
Fax:
(916) 786-5311
E-mail:
rfg@monkeys.com
Contact:
Ronald F. Guilmette
Type of support:
In-house and on-site.
Special expertise:
Maintenance and enhancement of GNU software development tools.
Sample prices:
Upon request.
Last modified:
June 22, 1997.

Bill Rousseau
842 Lucille Street, Livermore, CA 94550-3519
Phone:
(510) 455-8008
Fax:
(510) 455-8008

E-mail:
rousseau@aimnet.com
URL:
Look me up at www.ieee-sv-consult.org which I maintain.
Contact:
Bill Rousseau
Type of support:
Phone, e-mail, and on-site.
Special expertise:
Software development is off-site as much as possible. Training is available if there is sufficient interest.
Sample prices:
General computing consulting (Unix, Linux, network configuring, software development) US$100/hour. Support for individuals attempting to install or configure Linux for their own use or for work that promises to benefit the Linux community may be offered at much lower prices or for free in special cases.
Last modified:
June 22, 1997.

Sifry Consulting
6034 Fulton Street, San Francisco, CA 94121
Phone:
(415) 831-9507
Fax:
(415) 831-9763
E-mail:
david@sifry.com
URL:
www.sifry.com
Contact:
David Sifry
Type of support:
Phone, e-mail, remote network administration, and on-site.
Special expertise:
Internet-related services. Global experience in connecting businesses using the Internet. Cost-benefit analysis of business communication structures. Virtual private network setups and installations. Internet connections and firewall systems, Web servers, FTP servers, NNTP servers, SMTP servers, etc. Custom software development in C, C++, and Perl, development and deployment of the Concept series of Web

robots, intelligent agents, and search engines. Consulting is available in both English and Japanese.

Sample prices:

Upon request.

Last modified:

October 25, 1998.

Softcraft Impresa

2923 Cohansey Drive, San Jose, CA 95132

Phone:

(408) 251-9820

E-mail:

sales@softcraft.com

URL:

www.softcraft.com

Contact:

Mauro DePalma

Type of support:

Linux Generations (see the following) installs are supported, within reasonable expectations, for one year, at no additional cost.

Special expertise:

Using our own Linux Generations secure operating environment, we provide custom/turnkey solutions which work and have, in most cases, more functionality than similar, if any, legacy solutions at prices only possible with freely distributed software; close to the time and effort of the specific solution.

Sample prices:

US$90/hour. Depends on the kind of work and duration.

Last modified:

June 25, 1997.

Earl A. Stutes, Inc.

5156 Elrose Avenue, San Jose, CA 95124

Phone:

(408) 448-1089

Fax:

(408) 448-7864

E-mail:

estutes@eas.san-jose.ca.us

URL:

www.eas.san-jose.ca.us

Contact:
Earl Stutes
Type of support:
Phone, e-mail, and in-house.
Special expertise:
Web engineering, Internet security, Perl and C++ programming.
Sample prices:
Upon request.
Last modified:
November 3, 1997.

Tech Support
8527 Whittier Boulevard, Suite 11, Pico Rivera, CA 90660
Fax:
(562) 464-0468
E-mail:
rjayasin@zdnetmail.com
Contact:
Ruwan Jayasinghe
Type of support:
E-mail, remote network administration, in-house, and on-site (LA area only).
Special expertise:
Installation, systems administration, Internet and intranet connectivity, firewall installation, troubleshooting, training, Appleshare, Windows NT, Windows 95, and Linux Integration, DNS.
Sample prices:
Upon request.
Last modified:
September 26, 1998.

Vennerable Consultants
1563 Solano Avenue, Suite 516, Berkeley, CA 94707
Phone:
(510) 528-8072
Fax:
(510) 528-8072
E-mail:
jason@vennerable.com
URL:
www.vennerable.com

Contact:
Jason Venner
Type of support:
Phone, e-mail, remote network administration, and in-house.
Special expertise:
Linux, FreeBSD, X11 (servers and applications), C, C++, Perl, tcl/tk, java applications and FastCGI, Web support services, secure Web servers, and distributed systems.
Sample prices:
Upon request.
Last modified:
February 14, 1998.

Gregg Weber
1076 Carol Lane #3, Lafayette, CA 94549
Phone:
(510) 283-6264
E-mail:
gregg@netcom.com
Contact:
Gregg Weber
Type of support:
On-site in SF Bay area or can travel for big jobs.
Special expertise:
Installation, C programming services, UUCP for Netware networks, troubleshooting.
Sample prices:
US$55/hour.
Last modified:
February 19, 1997.

Yggdrasil Computing, Inc.
4880 Stevens Creek Boulevard, Suite 205, San Jose, CA 95129-1034
Phone:
(800) 261-6630
Fax:
(408) 261-6631
E-mail:
tech-support@yggdrasil.com
URL:
www.yggdrasil.com

Contact:

Bill Selmeier

Type of support:

Phone, e-mail, and remote network administration.

Special expertise:

We are also able to use our T1 Internet connection to solve your problem online (if your machine is also on the Internet).

Sample prices:

US$25 for a 15-minute support call guaranteed to solve your problem. Other arrangements are available.

Last modified:

June 23, 1997.

Colorado Computer Consultants

615 Quartz Way, Broomfield, CO 80020-1727

Phone:

(303) 404-9589

Fax:

(303) 404-9588

E-mail:

co3-info@co3.com

URL:

www.co3.com

Contact:

Robert Kaczanowsk

Type of support:

Phone, e-mail, and on-site.

Special expertise:

Installation.

Sample prices:

US$35/hour for individuals (appointment required); US$55/hour for individuals (immediate dispatch); US$45/hour for small business (appointment required); US$65/hour for small business (immediate dispatch); US$55/hour for corporates (appointment required); US$100/ hour for corporates (immediate dispatch); contract prices available. May be subject to additional charges. Mileage: US$0.26 per mile over 5 miles; parking as necessary. Permits and fees as necessary. Additional supplies as necessary.

Last modified:

March 18, 1997.

ComputerCrafts

P.O. Box 4349, Woodland Park, CO 80866; 111 North Center Street, Suite C, Woodland Park, CO 80863

Phone:
(719) 687-6687
E-mail:
info@computercrafts.net
Contact:
Alan White, Gwen Todd
Type of support:
Phone, e-mail, remote network administration (24/7), and on-site.
Special expertise:
Software development including architecture/design, test and documentation; solution to Year 2000 issues; networking; client/server; middleware messaging; business process reengineering; Web design, development, and hosting; systems administration; technology training.
Sample prices:
Fixed price, or time and material, rates from US$90–$125 depending on customer's statement of work.
Last modified:
December 31, 1997.

Dale K. Hawkins

4979 S. Prince Ct #302, Littleton, CO 80123
Phone:
(303) 794-4518
Fax:
Available to clients.
E-mail:
dhawkins@rmas.com
Contact:
Dale K. Hawkins
Type of support:
Phone, e-mail, remote network administration, in-house and on-site.
Special expertise:
Programming services (including scripting, system programming, or low-level development), systems administration, Internet and intranet connectivity, troubleshooting, training.
Sample prices:
Upon request.

Last modified:
August 15, 1998.

Daylight Software
1062 Lexington Lane, Estes Park, CO 80517
Phone:
(970) 685-6058
E-mail:
daylight@frii.net
URL:
www.frii.net/~daylight
Contact:
Chris Howard
Type of support:
Phone and remote network administration.
Special expertise:
Administration and programming.
Sample prices:
US$65/hour.
Last modified:
August 5, 1997.

Eklektix, Inc.
5624 Rim Rock Court, Boulder, CO 80301-3553
Phone:
(303) 581-0750
Fax:
(303) 581-0385
E-mail:
info@eklektix.com
URL:
www.eklektix.com
Contact:
Elizabeth O. Coolbaugh
Type of support:
Phone, e-mail, remote network administration, in-house, and on-site.
Special expertise:
Red Hat Linux Support Partner (annual contracts available). Systems administration, Web site installation, Internet gateway systems, Perl, python, C, or C++ programming services, troubleshooting, and training.

Sample prices:
Upon request.
Last modified:
May 19, 1998.

Electronic Oasis Consulting, Inc.
1110 Boston Avenue, Suite 203, Longmont, CO 80501
Phone:
(303) 415-0777
Fax:
(303) 415-0807
E-mail:
blaine@e-oasis.com
URL:
www.e-oasis.com
Contact:
Blaine Berger
Type of support:
Phone, e-mail, fax, remote network administration, and on-site.
Special expertise:
How to displace or coexist with Windows NT using Linux. How to use
Linux to set up your intranet or extranet.
Sample prices:
Upon request.
Last modified:
December 23, 1997.

Kevin Fenzi
10332 Federal #172, Denver, CO 80221
Phone:
Available to clients.
Fax:
Available to clients.
E-mail:
kevin@scrye.com
URL:
scrye.com/~kevin
Contact:
Kevin Fenzi
Type of support:
E-mail, remote network administration, in-house, and on-site.

Special expertise:
Familiar with most topics, emphasis on security.
Sample prices:
Upon request.
Last modified:
October 12, 1997.

Granite Computing Solutions
P.O. Box 270103, Fort Collins, CO 80527-0103
Phone:
(970) 225-2370
E-mail:
granite@SoftHome.net
URL:
www.SoftHome.net/granite
Contact:
Brian Grossman <brian@SoftHome.net>
Type of support:
Phone, e-mail and remote network administration, on-site, if you are
close enough.
Special expertise:
Web CGI programming; integration of Linux with other platforms.
Sample prices:
US$45/hour for technical support.
Last modified:
August 7, 1997.

The HELP! desk
125 Franklin Avenue #405, Grand Junction, CO 81505
Phone:
(970) 245-0102
E-mail:
swilliamson@usa.net
Contact:
Shawn Williamson
Type of support:
E-mail, remote network administration, and on-site.
Special expertise:
Installation, systems administration, connectivity, Mars Novel emula-
tor, e-mail systems.

Sample prices:
US$25/hour.
Last modified:
August 9, 1997.

Linux Technologies, Inc.
6834 S. University Boulevard, Suite 228, Littleton, CO 80122; 7419 Metcalf Avenue, Suite 101, Overland Park, KS 66204
Phone:
(888) Linux OS
Fax:
(303) 471-1344 (Colorado); (913) 789-7194 (Kansas)
E-mail:
info@linuxtek.com
URL:
www.linuxtek.com
Contact:
Sharif J. Awad
Type of support:
Phone, e-mail, remote network administration (24/7), and on-site.
Special expertise:
Internet and intranet connectivity, turnkey Linux-based Internet solutions, network integration solutions, application development, systems support and administration.
Sample prices:
Upon request.
Last modified:
November 8, 1998.

Sehnert Engineering
2536 Sweetwater Circle, Lafayette, CO 80026
Phone:
(303) 665-2262
E-mail:
bsehnert@carrieraccess.com
Contact:
Bill Sehnert
Type of support:
Phone, e-mail, and remote network administration.

Special expertise:
Design and development of embedded Linux kernels for industrial controllers, monitor and measurement equipment. Web-based interfaces for controlling and monitoring equipment.
Sample prices:
Upon request.
Last modified:
November 8, 1998.

David J. Lloyd
1960 Bavaria Drive #208, Colorado Springs, CO 80918-8264
Phone:
(719) 548-1658
Fax:
(719) 548-1658 (call before faxing)
E-mail:
sdjl@teal.csn.net
URL:
www.csn.net/~sdjl
Contact:
David Lloyd
Type of support:
Phone, e-mail, and on-site.
Special expertise:
Installation, Samba, programming services (Unix in general, Motif, pthreads, Sybase), systems administration.
Sample prices:
Upon request.
Last modified:
September 30, 1998.

Tummy.com,ltd.
5400 Fossil Court North, Fort Collins, CO 80525
Phone:
(970) 223-8215
Fax:
(408) 490-2728
E-mail:
info@tummy.com

URL:
www.tummy.com
Contact:
Sean Reifschneider
Type of support:
Phone, e-mail, in-house.
Special expertise:
Python, PHP, PostreSQL, custom programming, firewall setup, general Unix and Linux consulting.
Sample prices:
Upon request.
Last modified:
May 15, 1998.

Worldwide Solutions, Inc.
4450 Arapahoe Avenue, Suite 100, Boulder, CO 80303
Phone:
(303) 581-0800
Fax:
(303) 530-0191
E-mail:
info@wwsi.com
URL:
www.wwsi.com
Contact:
Steve Hultquist, Bob Davenport
Type of support:
Phone, e-mail, remote network administration, and on-site.
Special expertise:
High-speed networking, Internet-connected systems, IP networking, training, installations, configuration, specification, architecture, engineering, integration.
Sample prices:
Variable. Monthly support agreements or project-based statement of work pricing preferred. Standard hourly rates available for those with specific requirements.
Last modified:
November 4, 1997.

B.P.S. Technologies, Inc.
1255 Middlebury Road, Middlebury, CT 06762

Phone:
(203) 598-7327
Fax:
(203) 598-3406
E-mail:
bpsinc@juno.com
Contact:
Chris Salinardi
Type of support:
Phone, e-mail, in-house, and on-site.
Special expertise:
Advanced Linux system and network installation, systems administration training, Internet connectivity, firewall installation, and troubleshooting for all Linux systems.
Sample prices:
Upon request.
Last modified:
April 17, 1997.

78.2. BRT Technical Services Corporation

50 Newtown Road, Danbury, CT 06810
Phone:
(203) 748-5100
Fax:
(203) 796-7679
E-mail:
info@brttech.com
URL:
www.brttech.com
Contact:
Chad Robinson
Type of support:
Phone, e-mail, in-house, and on-site.
Special expertise:
Consulting services, installation, and maintenance, MIS outsourcing.
Sample prices:
Upon request.
Last modified:
July 18, 1997.

Collective Systems, LLC
P.O. Box 310379, Newington, CT 06131-0379
Phone:
(860) 666-7101
Fax:
(860) 666-2605
E-mail:
info@collsys.com
URL:
www.collsys.com
Contact:
Rob Casey
Type of support:
Phone, in-house, and on-site.
Special expertise:
Systems administration, firewalls, and network security.
Sample prices:
Upon request.
Last modified:
September 25, 1998.

Creative Systems
Clearview Knoll, Middlebury, CT 06762
Phone:
(203) 598-3690
Fax:
(203) 377-7931
E-mail:
creative@stratgrp.com
URL:
www.creative.stratgrp.com
Contact:
Silas Moeckel
Type of support:
Phone, e-mail, remote network administration, in-house, and on-site.
Special expertise:
Installation, programming services, systems administration, Internet connectivity, troubleshooting, and training.
Sample prices:
US$100/hour for troubleshooting (four-hour minimum); US$50/hour for programming and porting.

Last modified:
February 25, 1997.

Darcom Systems Ltd
11 Wall Street, Suite 6, Milford, CT 06460
Phone:
(203) 878-6640
E-mail:
info@darcom.dyndns.com
URL:
http://darcom.dyndns.com
Contact:
Peter D'Arco
Type of support:
Phone, e-mail, remote network administration, in-house, and on-site.
Special expertise:
Installation, systems administration, Internet and intranet connectivity, firewall installation, troubleshooting, training, complex mail systems, DNS, NIS, network infrastructure.
Sample prices:
US$50–$150/hour.
Last modified:
August 4, 1997.

DownCity, LLC
31 Broadway, Norwich, CT 06360
Phone:
(800) 954-INET; (860) 823-3000
E-mail:
sales@downcity.net
URL:
www.downcity.net
Contact:
Robert Szarka
Type of support:
Phone and on-site.
Special expertise:
Internet and intranet connectivity, Web, training.
Sample prices:
Upon request.
Last modified:
August 1, 1998.

Kracked Rock Komputing, LLC
13 Fleetwood Drive, Danbury, CT 06810-7009
Phone:
(203) 778-6269
Fax:
(203) 778-6292
E-mail:
ken@eci.com
Contact:
Kenneth E. Nawyn
Type of support:
Phone, e-mail, and in-house.
Special expertise:
Systems administration, system configuration, and technical support
for Linux and FreeBSD. Over ten years of Unix systems administration
experience along with Perl and C coding experience. For more
detailed description of our experience and services, please contact us.
Sample prices:
Upon request.
Last modified:
March 27, 1997.

Tempest Harding Incorporated
322 Main Street, Willimantic, CT 06226
Phone:
(860) 456-3639
Fax:
(860) 456-2814
E-mail:
info@thinc.net
URL:
www.thinc.net
Contact:
Mike Stella
Type of support:
Phone, e-mail, fax, remote network administration, in-house, and on-
site.
Special expertise:
Firewall installation, Internet and intranet connectivity, systems
administration, troubleshooting, programming services, application

design, network installation (hardware and software), custom-designed computer systems.

Sample prices:

US$95/hour on-site; US$75/hour off-site for consulting; US$95/hour for programming services; US$65/hour for phone support; US$30/hour for travel (car); US$30/hour plus expenses paid for travel (other).

Last modified:

May 2, 1997.

CE Computers

418B North Dupont Hwy, US 113, Georgetown, DE 19947

Phone:

(302) 855-0941

Fax:

(302) 855-1248

E-mail:

nick@ce.net, steve@ce.net

URL:

www.cecomputers.com

Contact:

Nick Mitchell, Steve Robison

Type of support:

All types.

Special expertise:

Familiar with most topics.

Sample prices:

Upon request.

Last modified:

November 8, 1998.

Al Guerra Enterprises, Inc.

7636 NW 2 Terrace, Miami, FL 33126

Phone:

(305) 264-4199

E-mail:

mclinux@gate.net

URL:

www.gate.net/~mclinux

Contact:

Al Guerra

Type of support:
Phone, e-mail, IRC.
Special expertise:
Familiar with most topics.
Sample prices:
Upon request.
Last modified:
May 6, 1998.

Anthony Awtrey Consulting
781 Marsaille Drive, Suite D, Indialantic, FL 32903
Phone:
(407) 777-7164
Fax:
(407) 779-7269
E-mail:
tony@awtrey.com
URL:
www.awtrey.com
Contact:
Anthony Awtrey
Type of support:
Support available via Web site–based discussion group, through
e-mail, phone, and on-site customer support.
Special expertise:
Anthony Awtrey is both an experienced Linux systems administrator
and delevoper and an MCSE. This allows AAC to provide expert integration of Linux and Windows 95, 98, and NT systems in a mixed
environment. On Linux specifically, we support initial system installa-
tion, software and hardware upgrades, and application installation.
We also have experience in setting up and tuning database and Web
performance and developing or customizing system applications. This
also includes Web-based database integration and advanced Web programming based on PHP and CGI programs. We do not do Web page
design or hosting.
Sample prices:
Upon request.
Last modified:
November 8, 1998.

Mark A. Richman
10818 Cypress Glen Drive, Coral Springs, FL 33071
Phone:
Available to clients.
Fax:
(954) 227-3425
E-mail:
mark@programmer.net
URL:
www.li.net/~mrichman
Contact:
Mark A. Richman
Type of support:
Phone, e-mail, fax, in-house, and on-site.
Special expertise:
Familiar with most topics.
Sample prices:
Upon request.
Last modified:
September 25, 1998.

Progressive Computer Concepts, Inc.
1371 Cassat Avenue, Jacksonville, FL 32205
Phone:
(800) 580-2640
Fax:
(904) 389-6584
E-mail:
info@progressive-comp.com
URL:
www.progressive-comp.com
Contact:
Lester Hightower
Type of support:
Phone, e-mail, remote network administration, and on-site.
Special expertise:
Linux consulting, installations, and turnkey networks. Systems programming, applications programming, system installation, and administration, Internet and intranet connectivity, LAN and WAN,

firewall installation, security, troubleshooting, and training, Samba SMB networking support, custom LAN, WAN, and intranet business systems development, Web and CGI development (e.g., database gateways, catalogs).
Sample prices:
US$52/hour off-site, $60 on-site for installation and administration; US$60/hour for programming; US$52/hour off-site, $60 on-site for LAN/WAN consulting; US$60/hour for Internet and intranet; US$45/hour for e-mail support
Last modified:
June 23, 1997.

Fly-By-Day Consulting, Inc.
4642 Bentley Place, Duluth, GA 30096
Phone:
(770) 662-8321
Fax:
Available to clients.
E-mail:
bob@cavu.com
URL:
www.mindspring.com/~cavu
Contact:
Bob Toxen
Type of support:
Phone, e-mail, fax, remote network administration, in-house, and on-site.
Special expertise:
Porting, developing client-server applications, systems administration, networking (Internet and intranet), Web setup, filesystem repair, Linux setup. Twenty-two years of Unix and C experience, reasonable rates.
Sample prices:
Upon request.
Last modified:
August 6, 1998.

Hacom
2477 Wrightsboro Road, Augusta, GA 30904
Phone:
(706) 736-8717

Fax:
Available to clients.
E-mail:
info@hacom.net
URL:
www.hacom.net
Contact:
Bao Ha <bao@hacom.net>
Type of support:
Phone, e-mail, and on-site.
Special expertise:
Installation, configuration, systems administration, Internet and intranet connectivity, Internet and intranet application development, and training. We are both an Internet service and Web presence provider.
Sample prices:
US$65–$120/hour depending on job and requirements. Free initial consultation.
Last modified:
February 23, 1998.

QWK.Net Communications
1441 E. Carter Lane, Boise, ID 83706
Phone:
(800) 720-2212
E-mail:
info@qwk.net
URL:
www.qwk.net
Contact:
Travis Burnside
Type of support:
Phone, e-mail, in-house, and on-site.
Special expertise:
Installation, programming services, systems administration, Internet and intranet connectivity, firewall installation, Web and database servers, troubleshooting, training.
Sample prices:
Upon request.

Last modified:
September 26, 1998.

Rahim Azizarab
1925 S. 3rd Avenue, Maywood, IL 60153
Phone:
(708) 344-6994
E-mail:
rahim@megsinet.net or ray@tezcat.com
Contact:
Rahim Azizarab
Type of support:
Phone, e-mail, and in-house.
Special expertise:
Installation, programming services, systems administration, Internet
and intranet connectivity, firewall installation, troubleshooting, and
training.
Sample prices:
Free for individuals.
Last modified:
August 5, 1997.

Extreme Systems Consulting
1730 N 12 Street, Quincy, IL 62301
Phone:
(217) 222-7345
Fax:
(217) 222-7634
E-mail:
esc@haruchai.rnet.com
URL:
haruchai.rnet.com/esc
Contact:
Aaron Baugher
Type of support:
Phone, e-mail, remote network administration, and on-site.
Special expertise:
Installation, systems administration, programming, Internet program-
ming.
Sample prices:
US$60/hour plus expenses.

Last modified:
February 28, 1998.

FourThought LLC
614 W Giles Lane, B, Peoria, IL 61614
Phone:
(309) 689-1159
Fax:
(309) 669-4808
E-mail:
sales@fourthought.com
URL:
fourthought.com
Contact:
Brian Butte
Type of support:
Phone, e-mail, in-house, and on-site.
Special expertise:
Internet, intranet, and extranet development, systems integration, training, troubleshooting.
Sample prices:
Upon request.
Last modified:
June 26, 1998.

Tony Mendoza
6694 Double Eagle Drive #302, Woodridge, IL 60517
Phone:
(630) 493-0639
E-mail:
tmendoza@aol.com
Contact:
Tony Mendoza
Type of support:
Phone, e-mail, and on-site.
Special expertise:
Installation, programming services, systems administration, Internet and intranet connectivity, troubleshooting, training.
Sample prices:
Upon request.

Last modified:
August 15, 1998.

onShore, Inc.
1407 W. Chicago, Chicago, IL 60622
Phone:
(312) 850-5200
Fax:
(312) 850-5208
E-mail:
sales@onshore.com
URL:
www.onshore.com
Contact:
Stelios Valavanis
Type of support:
Phone, e-mail, and in-house.
Special expertise:
In-house installation and support of Linux for custom solutions such as routing, firewall, e-mail, Web serving, etc. Custom solutions for job tracking, print spooling/processing, intranet, etc.
Sample prices:
US$125/hour for support; US$150/hour for software development.
Last modified:
July 2, 1997.

Promethan Consulting
18 Skyview Drive, Springfield, IL 62702
Phone:
(217) 698-6234
Fax:
(217) 698-6234
E-mail:
jeff@luci.org
URL:
www.luci.org/~jeff/promethan
Contact:
Jeff Licquia
Type of support:
All types.

Special expertise:
Specializing in open source solutions. Internet and intranet, database, other custom programming, Internet access, LAN/WAN setup, design, and installation, integration, and bridging Linux, Windows NT, and Novell.
Sample prices:
Upon request.
Last modified:
September 30, 1998.

WellThot Inc.
305 Van Damin Avenue, Glen Ellyn, IL 60137-5215
Phone:
(630) 545-1470
Fax:
(630) 545-1471
E-mail:
linux@wellthot.com
URL:
www.wellthot.com/Linux.html
Contact:
Mark A. Schwenk
Type of support:
Phone, e-mail, remote network administration, in-house, and on-site.
Special expertise:
Programming services, systems administration, Internet and intranet connectivity, firewall installation.
Sample prices:
Upon request.
Last modified:
August 9, 1998.

Citadel
241 East Eleventh Street, P.O. Box 407, Brookville, IN 47012-0407
Phone:
(765) 647-4720
Fax:
(765) 647-6059
E-mail:
lfrost@cnz.com

URL:
www.cnz.com
Contact:
Lyle Frost
Type of support:
Remote network administration, in-house, and on-site.
Special expertise:
Citadel provides a complete line of information technology services, including network and Internet and intranet consulting, design, installation, security, maintenance, and administration, as well as software development, training, and technical writing.
Sample prices:
Upon request.
Last modified:
November 3, 1997.

WSI.com Consulting
27998 McQueen Road, West Harrison, IN 47060
Phone:
(812) 637-6681
E-mail:
sales@wsicnslt.com
URL:
www.wsicnslt.com
Contact:
Shane Shuler
Type of support:
Phone, e-mail, remote network administration.
Special expertise:
We specialize in Internet connectivity, custom Web site development, intranet development.
Sample prices:
Upon request.
Last modified:
February 14, 1998.

JEONET
P.O. Box 1282, Iowa City, IA 52244
Phone:
(319) 338-6353; (888) 8JEONET

Fax:
(319) 338-6353; (888) 8JEONET
E-mail:
afan@jeonet.com
URL:
www.jeonet.com/jeonet
Contact:
Afan Ottenheimer
Type of support:
Phone, e-mail, fax, remote network administration, in-house, and on-site.
Special expertise:
NT-Linux integration (Samba and NFS), installation, Web databases, Perl, cron, sendmail, systems administration, Internet and intranet connectivity, Linux firewalls, troubleshooting, training.
Sample prices:
Upon request.
Last modified:
April 22, 1998.

Linux Technologies, Inc.
6834 S. University Boulevard, Suite 228, Littleton, CO 80122; 7419 Metcalf Avenue, Suite 101, Overland Park, KS 66204
Phone:
(888) Linux OS
Fax:
(303) 471-1344 (Colorado); (913) 789-7194 (Kansas)
E-mail:
info@linuxtek.com
URL:
www.linuxtek.com
Contact:
Sharif J. Awad
Type of support:
Phone, e-mail, remote network administration (24/7), and on-site.
Special expertise:
Internet and intranet connectivity, turnkey Linux-based Internet solutions, network integration solutions, application development, systems support and administration.

Sample prices:
Upon request.
Last modified:
November 8, 1998.

NT Integrators
2400 W. 31st Street, Lawrence, KS 66046
Phone:
(913) 842-1100
E-mail:
watts@sunflower.com
URL:
www.ntintegrators.com
Contact:
Jeffrey Watts
Type of support:
Remote network administration and on-site.
Special expertise:
Installation of networks, Internet and intranet connectivity, custom
programming. Custom Web database solutions.
Sample prices:
US$75/hour.
Last modified:
June 13, 1997.

THEBUC.COM
11146 Nieman Road #102, Overland Park, KS 66210
Phone:
(913) 791-6946
E-mail:
consulting@thebuc.com
URL:
www.thebuc.com
Contact:
Bryan Jones
Type of support:
Phone and e-mail.
Special expertise:
Linux administration, Web hosting, Internet and intranet setup, Web
design, system setup. Shell scripting (Perl, Korn, and bash/bourne).

Sample prices:
Upon request.
Last modified:
February 23, 1998.

CMT Consulting
5609-D Salmen Street, Harahan, LA 70123
Phone:
(504) 258-0689
Fax:
(504) 733-6904
E-mail:
genejr@cmtconsulting.com
URL:
www.cmtconsulting.com
Contact:
William Billingsley
Type of support:
Phone, e-mail, remote network administration, and on-site. Two-hour on-site guarantee anywhere in Louisiana and Mississippi Gulf Coast.
Special expertise:
Year 2000 compliance, installation, programming services, systems administration, Internet and intranet connectivity, firewall installation, troubleshooting, training. Turnkey ISP solutions.
Sample prices:
US$125/hour. Quarterly, biannual, and yearly contracts available.
Last modified:
October 24, 1997.

Midcoast Internet Solutions
P.O. Box 669, Rockland, ME 04841
Phone:
(207) 594-8277
Fax:
(207) 596-7248
E-mail:
webmaster@midcoast.com
URL:
www.midcoast.com/mis
Contact:
Jason Philbrook

Type of support:
Phone, e-mail, remote network administration, and on-site.
Special expertise:
Connectivity, troubleshooting, system setups.
Sample prices:
US$50/hour minimum.
Last modified:
March 12, 1997.

89. USA - Maryland 89.1. I-Link, Inc.
136 Forests Edge Place, Laurel, MD 20724
Phone:
(301) 604-8411
Fax:
(301) 604-8411
E-mail:
fbennett@i-linkcom.com
URL:
i-linkcom.com
Contact:
Fred Bennett
Type of support:
Phone, e-mail, and in-house.
Special expertise:
We create Linux Internet, Web, and mail servers. We also support software from Red Hat Software, InfoMagic, Walnut Creek, and Caldera. We are an authorized Caldera Channel partner.
Sample prices:
US$50–$100/hour.
Last modified:
August 7, 1997.

JAMUX
4520 Yates Road, Beltsville, MD 20705-2629
Phone:
(301) 595-2013
E-mail:
jam@jamux.com
URL:
www.tux.org/~jam/jamux

Contact:
John A. Martin
Type of support:
Phone, e-mail, remote network administration, in-house, and on-site.
Special expertise:
Systems engineering, Linux installation, administration, support, networking, security. Red Hat Linux. Authorized Caldera Channel partner.
Sample prices:
Upon request.
Last modified:
November 14, 1997.

Matthew Kaylor
13639 Barnhart Road, Clear Spring, MD 21722
Phone:
(301) 733-2922
E-mail:
maxit@nfis.com
URL:
www.nfis.com/~maxit
Contact:
Matthew Kaylor
Type of support:
Phone, e-mail, IRC, and worldwide travel for on-site support.
Special expertise:
Linux system setup (remote or in-house) to commercial networked Internet servers (complete). Personal or group Linux training courses.
Sample prices:
US$5000/month; US$300/day; US$40/hour; negotiated pricing based on needs for individuals.
Last modified:
June 22, 1997.

Core Secure
49 Mountaingate Road, Ashland, MA 01721-2339
Phone:
(508) 881-5740
Fax:
(508) 881-1566

E-mail:
dave@coresecure.com
URL:
www.coresecure.com
Contact:
Davide De Santis
Type of support:
E-mail, remote network administration, and on-site.
Special expertise:
Web-based application development, Internet and intranet connectivity, firewall configuration and setup, troubleshooting, install, setup, and configuration of Linux as CSU/DSU and router for a dedicated frame relay connection, DNS configuration, and more.
Sample prices:
Upon request.
Last modified:
October 25, 1998.

NetInterface Consulting
56 Houghton Street, Hudson, MA 01749
Phone:
(978) 567-0972
Fax:
(978) 567-0972
E-mail:
sales@netinterface.com
URL:
www.netinterface.com
Contact:
Leonard Forziati
Type of support:
Phone, e-mail, remote network administration, in-house, and on-site.
Special expertise:
Installation, database configuration, systems administration, Internet and intranet connectivity, firewall installation, troubleshooting.
Sample prices:
Upon request.
Last modified:
October 25, 1998.

Worldmachine Technologies Corporation
44 Winter Street, Boston, MA 02108-4745
Phone:
(617) 357-4040
Fax:
(617) 357-4949
E-mail:
info@worldmachine.com
URL:
www.worldmachine.com
Contact:
Eric J. Hansen <eric@worldmachine.com>
Type of support:
Phone, e-mail, emergency 24/7 pager, remote network administration, in-house, and on-site.
Special expertise:
Familiar with most topics.
Sample prices:
US$90–$150/hour (depending on services). Our normal hourly rates are provided at a discount for maintenance contract customers. We will also provide fixed-price bids for design and development projects.
Last modified:
December 31, 1997.

Working Version
31 Shea Road, Cambridge, MA 02140
Phone:
Scheduled phone calls by appointment; please use e-mail, generally.
Fax:
Scheduled fax reception by appointment; please e-mail PostScript generally.
E-mail:
bb@wv.com
URL:
www.wv.com
Contact:
Brian Bartholomew
Type of support:
Phone, e-mail, fax, remote network administration, in-house, and on-site.

Special expertise:
We generally do contract program development, Unix toolsmithing, Unix piecework, and version-control infrastructure consulting, but we're very flexible and highly negotiable. Here are some keywords to describe our expertise base: configuration management, version control, ClearCase, telco, tariffs, Internet service provider, move planning and execution, ISP cutover, vendor management, systems architect, systems analysis and planning, systems design, feasibility and cost benefit studies, business process reengineering, enterprise integration, technology infrastructure requirements determination, project planning and scheduling, prototyping and evaluation, requirements determination, toolsmithing, network design and implementation, network monitoring, network mapping, network visualization, facilities planning, machine room layout, data center design, automated regression testing, build systems, financial, trading floor, distributed systems, database design, Unix systems administration.

Sample prices:
US$65–$250/hour. Please e-mail requirements for a quote on fixed-price development projects.

Last modified:
November 3, 1997.

Nugent Telecommunications
3081 Braeburn Circle, Ann Arbor, MI 48108
Phone:
(734) 971-1076
Fax:
(734) 971-4529
E-mail:
jjn@nuge.com
URL:
www.nuge.com
Contact:
Jay Nugent
Type of support:
Phone, e-mail, remote network administration, in-house, and on-site.
Special expertise:
Assisting ISPs and small businesses with Web, e-mail, and DNS servers, systems administration, security, SNMP management and

monitoring, training and seminars, Internet access (PPP, ISDN, T1, Frame Relay, ATM, and wireless).
Sample prices:
US$50–$125/hour.
Last modified:
March 27, 1998.

PIR Consulting
625 Barber Avenue, Ann Arbor, MI 48103
Phone:
(734) 741-0202
Fax:
(734) 761-6865
E-mail:
pir@pirconsulting.com
URL:
www.pirconsulting.com
Contact:
Andrew Caird, Kip Cranford
Type of support:
E-mail, remote network administration, and on-site.
Special expertise:
PIR Consulting offers installation, programming, systems administration, Internet and intranet connectivity, troubleshooting, and training for Linux.
Sample prices:
Upon request.
Last modified:
October 25, 1998.

Waypointe Information Technologies
1121 Ottawa Beach Road, Suite 200, Holland, MI 49424
Phone:
(616) 786-4488
Fax:
(616) 786-4499
E-mail:
pete@waypointe.com
URL:
www.waypointe.com

Contact:
Pete Hoffswell
Type of support:
Phone, e-mail, remote network administration, in-house, and on-site.
Special expertise:
Server installation and configuration, systems administration, security services, network connectivity, firewall installation.
Sample prices:
Upon request.
Last modified:
July 18, 1997.

Jim Willette
18190 - 15 Mile Road, Big Rapids, MI 49307
Phone:
(616) 592-3119
E-mail:
jimw@ctec.net
URL:
www.netonecom.net/~jimw, http://www.ctec.net
Contact:
Jim Willette
Type of support:
Phone, e-mail, remote network administration, and in-house.
Special expertise:
Specialties include Internet firewalls, proxy servers, Web servers, domain name servers (DNS), Linux terminal servers, Internet connectivity networking, NFS, and more.
Sample prices:
US$45/hour for phone support; US$55/hour for on-site plus expenses and travel time (negotiable).
Last modified:
March 27, 1997.

MaxBaud.Net
4940 S. Peck Avenue, Independence, MO 63031
Phone:
(816) 478-7078
Fax:
(816) 350-7001

E-mail:
ccav@maxbaud.net
URL:
www.maxbaud.net
Contact:
Chris Caviness
Type of support:
Phone, e-mail, remote network administration, in-house, and on-site.
Special expertise:
Installation, programming services, systems administration, Internet
and intranet connectivity, firewall installation, troubleshooting, training.
Sample prices:
US$65/hour.
Last modified:
March 27, 1998.

Internet Gateway Inc.
#12 Plaza 94, Suite 108, St. Peters, MO 63367
Phone:
(314) 936-8655
Fax:
(314) 936-0054
E-mail:
sales@igateway.net
URL:
www.igateway.net
Contact:
Tim Jung
Type of support:
Phone, e-mail, remote network administration, in-house, and on-site.
Special expertise:
Installation, systems administration, Internet and intranet connectivity,
firewall installation, troubleshooting. Training, e-commerce, security
audits, enterprise network planning, design, management, and inte-
gration. ISP consulting and support, WAN/LAN configuration and
setup.
Sample prices:
Upon request.
Last modified:
October 14, 1998.

Reboot Inc.
579 Rue St., Ferdinand Florissant, MO 63031
Phone:
(314) 830-0427
Fax:
(314) 830-0427
E-mail:
reboot@cyberusa.com
URL:
www.cyberusa.com/~reboot
Contact:
Zubin Chandran
Type of support:
Phone, e-mail, and on-site to the 314 and 618 area codes.
Special expertise:
Training on-site as well as hardware upgrades and sales.
Sample prices:
Call for special pricing and promotional deals. US$40/hour for commercial clients, and US$30/hour for residential clients. Minimum one-hour charge per visit. Promotional deals available.
Last modified:
September 23, 1997.

Damon C. Richardson
St. Louis, MO
E-mail:
mercybeat@earthlink.net
URL:
home.earthlink.net/~mercybeat/linux
Contact:
Damon C. Richardson
Type of support:
E-mail and on-site.
Special expertise:
Installation, programming services, client/server database programming, systems administration, Internet and intranet connectivity, firewall installation, troubleshooting, training.
Sample prices:
Upon request.

Last modified:
November 21, 1997.

Cottonwood Computer Solutions
5285 River Road, Laurel, MT 59044
Phone:
(406) 698-2145
E-mail:
ccsolutions@imt.net
URL:
www.imt.net/~ccsolutions
Contact:
Brock Williams
Type of support:
Phone and on-site.
Special expertise:
Installation, programming, cross-platform network integration.
Sample prices:
US$40/hour general, programming negotiable, or bid per job.
Last modified:
February 11, 1998.

Jinn Enterprises
P.O. Box 22174, Lincoln, NE 68542
Phone:
(402) 440-3225
E-mail:
jinn@irony.org
URL:
www.irony.org/linux
Contact:
Marina Gandelsman
Type of support:
Phone, e-mail, remote network administration, in-house, and on-site
(within 60 miles of Lincoln).
Special expertise:
Installation, systems administration, Internet connectivity, firewall
installation, training.
Sample prices:
Upon request.

Last modified:
September 25, 1998.

Morton Technologies
5112 W. Kent Street
Phone:
(402) 470-3243; (402) 890-4328
E-mail:
mmorton@binary.net
URL:
www.binary.net/mmorton/morton.html
Contact:
Matt Morton
Type of support:
Phone, e-mail, remote Web site administration, in-house, and on-site.
Special expertise:
Installation, programming services, systems administration, Internet and intranet connectivity, firewall installation, troubleshooting, training. Also printed circuit board design and custom system development.
Sample prices:
Upon request.
Last modified:
May 30, 1998.

Paktronix Systems, LLC
1506 North 59th Street, Omaha, NE 68104
Phone:
(402) 932-7250
Fax:
(402) 932-7258
E-mail:
tech@paktronix.com
URL:
www.paktronix.com, www.midwestlinux.com
Contact:
Matthew G. Marsh
Type of support:
Phone, e-mail, remote network administration, in-house, on-site.
Special expertise:
Network security, virtual private networks, firewall installation, systems administration, Internet and intranet connectivity, troubleshoot-

ing. Nebraska's oldest and largest Linux source. Authorized Caldera Channel partner, Authorized Red Hat Reseller, Authorized S.u.S.E. Reseller, and Novell Authorized partner.
Sample prices:
Upon request.
Last modified:
October 25, 1998.

Steve Hedlund
Las Vegas, NV
Phone:
(702) 254-6749
E-mail:
ssh@dpn.com
URL:
www.usnetworking.com
Contact:
Steve Hedlund
Type of support:
Phone, e-mail, and in-house.
Special expertise:
Internet and intranet connectivity, installation, programming services, systems administration, firewall installation, troubleshooting, virtual addressing, IP masquerading (for connecting networks to the Internet).
Sample prices:
US$25–$40/hour.
Last modified:
March 19, 1998.

CodeMeta, Inc.
795 Elm Street, #508, Manchester, NH 03101
Phone:
(800) 354-2209; (603) 625-1493
E-mail:
info@codemeta.com
URL:
http://linux.codemeta.com
Contact:
Tom Albright
Type of support:
Phone, e-mail, on-site, and in-house.

Special expertise:
Installation and configuration of Internet and intranet servers, Web and database integration, debugging, systems administration, Red Hat Linux.
Sample prices:
Upon request.
Last modified:
August 9, 1998.

Juan Daugherty
633 Franklin Avenue, Nutley, NJ 07110
Phone:
(973) 340-3002
Fax:
(973) 340-2685
E-mail:
juan@acm.org
URL:
www.kybernet.com
Contact:
Juan Daugherty
Type of support:
Phone and e-mail.
Special expertise:
Systems and application development.
Sample prices:
Upon request.
Last modified:
January 16, 1998.

Etc Services
31 N. Vivyen Street, Bergenfield, NJ 07621-1529
Phone:
(201) 385-7113; pager: (800) 379-2402
E-mail:
swebster@carroll.com
Contact:
Scott D. Webster
Type of support:
Phone, e-mail, fax, remote network administration, in-house, and on-site.

Special expertise:
System setup and administration, TCP/IP network configuration, Web server setup (not content creation), Linux LAN servers, DNS configuration, experience with Linux on x86, Linux on Digital Alpha (AXP).
Sample prices:
Upon request.
Last modified:
December 18, 1997.

ZEI Software
2713 State Hwy 23 South, Newfoundland, NJ 07435
Phone:
(201) 208-8800
Fax:
(201) 208-1888
E-mail:
art@nji.com
Contact:
Arthur Zysk
Type of support:
Phone, e-mail, in-house, and on-site.
Special expertise:
Senior project managers with 25 years of experience. C, C++, Sybase, kernel drivers, Internet connectivity. Mission-critical project management services.
Sample prices:
Upon request.
Last modified:
June 24, 1997.

Crynwr Software
521 Pleasant Valley Road, Potsdam, NY 13676
Phone:
(315) 268-1925
Fax:
(315) 268-9201
E-mail:
info@crynwr.com
URL:
www.crynwr.com

Contact:
Russell Nelson
Type of support:
All types.
Special expertise:
Qualified to do any kind of support; specializing in networking drivers.
Sample prices:
US$100/hour; fixed-price quotes for your task.
Last modified:
June 22, 1997.

Evantide Graphical
15 Thornridge Lane S., Setauket, NY 11720
Phone:
(516) 246-8212
Fax:
(516) 246-8212
E-mail:
staff@evantide.com
URL:
www.evantide.com
Contact:
Anders Brownworth
Type of support:
Remote network administration and on-site.
Special expertise:
Soup to nuts, qualified for any task; we excel in emergency situations.
We cover clients on Long Island, west to Gotham and east to the
Hamptons.
Sample prices:
US$125/hour plus expenses.
Last modified:
December 31, 1997.

Lrw.Net
188 2nd Avenue, #9, New York, NY 10003
Phone:
(212) 254-3551
Fax:
(212) 254-8176

E-mail:
rw26@lrw.net
URL:
http://lrw.net
Contact:
Randy Wright
Type of support:
Phone, e-mail, and remote network administration.
Special expertise:
Programming, server and network installations, training, Web administration and programming.
Sample prices:
Upon request.
Last modified:
October 2, 1998.

Psytronics
99 Leroy Street, Binghamton, NY 13905
Phone:
(607) 724-3240
Fax:
(516) 598-4619
E-mail:
info@psytronics.com
URL:
www.psytronics.com
Contact:
Jaron Rubenstein
Type of support:
All types. Support contracts available.
Special expertise:
Familiar with most topics. Specializing in Linux/Windows heterogeneous network integration, custom programming, and Internet and intranet server configuration. Authorized Red Hat Reseller and authorized Red Hat Support Partner.
Sample prices:
Upon request.
Last modified:
October 13, 1998.

David Wood
157 Ludlow Street, 6th Floor, New York, NY 10002
Phone:
(212) 982-9360
Fax:
(212) 982-9370
E-mail:
dwood@templar.com
URL:
www.templar.com
Contact:
David Wood
Type of support:
Phone, e-mail, remote network administration, in-house, and on-site.
Available in New York City.
Special expertise:
Installation, systems administration, Internet and intranet connectivity,
firewall installation, troubleshooting, training.
Sample prices:
Upon request.
Last modified:
May 28, 1998.

Model-View-Computing
1007 N. Buchanan Boulevard, Durham, NC 27701-1139
Phone:
(919) 286-1441
Fax:
(919) 286-1441
E-mail:
biggers@gooey.mvc.com.inter.net, biggers@saiph.com
Contact:
Mark Biggers
Type of support:
Phone, e-mail, remote network administration, IRC (local server, by
arrangement), in-house, and on-site.
Special expertise:
Nine years X/Motif development, consulting experience. Two years of
networking and Web intranet and Internet development experience;
see www.unitedmedia.com/store for an example. Thirteen years C,

Unix, and Linux applications and system programming, three years C++ programming and OOD. Most familiar with Red Hat Linux. Two years Python language programming. Experienced trainer: X-Window System introduction, X/Motif programming, Linux/Unix introduction, C++ introduction.

Sample prices:
US$0–$125/hour. Pricing varies, based on duration and complexity of projects. Flexible pricing for individuals and nonprofit organizations.
Last modified:
April 30, 1997.

The Cleveland Internet Association
4876 E. 85th Street, Cleveland, OH 44125
Phone:
(216) 552-4368
E-mail:
jeff@cia.net
URL:
www.cia.net
Contact:
Jeff Garvas
Type of support:
Phone, e-mail, remote administration, in-house, and on-site. Flexible, available 24/7 with retainer. Willing to travel.
Special expertise:
Installation, consultation, programming, Web design, CGI authoring, database integration, systems administration, Internet and intranet connectivity, troubleshooting, training, network monitoring and alpha-paging automation installation. We also support operating systems besides Linux, and the intergration between them.
Sample prices:
Prices vary depending upon type of help needed and our current availability. We are flexible for nonprofit, government, and educational institutions. Free estimates and/or quotes in most cases.
Last modified:
August 9, 1997.

The Computer Underground, Inc.
1357 West Lane Avenue, Suite 210, Columbus, OH 43221
Phone:
(614) 485-0506; (888) 485-5865

E-mail:
president@tcu-inc.com
URL:
www.tcu-inc.com
Contact:
Mark Nielsen
Type of support:
E-mail and remote network administration.
Special expertise:
Preinstalled Linux computers, programming, Web, database, networking, configuration. Apache, Perl, Embperl, ePerl, mod_perl, PostgreSQL, integrating various platforms and operating systems with Linux in a network environment.
Sample prices:
Upon request.
Last modified:
September 26, 1998.

DESIGN SCIENCE LABS
P.O. Box 542, Berea, OH 44017-0542
Phone:
(216) 243-1346
Fax:
(216) 524-0979
E-mail:
stutz@dsl.org
URL:
http://dsl.org
Contact:
Michael Stutz
Type of support:
Phone and e-mail.
Special expertise:
Music/CD-R production, tech writing, Web design, training.
Sample prices:
Billing by project or hourly, US$50/hour.
Last modified:
June 29, 1997.

Intelligent Algorithmic Solutions (Intalsol)
1727 Messner Drive, Hilliard, OH 43026

Phone:
(614) 529-1472
E-mail:
Sean-Walton@technologist.com
Contact:
Sean Walton
Type of support:
E-mail, in-house, and on-site.
Special expertise:
Programming services (languages, AI, general algorithms), Linux installation, setup, LAN, Web site administration, and troubleshooting.
Sample prices:
US$45–$70/hour for programming (fully designed, documented fault-tolerant); US$35–$45/hour for Linux installation (includes training); US$35–$50/hour for Linux administration and troubleshooting; US$35/hour for Linux training; US$45–$60/hour for Linux Web site installation (includes homepage—must provide own ISP).
Last modified:
August 13, 1997.

Internet Robotics
131 Willow Lane, Floor 2, Oxford, OH 45056
Phone:
(513) 523-7621
Fax:
(513) 523-7501
E-mail:
support@bill.iac.net
URL:
www.minivend.com
Contact:
Mike Heins
Type of support:
Phone and e-mail, will travel for training courses.
Special expertise:
Specializing in online shopping with MiniVend, the GPL shopping cart. Expertise in all aspects of Linux, Web administration, shell and Perl scripting, and network configuration. Performance tuning.
Sample prices:
US$100/hour for contract shopping site HTML design; US$100 for monthly retainer (includes first hour); US$85/hour for contract techni-

cal support (with retainer); US$100/hour for contract shopping soft-ware design; US$85/hour for contract technical support (with retainer at monthly minimum of one hour); US$100/hour for expert technical support (uncontracted).
Last modified:
August 4, 1997.

Bradley M. Kuhn
P.O. Box 20042, Cincinnati, OH 45220
Phone:
(513) 475-0311
E-mail:
bkuhn@ebb.org
URL:
www.ebb.org/bkuhn/resume
Contact:
Bradley M. Kuhn
Type of support:
Phone, e-mail, and on-site.
Special expertise:
Installation, integration, Perl development, systems administration, GPL software development.
Sample prices:
US$25–$45/hour depending on work. Substantially less for nonprofit organizations.
Last modified:
May 16, 1998.

Life & Energy Systems
700 West Pete Rose Way, Cincinnati, OH 45203
Phone:
(513) 721-4055; (800) 775-0977
Fax:
(513) 421-7711
E-mail:
graham@techgallery.com
URL:
www.techgallery.com
Contact:
Graham Cebulskie, David Powell

Type of support:
Phone, e-mail, remote network administration, in-house, and on-site.
Special expertise:
Setup and configuration of light- and heavy-duty (multiprocessor) Linux servers, RAID configurations, database installation and configuration (PostgreSQL, MySQL, msql, Sybase, Informix), CGI (PHP, Perl, tcl, C/C++, java), remote and on-site systems administration, firewalling, IP masquerading, custom router configuration, mail systems (POP, IMAP), directory services (LDAP), DNS, Web server (Apache, NCSA, Netscape FastTrack), on-site training, troubleshooting. Certifications: Netscape Solution Expert.
Sample prices:
Upon request.
Last modified:
October 25, 1998.

MaDCreW Organization
1446 West River RD Suite G, Elyria, OH 44035
Phone:
(440) 324-7317
Fax:
(440) 324-7323
E-mail:
dice@mcfounders.com
Contact:
Chris Rhame
Type of support:
Phone, e-mail, remote network administration, in-house, and on-site.
Special expertise:
Internet and intranet connectivity, security, firewall, troubleshooting, installation and setup, training, administration, Web development, DNS, FTP, mail, news, IRC servers. Full ISP setup and administration.
Sample prices:
Upon request.
Last modified:
December 12, 1997.

Mythical Solutions
3344 Chetwood Place, Dublin, OH 43017
Phone:
Available to clients.

E-mail:
ximenes@mythic.net
URL:
www.mythic.net/consult.html
Contact:
Ximenes Zalteca
Type of support:
Phone, e-mail, remote network administration, and on-site.
Special expertise:
Systems administration, DNS, Web, FTP, qmail, Red Hat Linux, troubleshooting, security, installation, hardware, HTML, and more. It is highly likely that whatever you want, we can do for you.
Sample prices:
Depends highly upon the type of work. A remote administration job would go for US$300/day or so. Prices are negotiable, as well as the method of determining the price (per day, per hour, per week, etc.).
Last modified:
October 12, 1997.

New Age Consulting Service, Inc.
815 Superior Avenue #425, Cleveland, OH 44114
Phone:
(216) 619-2000
Fax:
(216) 619-2004
E-mail:
support@nacs.net
URL:
www.nacs.net
Contact:
Gregory Boehnlein
Type of support:
Phone, e-mail, remote network administration, and on-site.
Special expertise:
Familiar with most topics. Use Linux for large-scale firewall and Internet service provisioning.
Sample prices:
Upon request.
Last modified:
October 1, 1998.

Practical Network Design
9 Chambers Road, Mansfield, OH 44906-1302
Phone:
(419) 529-3841
Fax:
(419) 529-3625
E-mail:
info@practical.net
URL:
www.practical.net
Contact:
Chuck Stickelman
Type of support:
Phone, e-mail, and on-site.
Special expertise:
PND specializes in Unix-based solutions, with a strong emphasis on
Linux. We provide system and network planning, sales, installation,
support, and administration. Custom programming and application
development is also available, as well as training for systems and net-
work administration. Hardware service and support is available to
clients in the North-Central Ohio area.
Sample prices:
US$50/hour for phone, dial-up, and Internet support (one-hour mini-
mum); on-site support can be contracted on an hourly basis at
US$100/hour (two-hour minimum) or by half-day/full-day or per
project basis.
Last modified:
March 18, 1997.

Paul J. Mech
477 S. Napoleon, Columbus, OH 43213
Phone:
(614) 237-0261
E-mail:
paul@coil.com
Contact:
Paul J. Mech
Type of support:
Phone, e-mail, remote network administration, and on-site.

Special expertise:
Programming services (C, C++, Shell), systems administration, security, telephony, small business applications, scientific and engineering applications.
Sample prices:
US$75–$150/hour depending on the work involved. Project rates and retainer rates are negotiable.
Last modified:
July 11, 1997.

TES, Inc.
2903 Ravogli Avenue, Cincinnati, OH 45211-7848
Phone:
(513) 661-3200
Fax:
(513) 661-3732
E-mail:
info@tesnet.com
Contact:
Larry Townsend
Type of support:
Phone, e-mail, in-house, and on-site.
Special expertise:
TES has been in business since 1989. We have extensive experience both in the United States and internationally in all of the following areas: software and hardware development for industrial and laboratory applications, data acquisition and signal processing, embedded systems design, servo control and vibration test systems, system integration.
Sample prices:
Upon request.
Last modified:
October 24, 1997.

TraiCom Services, Inc.
217 Vine Street, Pataskala, OH 43062
Phone:
(614) 207-1909
Fax:
(614) 825-2034
E-mail:
gravesp@traicom.interhack.net

URL:
www.traicom.interhack.net
Contact:
Paul L. Graves
Type of support:
Phone, e-mail, remote network administration, in-house, and on-site.
Special expertise:
Systems integration, installation, Web and CGI programming services, systems administration, Internet and intranet connectivity, firewall installation, troubleshooting, training.
Sample prices:
Upon request.
Last modified:
October 25, 1998.

Tri-State Networking Technologies, Ltd.
2603 Pancoast Avenue, Cincinnati, OH 45211
Phone:
(513) 662-4700
E-mail:
Joe.Filbrun@tnt-online.com
URL:
www.tnt-online.com
Contact:
Joe Filbrun, Dave Buffington
Type of support:
Phone, e-mail, remote network administration, in-house, and on-site.
Special expertise:
Installation, configuration and customization, troubleshooting, network connectivity, training, and application support.
Sample prices:
By project or hourly, depending on project. Estimates available upon request.
Last modified:
January 16, 1998.

After Hours Computer Consulting, LLC.
2301 West Galveston Street, Broken Arrow, OK 74012
Phone:
(918) 258-9842

E-mail:
support@ahcctulsa.com
URL:
www.ahcctulsa.com
Contact:
Kenneth Hess
Type of support:
Phone, e-mail, remote network administration, in-house, and on-site.
Special expertise:
Installation, systems administration, Internet and intranet connectivity, troubleshooting, training.
Sample prices:
US$50/hour.
Last modified:
July 12, 1997.

Bailey and Associates
2810 S. Hudson, Tulsa, OK 74114
Phone:
(918) 749-9304
E-mail:
cbailey@galstar.com
Contact:
Cliff Bailey
Type of support:
Phone, e-mail, remote network administration, in-house, and on-site.
Special expertise:
Installation, programming services, systems administration, Internet and intranet connectivity, troubleshooting, training.
Sample prices:
US$75/hour or monthly retainer.
Last modified:
February 11, 1998.

Rueb Group Ltd
917 NW 59, Oklahoma City, OK 73118
Phone:
(405) 840-9221
E-mail:
markg@netplus.net

URL:
www.netplus.net
Contact:
Tom Rueb, Mark Grennan
Type of support:
Remote network administration, in-house, and on-site.
Special expertise:
Network administration of all types, firewall installation (Mark Grennan is the author of the Firewall HOWTO), systems administration.
Sample prices:
US$75/hour.
Last modified:
April 24, 1997.

F.M. Taylor & Associates
123 Kenwood Avenue, Medford, OR 97501
Phone:
(541) 776-3283
E-mail:
taylor@jeffnet.org
URL:
www.jeffnet.org/fmta
Contact:
Mike Taylor
Type of support:
Phone, e-mail, remote network administration, in-house, and on-site.
Special expertise:
Installation, programming services, systems administration, Internet and intranet connectivity, firewall installation, troubleshooting, training.
Sample prices:
US$20/hour.
Last modified:
August 4, 1997.

Hurrah Internet Services
18850 SW Sieffert, Sherwood, OR 97140
Phone:
(503) 380-3218
E-mail:
webgurus@hurrah.com

URL:
www.hurrah.com/HIS
Contact:
Tracy Camp
Type of support:
E-mail and remote network administration.
Special expertise:
Setup, configuration, programming, and general problem solving help. Linux-based server configuration, technical support.
Sample prices:
Varies upon service, generally between US$20–$30/hour.
Last modified:
September 9, 1997.

Kymsoft Consulting
745 Foothill Drive, Eugene, OR 97405
Phone:
(541) 465-9008
Fax:
(541) 465-9052
E-mail:
rick@efn.org
URL:
www.efn.org/~rick
Contact:
Rick Bronson
Type of support:
Phone, e-mail, and in-house.
Special expertise:
Twelve years Unix experience.
Sample prices:
US$65/hour.
Last modified:
June 22, 1997.

Naked Ape Consulting
3203 SE Woodstock Boulevard #1300, Portland, OR 97202
Phone:
(503) 517-5248

E-mail:
wcooley@nakedape.ml.org
URL:
nakedape.ml.org
Contact:
Wil Cooley
Type of support:
Phone, e-mail, and on-site.
Special expertise:
Red Hat Linux installation and support, small office networking
(including PPP), RPM packaging, Web scripting (PHP, Perl, SQL).
Sample prices:
Upon request.
Last modified:
November 8, 1998.

NET-Community
522 SW 5th Avenue, Suite 1105, Portland, OR 97204
Phone:
(800) 919-0060; (503) 274-4423
Fax:
(503) 953-5829
E-mail:
sales@net-community.com
URL:
www.net-community.com
Contact:
Scott Christley
Type of support:
Phone and e-mail.
Special expertise:
NET-Community specializes in support for GNUstep and MediaBook.
Our Web site has details regarding the support plans.
Sample prices:
US$50/year for GNUstep Developer (e-mail only); US$200/year for
GNUstep Corporate (e-mail only); US$2500/year for MediaBook Com-
prehensive (e-mail and phone).
Last modified:
June 22, 1997.

Zot Consulting, Inc.
353 G Avenue Lake Oswego, Lake Oswego, OR 97034-2331
Phone:
(503) 635-9792
Fax:
(503) 697-8047
E-mail:
info@zotconsulting.com
URL:
www.zotconsulting.com
Contact:
Zot O'Connor
Type of support:
Phone, e-mail, remote network administration, and on-site.
Special expertise:
Security (physical and network), installation, large-scale systems design, e-commerce, credit cards, connectivity, training software use, policy writing. We work with large Fortune 100 companies and startups.
Sample prices:
Upon request.
Last modified:
September 26, 1998.

Robert Dale
2850 Broadway Avenue, APT 3, Pittsburgh, PA 15216
Phone:
(412) 388-0541
E-mail:
rob@nb.net
URL:
www.nb.net/~rob
Contact:
Robert Dale
Type of support:
On-site.
Special expertise:
Programming services, Internet and intranet connectivity, installation, and troubleshooting.
Sample prices:
Upon request.

Last modified:
September 25, 1998.

Eonova
1530 Locust Street #7, Philadelphia, PA 19102
Phone:
(215) 985-4317
E-mail:
mk@eonova.com
URL:
www.eonova.com
Contact:
Mike Knerr
Type of support:
Phone, e-mail, remote network administration, and in-house.
Special expertise:
Server design, administration, configuration, custom software engineering.
Sample prices:
Upon request.
Last modified:
October 2, 1998.

Christopher J. Fearnley
4807 Chester Ave. Apt. 207, Philadelphia, PA 19143-3441
Phone:
(215) 724-2265
E-mail:
cjf@netaxs.com
URL:
www.netaxs.com/~cjf
Contact:
Chris Fearnley
Type of support:
Phone, ssh-based remote network administration, and on-site.
Special expertise:
Debian GNU/Linux configurations for TCP/IP networks. Installation and maintenance of various types of Internet servers including Web, news, and mail. Business and technical consulting for ISPs.
Sample prices:
US$500/day; US$65/hour.

Last modified:
June 24, 1997.

Filmore St. Consultants
4634 Filmore Street, Pittsburgh, PA 15213
Phone:
(412) 621-2786
Fax:
(412) 683-8179
E-mail:
info@filmore.com
URL:
www.filmore.com
Contact:
Jeffrey Eaton
Type of support:
Phone, remote network administration, and on-site.
Special expertise:
Internet and intranet connectivity; security and firewalls; Web, news, and mail servers.
Sample prices:
US$50/hour or US$250/day.
Last modified:
September 27, 1997.

Steven Jackson
23 Boxwood Lane, Langhorne, PA 19047
Phone:
(215) 702-7011
E-mail:
steve@slac.com
Contact:
Steve Jackson
Type of support:
E-mail, on-site between Philadelphia and New York, small office and weekends preferred.
Special expertise:
LAN design, installation, configuration, mail, Internet and intranet, NT integration, proxy and firewall.

Sample prices:
Upon request.
Last modified:
May 19, 1998.

PA dot NET
401 East Louther, Suite 223, Carlisle, PA 17013
Phone:
(717) 249-7270
Fax:
(717) 258-0975
E-mail:
info@pa.net
URL:
www.pa.net
Contact:
Patrick Haller
Type of support:
Phone, e-mail, fax, remote network administration, in-house, and on-site.
Special expertise:
Unix/NT integration, Linux design, build, installation, Internet and intranet networking services, including firewall design and implementation.
Sample prices:
US$40/hour plus expenses.
Last modified:
December 15, 1997.

Westphila.net
922 S. 46th Street, Philadelphia, PA 19143
Phone:
(215) 222-6441
E-mail:
support@westphila.net
URL:
westphila.net
Contact:
Michael Jastremski

Type of support:
Remote network administration, on-site, and in-house.
Special expertise:
Apache Web servers, custom Perl, network administration, network security, network connectivity, SMB/AFP file servers, general hackery, systems administration, online shopping.
Sample prices:
Upon request.
Last modified:
April 6, 1998.

Crux
729 Martin Road, Starr, SC 29684
Phone:
(864) 375-0377
Fax:
(864) 375-0377
E-mail:
carlk@carol.net
URL:
members.carol.net/~carlk
Contact:
Carl A. Kolasky
Type of support:
Phone, e-mail, remote network administration, in-house, and on-site.
Special expertise:
Installation, programming services, systems administration, Internet and intranet connectivity, troubleshooting, training, C, C++, Forth, Java, HTML, BAL, custom device drivers, custom communication solutions, tool services. Twenty-seven years commercial experience from mainframe to micro machines.
Sample prices:
US$50–$100 depending on services provided.
Last modified:
August 5, 1997.

GAME.NET, Inc
1209 Midvale Avenue, Charleston, SC 29412
Phone:
(803) 762-7131

Fax:
(803) 762-7131
E-mail:
info@game.net
URL:
http://game.net
Contact:
Jim Sims
Type of support:
Phone, e-mail, remote network administration, in-house, and on-site.
Special expertise:
Systems administration, Internet, training.
Sample prices:
US$50–$150/hour.
Last modified:
December 14, 1997.

JobSoft Design and Development, Inc.
118 South Maple Street, Murfreesboro, TN 37130
Phone:
(615) 904-9559; (615) 904-9562
Fax:
(615) 890-8941
E-mail:
linux@jobsoft.com
URL:
www.jobsoft.com
Contact:
Mark J. Bailey, James M. Nelson, Steven Edwards
Type of support:
Phone, e-mail, remote network administration, and on-site.
Special expertise:
Strategic consultation, installation, programming design and development, Internet and intranet, firewalls, troubleshooting, Web application development, database servers (Oracle, PostgreSQL, etc.), Enterprise e-mail servers, HylaFax (fax, data, alphapaging), Samba, Java, JDBC.
Sample prices:
Upon request.

Last modified:
March 13, 1998.

Sheer Genius Consulting
2016 Rosecliff Drive, Nashville, TN 37206
Phone:
(615) 226-4040
Fax:
(615) 228-1819
E-mail:
consulting@sheergenius.com
URL:
www.sheergenius.com
Contact:
Matt Kenigson <matt@sheergenius.com>
Type of support:
Phone, e-mail, and remote network administration. Limited on-site
support in the Nashville area.
Special expertise:
Programming services (C, Perl, SQL, xBase), database programming
and administration, systems administration, Internet and intranet con-
nectivity, commerce solutions, Web hosting and design, troubleshoot-
ing, training, integration and migration services, security, LAN and
WAN setup and tuning.
Sample prices:
Depends on type of work. Most jobs US$60/hour plus travel and
expenses, if outside Nashville.
Last modified:
March 5, 1998.

Aegis Data Systems
P.O. Box 28554, Dallas, TX 75228
Phone:
(972) 922-8253
Fax:
(214) 634-8844
E-mail:
operations@aegisdata.com
URL:
www.aegisdata.com

Contact:
Mark Stingley
Type of support:
Phone, e-mail, remote network administration, in-house, and on-site.
Special expertise:
Installation, programming services, systems administration, Internet and intranet connectivity, firewall installation, troubleshooting, training, Web server setup and administration.
Sample prices:
Upon request.
Last modified:
April 6, 1998.

AustinTX.COM
P.O. Box 81158, Austin, TX 78708-1158
Phone:
(512) 835-8005
Fax:
(512) 485-8661
E-mail:
sales@austintx.com
URL:
www.austintx.com
Contact:
David Himawan
Type of support:
Phone and e-mail.
Special expertise:
Networking, LAN/WAN, Internet services, installation, administration, support, hardware and software sales.
Sample prices:
US$90/hour or negotiated service contract.
Last modified:
February 28, 1998.

Bobcat Open Systems, Inc.
Rt. 2, Box 68, Cumby, TX 75433-9707
Phone:
(800) 929-5513; (972) 490-5738

Fax:
(972) 490-5053
E-mail:
bmcclure@cyberramp.net
Contact:
Bob McClure, Jr.
Type of support:
Phone, e-mail, in-house, and on-site.
Special expertise:
Installation, programming services, systems administration, trouble-shooting, training.
Sample prices:
US$90/hour or firm fixed price.
Last modified:
November 21, 1997.

Cymitar Technology Group, Inc.
9828 Lorene Lane, San Antonio, TX 78216-4450
Phone:
(210) 892-4000
Fax:
(210) 892-4329
E-mail:
info@cymitar.com
URL:
www.cymitar.com
Contact:
Dirk Elmendorf
Type of support:
Phone, e-mail, remote network administration, and on-site.
Special expertise:
Network design, installation and support, LAN/WAN, Internet services, custom software development, database integration, e-commerce solutions.
Sample prices:
US$125/hour or negotiated service contract.
Last modified:
March 13, 1998.

Kyle Davenport Consulting
5711 Preston Oaks, #1727, Dallas, TX 75240

Phone:
(972) 503-3958
Fax:
(972) 503-3957
E-mail:
kdd@onramp.net
Contact:
Kyle Davenport
Type of support:
E-mail, remote network administration, and on-site.
Special expertise:
Twenty years computer industry experience, seven years Unix systems administration, four years experience administration and utilization of Linux. All types of programming, system design, and integration.
Sample prices:
Upon request.
Last modified:
October 1, 1998.

Deep Eddy Internet Consulting
609 Deep Eddy Avenue, Austin, TX 78703-4513
Phone:
(512) 432-4046
Fax:
(512) 499-0252
E-mail:
sales@DeepEddy.Com
URL:
www.DeepEddy.Com
Contact:
Chris Garrigues
Type of support:
Remote network administration, in-house, and on-site.
Special expertise:
Installation, systems administration, Internet and intranet connectivity, firewalls, security, troubleshooting, training, Perl, qmail, mh, MkLinux, amanda, PGP, also know routers and many commercial Unixes.
Sample prices:
US$90/hour; may discount for large projects.

Last modified:
October 24, 1997.

Heights Computer Center
517 Harvard Street, Houston, TX 77007
Phone:
(713) 864-5676
Fax:
(713) 864-0072
E-mail:
hcc@netservers.com
URL:
hcc.netservers.com
Contact:
Perry Piplani
Type of support:
Phone, e-mail, remote network administration, in-house, and on-site.
Special expertise:
Network design, setup, and support; Linux installation, setup, and troubleshooting; systems administration and programming; Internet connectivity.
Sample prices:
Upon request.
Last modified:
April 6, 1998.

J-Quad & Associates, Ltd.
LBJ Freeway, Suite 504, Dallas, TX 75244
Phone:
(972) 661-5313
Fax:
(972) 661-5443
E-mail:
sanfordj@jquad.com
URL:
www.jquad.com
Contact:
Jerry Sanford
Type of support:
All types.

Special expertise:
Installation, systems administration, troubleshooting, training.
Sample prices:
Upon request.
Last modified:
September 30, 1998.

Magpies
P.O. Box 984, Converse, TX 78109
Phone:
(210) 408-2558; (888) 467-4070
Fax:
Available to clients.
E-mail:
sales@magpies.com
URL:
www.magpies.com
Contact:
Michael Masoni
Type of support:
Phone, e-mail, in-house, and on-site.
Special expertise:
Installation, systems administration, Internet connectivity, training,
Web server setup.
Sample prices:
US$60–$95/hour.
Last modified:
January 23, 1998.

Tom McDonald Consulting
8713 Sabinas Trail, Ft. Worth, TX 76118
Phone:
(818) 590-2929
E-mail:
mickeyd@airmail.net
Contact:
Tom McDonald
Type of support:
In-house and on-site.

Special expertise:
Installation, programming services, systems administration, trouble-shooting, training.
Sample prices:
US$90/hour.
Last modified:
August 9, 1997.

Net Resonance
P.O. Box 10248, Austin, TX 78766
Phone:
(512) 373-0091
E-mail:
jhemm@netresonance.com
URL:
www.netresonance.com
Contact:
Jason Hemmenway
Type of support:
Phone, remote network administration, and on-site.
Special expertise:
Internet connectivity and server administration, general systems administration.
Sample prices:
Upon request.
Last modified:
June 11, 1997.

Penguin Technical Services
800 Brazos, Suite 330, Austin, TX 78701
Phone:
(512) 464-TECH; (877) GO LINUX
Fax:
(512) 236-8272
E-mail:
tcameron@penguintech.com
URL:
www.penguintech.com
Contact:
Thomas Cameron

Type of support:
Phone, e-mail, and remote network administration.
Special expertise:
Networking (Internet and intranet), firewalls, sendmail, Perl, cgi-bin, e-commerce on Linux, Samba, DNS, calendaring software.
Sample prices:
Upon request.
Last modified:
October 25, 1998.

Three Point Consulting
3408 Los Alamos Lane, McKinney, TX 75070
Phone:
(972) 540-5278
E-mail:
info@threepoint.com
URL:
www.threepoint.com
Contact:
Dave Whitinger
Type of support:
E-mail, remote network administration, and on-site.
Special expertise:
Linux installation, Internet and intranet services, network administration, systems administration, Web site development, graphic design.
Sample prices:
Upon request.
Last modified:
August 2, 1998.

UHW Corporation
1540 Selene Drive, Suite 118, Carrollton, TX 75006
Phone:
(972) 242-0040
Fax:
(972) 323-0444
E-mail:
david@uhw.com
URL:
www.uhw.com

Contact:
Dave Stokes
Type of support:
Phone, e-mail, fax, remote network administration, in-house, and on-site.
Special expertise:
Internet, troubleshooting, install, and training.
Sample prices:
Upon request.
Last modified:
April 22, 1998.

WarpWare
3905 Country Place 907, Fort Worth, TX 76109
Phone:
(817) 315-2172
Fax:
(817) 315-2173
E-mail:
sales@warpware.com
URL:
www.warpware.com
Contact:
Sujay D'Souza <sad@warpware.com>
Type of support:
Phone, e-mail, remote network administration, in-house, and on-site.
Special expertise:
Installation, system integration, programming services, systems administration, Internet and intranet connectivity, firewall installation, troubleshooting, hardware server sales and support, and complete Linux solutions.
Sample prices:
Upon request.
Last modified:
November 8, 1998.

xprt Computer Consulting, Inc.
731 Voyager, Houston, TX 77062
Phone:
(281) 480-8649

Fax:
(281) 480-7357
E-mail:
jody@sccsi.com
URL:
zeus.xprt.com/~info/xprt.html
Contact:
Jody Winston
Type of support:
Phone, e-mail, and on-site.
Special expertise:
Training, custom software, custom device drivers, custom application development.
Sample prices:
Either by the hour starting at US$100 or a firm fixed price.
Last modified:
June 24, 1997.

Internet Connect
455 E 400 S, Suite #309, Salt Lake City, UT 84111
Phone:
(888) 364-4059
Fax:
(801) 364-4076
E-mail:
admin@inconnect.com
URL:
www.inconnect.com
Contact:
Dax Kelson
Type of support:
Phone, e-mail, remote network administration, and on-site.
Special expertise:
Database, NT/Netware Integration, dial-up, secure SMTP, installation, custom programming services, administration, Internet and intranet, security audits, firewall configuration and installation, troubleshooting, training.
Sample prices:
Upon request.

Last modified:
June 5, 1998.

TerraBytes Computers
P.O. Box 466, Williston, VT 05495
Phone:
(802) 863-6296
Fax:
(802) 864-8265
E-mail:
bennet@terrabytesweb.com
URL:
www.terrabytesweb.com
Contact:
Bennet Deliduka
Type of support:
Phone, e-mail, remote network administration, in-house, and on-site.
Special expertise:
Troubleshooting hardware issues, installation, script programming services, systems administration, Internet and intranet connectivity, firewall installation, troubleshooting, training.
Sample prices:
Upon request.
Last modified:
March 21, 1998.

Branch & Company
P.O. Box 547, Powhatan, VA 23139
Phone:
(804) 598-2153
Fax:
(804) 225-0167
E-mail:
branch@csi.com
Contact:
Carlisle Branch
Type of support:
Phone, e-mail, fax, remote network administration, in-house, and on-site.
Special expertise:
Installation, programming services, systems administration, Internet and intranet connectivity, troubleshooting.

Sample prices:
Upon request.
Last modified:
August 2, 1998.

Flamingo Internet Navigators
310-D Patriot Lane, Williamsburg, VA 23185-2055
Phone:
(757) 221-8095
Fax:
(757) 564-1340
E-mail:
sales@fini.net
URL:
www.fini.net
Contact:
Christopher Hicks
Type of support:
Remote network and systems administration, on-site (worldwide),
e-mail, phone. Support contracts with 24/7 access to a variety of technicians are available.
Special expertise:
FINI integrates a number of skillsets to provide a total solution. Expe-
rience includes Web development (HTML, CGI, graphics, etc.), sys-
tems administration (of many different operating systems), database
development (on Oracle, Sybase, MySQL, and PostgreSQL), software
development (under Linux, Windows, Unix), network design and
administration, training, and security auditing. This allows the appropriate solution to be provided by one firm.
Sample prices:
Upon request.
Last modified:
September 25, 1998.

GJR Software Products
P.O. Box 3416, Merrifield, VA 22116-3416
Phone:
(703) 934-1376
E-mail:
gjrsoft@world.std.com

URL:
world.std.com/~gjrsoft
Contact:
Gene J. Raymond
Type of support:
Phone, e-mail, remote network administration, and on-site.
Special expertise:
Installation, troubleshooting, training, systems administration, programming (shell, Perl, C), HTML.
Sample prices:
Upon request.
Last modified:
December 5, 1997.

Internet Systems and Services
6022 Rockton Court, Centreville, VA 22020
Phone:
(703) 222-4243
Fax:
(703) 222-7320
E-mail:
bass@silkroad.com
URL:
www.silkroad.com
Contact:
Tim Bass
Type of support:
Phone, e-mail, and in-house.
Special expertise:
Large-scale Internet systems, network security.
Sample prices:
US$85/hour plus travel expenses (80 hours normal minimum).
Last modified:
November 3, 1997.

NetTek, Inc.
700 Baker Road, Suite 106, Virginia Beach, VA 23462
Phone:
(757) 425-5950
Fax:
(757) 557-0754

E-mail:
mskar@nettek.net
URL:
http://oceanside.nettek.net
Contact:
Marc Skarshinski
Type of support:
Phone, remote network administration, and on-site.
Special expertise:
Installation, systems administration, Internet connectivity, firewall installation, troubleshooting.
Sample prices:
US$60–$90 depending on block of time purchased.
Last modified:
August 5, 1997.

Phaedo Consulting, Inc.
1022 Manning Drive, Fredericksburg, VA 22405; 829 N. Lexington Street, Arlington, VA 22205
Phone:
(540) 370-4184
Fax:
(540) 370-4185
E-mail:
info@phaedo.com
URL:
www.phaedo.com
Contact:
Ryan Quick
Type of support:
Phone, e-mail, remote network administration, in-house, on-site, disaster recovery, emergency response, full-time, contract, maintenance, time-and-materials.
Special expertise:
System installation, configuration, backup, recovery, disaster recovery and preparedness, Internet and intranet security, distributed computing (NIS, NIS+, DCE), troubleshooting, benchmarking and performance tuning, systems administration.
Sample prices:
Contracts vary, but standard fees range between US$100–$200/hour.

Last modified:
September 27, 1997.

SimsCon Services
3990 Gaskins Road, Richmond, VA 23233
Phone:
(804) 273-6331
Fax:
(804) 747-8628
E-mail:
phanty@wwwlab.com
URL:
http://nothing.but.net
Contact:
Tripp Sims
Type of support:
Phone, e-mail, remote administration.
Special expertise:
Installation, Perl, administration, routing, firewall, security.
Sample prices:
Upon request.
Last modified:
April 6, 1998.

Spectrum Office Systems, Inc.
1964 Gallows Road, Suite 300, Vienna, VA 22182
Phone:
(800) 929-3781; (703) 556-6511
Fax:
(703) 556-9002
E-mail:
spectrum@specnet.com
URL:
www.specnet.com
Contact:
Frank Araby
Type of support:
Phone, e-mail, remote network administration, in-house, and on-site.
Special expertise:
Training, PC, Unix and Linux connectivity.
Sample prices:
In-house technicians range from US$85–$130/hour.

Last modified:
August 4, 1997.

Cheek Consulting
620 5th Ave. W, Suite 309, Seattle, WA 98119
Phone:
(206) 282-2892
E-mail:
joseph@cheek.com
URL:
www.cheek.com/linux
Contact:
Joseph Cheek
Type of support:
Phone, e-mail, remote network administration, in-house, and on-site.
Special expertise:
Netware connectivity, also installation, administration, Internet and
intranet connectivity, retail and SOHO industries.
Sample prices:
Upon request.
Last modified:
April 22, 1998.

Cutting Edge Communications, Inc.
422 West Riverside, Suite 516, Spokane, WA 99201
Phone:
(509) 444-4638
Fax:
Available to clients.
E-mail:
roberth@cet.com
URL:
www.cet.com
Contact:
Robert Hanson
Type of support:
Phone, e-mail, remote network administration, and on-site.
Special expertise:
Programming, system installation and administration, Internet and
intranet connectivity, turnkey ISP solutions, LAN and WAN, security,
systems design, engineering and integration, troubleshooting, and
training.

Sample prices:
US$45/hour–$220/hour depending on client needs.
Last modified:
July 4, 1997.

TSCNet, Inc.
10049 Kitsap Mall Boulevard, Suite 104, Silverdale, WA 98383
Phone:
(360) 613-0708
Fax:
(360) 308-0185
E-mail:
mhjack@tscnet.com
URL:
www.tscnet.com
Contact:
Mike Jackson, Ron Tidd
Type of support:
Phone, e-mail, remote network administration, and on-site.
Special expertise:
TCP/IP networking, DNS, sendmail, firewalls, IP routing, subnetting, systems administration, security, modems and PPP, ISP services, PHP/FI and SQL Web programming, and client/server C programming.
Sample prices:
Upon request.
Last modified:
July 16, 1998.

Willson Consulting Services
Seattle, WA 98146-1724
Phone:
(206) 439-1164
Fax:
Available to clients.
E-mail:
cpu@ifixcomputers.com
URL:
www.ifixcomputers.com
Contact:
Bradley J. Willson

Type of support:
Phone (limited long-distance), e-mail, fax (limited long-distance), remote network administration, in-house, and on-site (within Puget Sound area).
Special expertise:
Installation, configuration, Internet and intranet connectivity, and systems administration.
Sample prices:
Upon request.
Last modified:
September 27, 1997.

Badger Data Solutions
433 N. Oneida Street, Suite A, Appleton, WI 54911
Phone:
(920) 832-0231; (800) 292-2359
E-mail:
info@badgerdata.com
URL:
www.badgerdata.com
Contact:
Garrett Meiers <Garrett@badgerdata.com>, Steve Wiater <Steve@ badgerdata.com>
Type of support:
Phone, e-mail, remote network administration, in-house, and on-site.
Special expertise:
Linux installation, support, Internet, networking, etc.
Sample prices:
US$35–$85/hour.
Last modified:
January 16, 1998.

Couvares Consulting
913 Erin Street, Madison, WI 53715
Phone:
(608) 256-6201
Fax:
(608) 256-6201
E-mail:
couvares@poboxes.com

Contact:
Peter Couvares
Type of support:
Phone, e-mail, remote network administration, and on-site.
Special expertise:
Consulting, design, and implementation of customized systems and software solutions for free and commercial Unix environments.
Sample prices:
US$60/hour for commercial clients; US$20–$60/hour sliding scale for private and nonprofit clients.
Last modified:
August 5, 1997.

Sean Harper
4163 N Stowell, Milwaukee, WI 53211
Phone:
(414) 963-0317
Fax:
(414) 963-0317
E-mail:
seanh@pitnet.net
Contact:
Sean Harper
Type of support:
Phone, e-mail, remote network administration, in-house, and on-site.
Special expertise:
Installation, systems administration, Internet and intranet connectivity, dial-up, HTML, Java and CGI, custom programming.
Sample prices:
US$20–$40/hour.
Last modified:
November 3, 1997.

Network Interation Services, Inc.
S29W30139 S. Bethesda Circle, Waukesha, WI 53188
Phone:
(414) 968-3044
Fax:
(414) 968-3044
E-mail:
nis@pobox.com

Contact:
Michael Bloxham
Type of support:
All types.
Special expertise:
Specializing in Internet and intranet connectivity including firewalls,
installation, systems administration, troubleshooting, and training.
Sample prices:
Upon request.
Last modified:
September 25, 1998.

Roger A. Prata
5134 Churchill Lane, Middleton, WI 53562
Phone:
(608) 446-3038
E-mail:
network-systems@usa.net
Contact:
Roger Prata
Type of support:
Phone, e-mail, fax, remote network administration, in-house, and on-
site.
Special expertise:
Installation, systems administration, Internet and intranet connectivity,
troubleshooting, training (no programming, or firewall).
Sample prices:
US$30–$60.
Last modified:
February 23, 1998.

The Rindy Corporation
W149 N6203 Pocahontas Drive, Milwaukee, WI 53051
Phone:
(414) 252-4273
Fax:
(414) 252-4274
E-mail:
info@rindy.com
URL:
www.rindy.com

Contact:
Troy Rindy
Type of support:
Phone, e-mail, remote network administration, in-house, and on-site.
Special expertise:
Familiar with most topics.
Sample prices:
Upon request.
Last modified:
August 5, 1997.

William Rozmiarek
1160 Langlade Avenue, Green Bay, WI 54304
Phone:
(920) 497-9623
E-mail:
wdroze@online.dct.com
Contact:
William Rozmiarek
Type of support:
Phone, e-mail, remote network administration, and on-site.
Special expertise:
Building custom Linux servers and workstations. Installing and troubleshooting the Linux operating system (all varieties). Integrating Windows clients and Linux servers (e-mail, intranet, file, and print services). File backup and disaster recovery assessment, planning, and implementation. PostgreSQL server installation, administration, and programming. On-site and off-site systems and network administration for small businesses, individuals, and NPOs.
Sample prices:
Upon request.
Last modified:
September 25, 1998.

WhitePine Consulting
P.O. Box 721, Madison, WI 53701; 606 N. Nain Street, Fall River, WI 53932
Phone:
(920) 484-6005
Fax:
(920) 484-6020

E-mail:
mjmc@whitepine.com
Contact:
Michael McEvoy
Type of support:
Phone, e-mail, remote network administration, and on-site.
Special expertise:
Consulting, design, and implementation of Internet and intranet and distributed computing applications.
Sample prices:
US$75/hour for commercial clients; US$25–$50/hour sliding scale for private and nonprofit clients. In-kind and pro bono work negotiable.
Last modified:
October 17, 1997.

Kuenzsoftware
1425 South Lowell Street, Casper, WY 82601
Phone:
(307) 266-3327
E-mail:
kuenzdc@wind.cc.whecn.edu
URL:
http://gtcs.com/assoc/ks/don
Contact:
Don Kuenz
Type of support:
Phone, e-mail, remote network administration, and on-site.
Special expertise:
Programming and systems administration.
Sample prices:
US$45/hour (scheduled); US$90/hour (emergency). Additional charges for travel and lodging.
Last modified:
August 9, 1997.

A

A. C. Technologies, 251

Access, multiple-user, 54–55

Access control lists (ACLs), 189

Addresses, IP, 81

Address Verification System (AVS), 217

Administration, 49–76. *See also* Linux
    administration
  advanced, 69–76
  costs of, 146–147
  tools for, 34

Adobe Acrobat Reader, 212–213

Aegis Data Systems, 330–331

After Hours Computer Consulting, LLC,
    319–320

AfterStep, 68

Al Guerra Enterprises, Inc., 281–282

Aliasing, 64

allmkprint script, 128

Amiga Fast File System (AFFS), 175

Andrew File System (AFS), 185

Anthony Awtry Consulting, 282

Apache Web server, 47, 60, 84–85, 89, 164,
    201, 203
  configuring, 161–162

API interface, 135

Appletalk, 119, 123

Application programming interfaces (APIs),
    181, 216. *See also* API interface

Applications, 52, 146
  business, 201–225
  custom, 74–75
  Internet, 79–100
  Linux, 37–48

Applix Anyware, 214

Applix Enterprise, 213

Applix Office Suite, 213–214

Applix TM1, 214

Applixware, 105, 144

Archive sites, Linux, 171

Archiving, 211–212

Arizona Network Engineering Services, 247

Arkeia network backup product, 204–206
  case study on, 206–212

Assembler language, 37

Asynchronous Routing Protocol (ARP), 70

Asynchronous Transfer Mode (ATM), 87

AustinTX.COM, 331

Automatic working-set trimming, 183

AX.25 protocol, 70

B

B.P.S. Technologies, Inc., 276–277

Background processing, 27

Backups, 62–63, 151
  incremental, 211

Backup server
  primary, 208–209
  secondary, 209

Backup software solutions, comparison of,
    207

Badger Data Solutions, 347

Bailey and Associates, 320

Barriers, corporate, 90

Bash, 58–59

Bastion hosts, 96–99

BayLinks Communications, 251–252

BB Stock Pro, 215, 233–237

BB Stock Tool, 236

Bidding, competitive, 46

Bill Rousseau Consulting, 264–265

Binaries, 186

Bobcat Open Systems, Inc., 331–332

BOOT.INI file, 151, 152
  adding DOS to, 157–158
  adding Linux to, 158
  adding other operating systems to, 158–159

BOOTPART, 155–156, 158, 159

Boot process, 31–34
BOOTP server, 135
BOOTSECT.DOS file, 151, 152–153
BOOTSECT.LNX file, 156, 158
Boot sector file, creating, 152–153
Bootup directory, 152
Bradley M. Kuhn Consulting, 314
Branch & Company, 340–341
Browsers, 83
BRT Technical Services Corporation, 277
Bugtraq, 76, 96
Bullet-proof networks, 71–74
Business. *See also* Corporations
  integrating of Linux solutions with,
    143–162
  Linux in, 22–23, 110–116, 170
Business models, intranet and extranet,
  88–91
Business products, Linux, 201–225

C
Caldera, 52, 104, 105
Carumba Inc., 252
Cascading Style Sheet (CSS), 66
Casey-Dakota, 252–253
CD-ROM
  Linux, 165
  software on, 233–238
CE Computers, 281
Central print server printing, 119–120
Central servers, multiple, 120–121
CERT, 96
CERT Advisory List, 76
Certificate, 66
Chat, 65–66
Checksum databasing, 98
Cheek Consulting, 345
Christopher J. Fearnley Consulting, 325–326
Cisco Systems, Linux print system at,
  116–137
Citadel, 289–290
Cleveland Internet Association, 311
Client LPR system, 123–124
Client/server model, 181
Client-to-printer printing, 118–119
Closed source companies, 199
CMT Consulting, 293
CodeMeta, Inc., 305–306
Code walk, 18
Collective Systems, LLC, 278

Collective Technologies AnswerDesk,
  240–241
Colorado Computer Consultants, 269
Columbia Appletalk Protocol (CAP), 125
Command resources, 55–56
Commands, piped, 52
Commercial software, 25–26
Common Gateway Interface (CGI), 11, 85,
  133
Communication, corporate, 89–90
Compatibility, software-systems, 187
ComputerCrafts, 270
Computer Oracle and Password System
  (COPS), 98
Computer Underground, Inc., 311–312
ComputerWorld Web site, 196
Configuration files, 52
Configuration scripts, 33
Consultants, Linux, 44, 239–351
Contract consultants, 44
Contractors, hiring, 14
Conversion tools, Windows NT to Linux, 185
Core Secure, 295–296
Corporate mission, 89, 229
Corporations. *See also* Business
  selling Linux to, 102–108
  use of Linux by, 110–116
Corprotech, Inc., 250–251
Costs, corporate operating system, 202–203
Cottonwood Computer Solutions, 303
Couvares Consulting, 347–348
cpio standard, 63
C programming language, 20–21, 37–38
C++ programming language, 162
CPU activity, scheduled, 26–27
Creative Systems, 278–279
Credit Card Verification System (CCVS), 215
cron command, 162
crontab-e routine, 162
Crux Consulting, 328
Crynwr Software, 307–308
C shell *csh*, 59
Custom applications, 74–75
Customization, in-house, 18–19
Customized solutions, 15–21
CustomLogic, 253
Cutting Edge Communications, Inc.,
  345–346
CyberNautix, Inc., 253–254
CyberShell Engineering, 254

cybertronics, 103, 104, 108
Cymitar Technology Group, Inc., 332

D

Dale K. Hawkins Consulting, 270–271
Damon C. Richardson Consulting, 302–303
Darcom Systems Ltd., 279
Data archiving, 211–212
DataCrest, Inc., 246
David Fetter Consulting, 256–257
David J. Lloyd Consulting, 275
David Wood Consulting, 310
Daylight Software, 271
DCA Online (Dutch Computer Association), 241–242
dd command, 156
DEBUG command, 152
Debuggers, 75
DEC Consulting, 254–255
Decision support. *See also* Support
  multidimensional analysis for, 214
  solutions for, 213–214
Deep Eddy Internet Consulting, 333–334
Default boot process, 32–33
Deja News, 112
DESIGN SCIENCE LABS, 312
Desktop capabilities, 22
Desktop operating systems, 101
  functionality with, 39
Desktop productivity tools, 213
Desktop Technology Group, 126, 128
Development kernel, 31
Development tools, 74
Development trees, feedback to, 47–48. *See also* Linux development
DHCP server, 137
Dialog Group, 261
Dial-up connectivity, 36
Digital Equipment Corporation, 180
Directory mirroring, 134
Disk space requirements, 174
Distributed computing, 36, 117, 181
Distributions, 203–204
Documentation, 146
  downloading, 173
Domain Name Service (DNS), 45, 81
Domains, Windows NT, 184
DOS
  accessing, 174–175
  adding to the BOOT.INI file, 157–158

DOS bootsector, 152–153
DOS diskettes, BOOTABLE, 151
DOS emulator, 170
DOS filesystem, 175
Dotted quad addresses, 81
DownCity, LLC, 279
dump, 63

E

Earl A. Stutes, Inc., 266–267
Edit tools, 53
Eklektix, Inc., 271–272
Electric Fence, 75
Electronic mail server, 111, 115, 138, 140
Electronic Oasis Consulting, Inc., 272
Emacs, 53
E-mail, 64–65, 82, 147. *See also* **sendmail**
Embedded Linux Kernel Subset (ELKS), 174
Empress Software, 168–169
Emulators, WISE, 186
Enterprise management, 11, 39–40
Eonova, 325
Etc Services, 306–307
Ethernet, 86–87, 98
EtherTalk, 125
Evantide Graphical, 308
Evolve Computer Solutions, 256
Extreme Systems Consulting, 286–287

F

F.M. Taylor & Associates, 321
Failover procedure, 135
Falkor Technology, 236–237
Fast Ethernet, 86–87
FAT-filesystem boot partition, 149, 154
fdisk, 61
fetchmail, 64
File metaphor, 182
File services file, 188
Filesystems, 22
  accessing, 174–176
  backup of, 210–211
Filesystem security, 71
  Linux, 190–191
File System Standard (FSSTND), 23
File Transfer Protocol (FTP), 57, 80
Filmore St. Consultants, 326
Firewalls, 70. *See also* Bastion hosts; Security
  setting up, 93–96
Flamingo Internet Navigators, 341

Floppy disk, booting from, 33
Fluke Corporation, use of Linux by, 137–139
Fly-By-Day Consulting, Inc., 284
Fork and exec, 35
Fork bomb, 35
FourThought, LLC, 287
Frame relay, 87
Free command, 56
Free Electron Labs, 242
Frequently Asked Questions (FAQ) lists, 42
FTP server, 111

G
GAME.NET, Inc., 328–329
Games, 107
Gardner, P. David, 176
Gatorboxes, 123, 125–126
gcc (Gnu C compiler), 73
gdb (GNU Debugger), 75
Gigabit Ethernet, 87
GJR Software Products, 341–342
Global mail service, 45
Global marketplace, 102
GNU Network Object Mode Environment
    (gnome), 69
GNU's Not Unix (GNU), 69–70
GNU's Not Unix (GNU) General Public
    License, 165, 168, 196
Granite Computer Solutions, 273
Graphical User Interface (GUI), 40, 67–69
Greg Weber Consulting, 268
Group accounts, managing, 54–55
Group ID (GID), 35, 55
Groups, creating, 71

H
Hacom Consulting, 284–285
Halloween documents, 196–197
Hamilton C Shell for NT, 185
Hard drive boot, 32
Hardware
    adding, 61–62
    backup, 63
    Linux-supporting, 173–174
Hardware platforms, porting Linux to, 23
Heights Computer Center, 334
HELP! desk, 273–274
Herlein Engineering, 257
Heterogeneous platforms, integration with,
    108–116

Hierarchical File System (HFS), 176
Hiverworld Consulting, 257–258
HKS Web site, 217
Host data restoration, 211
Hotmail, 203
HPFS, accessing, 175
Hurrah Internet Services, 321–322
HyperText Markup Language (HTML), 67
HyperText Transfer Protocol (HTTP), 45
HyperText Transfer Protocol Daemon
    (HTTPD), 83–84

I
IBM Corporation, 47
iConnect Corporation, 112–113
ifconfig command, 62, 161
I-Link, Inc., 294
IMAP (Internet Message Access Protocol), 66
Incremental backups, 211
inetd.conf file, 188
InfoMagic, 243
Information technology solutions, 15
In-house solutions, 41, 108–116
Init process, 34
Insignia Solutions, 186
Integrated Services Digital Network (ISDN), 87
Integration
    with business, 143–162
    with existing hardware, 18
    into existing networks, 37
    with existing platforms, 148–159
    with heterogeneous platforms, 108–116
    with Windows 98, 147–148
Integration Engineering, 258
Intelligent Algorithmic Solutions (Intalsol),
    312–313
Intel Pentium, 108
Inter@ctive Consulting Group, 258–259
Internal firewalls, 96
Internet applications, 79–100
Internet Connect Consulting, 339–340
Internet connectivity server, 29–30
Internet Gateway, Inc., 301
Internet Infrastructure Consulting, Inc., 259
Internet Printing Protocol (IPP), 137
Internet Relay Chat (IRC), 89–90
Internet Robotics, 313–314
Internet service providers (ISPs), linux use
    by, 201
Internet sites, Linux-based, 22

Internet support groups, 146
Internet Systems and Services, 342
Internet/Web-based resources, 231–232
Interoperability, 38–39, 90–91, 108
Inter-Process Communication (IPC)
    mechanisms, 187
Intranet business model, 88–91
Intranets, 66
Iomega Zip driver, 168–169
IP (Internet Protocol), 80, 81–82
IP filtering, 70
IP firewalls, 93–94
IPv4, 82
Ishmail, 218–220
ispell, 219
IT (information technology) departments, 50
IT marketplace, 197, 198

J

JAMUX, 294–295
Java, print queues using, 137
Java Script, 66
Jay Ts Consulting, 249–250
JEONET, 290–291
JetDirect interface, 125
Jim Willette Consulting, 300
Jinn Enterprises, 303–304
JobSoft Design and Development, Inc.,
    329–330
J-Quad & Associates, Ltd., 334–335
Juan Daugherty Consulting, 306

K

K Desktop Environment (KDE), 69
Kernel mode, 181
Kernel modularity, 29–31
Kernels. *See also* Linux kernels
    configurable, 29
    custom, 18
Kevin Fenzi Consulting, 272–273
Kill script, 33–34
Knox Software, 204, 206
Kracked Rock Komputing, LLC, 280
Kuenzsoftware, 351
Kyle Davenport Consulting, 332–333
Kymsoft Consulting, 322

L

Languages, for custom applications, 74–75
Laptops, using Linux on, 174

Legacy hardware, 18
Licensing issues, 17, 37
Life & Energy Systems, 314–315
LILO (Linux Loader), 32–33, 73, 152, 154,
    155
    removing from the master boot record,
        156–157
lilo.conf file, editing, 154–155
Linux. *See also* Integration; Linux operating
        system (LOS)
    adding to the BOOT.INI file, 158
    as an alternative, 145–147
    business advantages of, 101–141
    companies using, 108–116
    drawbacks of, 177–178
    flexibility of, 144–145, 147
    integrating with existing platforms,
        148–159
    integrating with Windows 98, 147–148
    integration with business, 143–162
    porting Windows-based applications to,
        185–187
    power of, 107
    running Windows programs under,
        176–177
    security of, 91–92, 190–191
    selling to corporations, 102–108
    as a server replacement, 164–178
    simplicity of, 104
    versus Windows NT, 179–191
Linux administration. *See also*
        Administration
    advanced, 69–74
    basic, 52–69
Linux Application Development (LAP)
        (Johnson and Troan), 31
Linux applications, 37–48, 52, 146
Linux Applications Development (Johnson
        and Troan), 37
Linux bootsector file, 158
    creating, 154–156
    updating, 155
Linux business model, 101–102
Linux business products, 201–225
linuxconf, 69
Linux consultants, 239–351
Linux Consultants HOWTO, 239–240
Linux-Consulting, 259–260
Linux culture, 43
Linux desktop, 178

Linux development. *See also* Development trees
  investment in, 168
  model for, 166
Linux distribution, items in, 165
Linux documentation, 146
Linux for manufacturing, 222–225
Linux GUI, 185
Linux Journal, 44, 117, 227
Linux kernels
  booting different, 32
  development of, 28
  overview of, 26–31
Linux Kernel Hackers Guide (Johnson), 31
Linux Manifesto, 195
Linux Network File System (NFS), 190–191
Linux Online site, 203, 206
Linux operating system (LOS), 3–12. *See also* Operating systems (OSs)
  in business, 170
  benefits of, 6–7
  decision making about, 16–17
  power of, 15–24, 165
  technical specifications of, 21–24
  transparency of, 14
  versus other operating systems, 167–169
Linux print server, cost of, 134
Linux resources, Internet/Web-based, 231–232
Linux revolution, 163
Linux Security Administrators Guide, 75
Linux server, 117
  adding hardware to, 61–62
  self-sustaining nature of, 51–52
Linux Services, 260–261
Linux support infrastructure, 12–14
Linux-supporting hardware, 173–174
Linux-supporting software, 170–173
Linux support solutions, 40–48
Linux systems, advantages of, 106
Linux Technologies, Inc., 274, 291–292
Linux tools, 19
  for Windows NT, 185
Linux training environment, 159–162
Load on demand, 30
Local first in, first out (FIFO) replacement, 183
Location codes (loccodes), 126–128, 130–131, 135
Locus Corporation, 186
LOD Communications, 248

Logging facilities, 98
Los Angeles Research Coalition, 261
lpq command, 126
LPR code, 135
LPR protocol, 125, 126
LPR system, 123–124
Lrw.Net, 308–309
LsaLoginUser process, 189–190

M
M. Cooper Consulting, 247–248
Mac filesystems, accessing, 176
Mach operating system, 181
MaDCreW Organization, 315
Magpies, 335
mail, 64
Mail, multimedia, 218
Mailing lists, 42
  internal, 83
Mail programs, 65
Mail server function, 111
Mail service, global, 45
Mailslot File System (MSFS), 187
Mail transport agent (MTA), 64
Maintenance-free processes, 162
Majordomo, 60, 83, 85
make, 72
make config command, 161
Management responsibilities, 89
Man pages, 66–67
Manufacturing, Linux for, 222–225
Mark A. Richman Consulting, 283
Master boot record, removing **LILO** from, 156–157
Master boot record (MBR), 154
Master configuration file, 125
Matthew Kaylor Consulting, 295
MaxBaud.Net, 300–301
Maxwell Word Processing, 220–221, 237–238
Mechanix Computer Consulting, 248–249
Memory management, 106
Mercedes-Benz AG Corporation, 110
Microchannel architecture (MCA), 173
Micro Channel Linux Web page, 174
Microsoft, open source project and, 196–199
Microsoft Knowledge Base, 148
Microsoft Office Suite, 144
Microsoft Windows binaries, emulator for, 171
Midcoast Internet Solutions, 293–294
mkfs tools, 61
mkprint command, 127, 135

mkprint program, 132, 133
mkprint script, 125
MKS Toolkit for NT, 185
Model-View-Computing, 310–311
Modem communications, 112, 140
Modular operating system, 181
Morton Technologies, 304
M&S Group, Inc., 249
Multibooting, 148
Multinational companies, 14
Multiplexing, 209–210, 211
Multiprocessing support, 177
Multitasking system, 21–22
Multiuser operating systems, 180–181
Multiuser support, Windows NT, 184
Multiuser system, 22
Mythical Solutions, 315–316

N
Naked Ape Consulting, 322–323
Named Pipe File System (NPFS), 187
Name File Server (NFS), 62
Name Interface Server (NIS), 57
NDA Consulting, 243–244
NetAtalk, 125–126
NET-Community, 323
Net Effect, LLC, 246–247
NetInterface Corporation, 296
Net news, 42, 65, 66
Net Resonance, 336
Netscape Communicator, 66, 82
Netscape Navigator, 83–84
Netstat-a utility, 188
NetTek, Inc., 342–343
Net use command, 189
Network addresses, 81–82
Network backup software, 209–212
Network connections, 36
Network Dynamic Data Exchange (NetDDE),
    187
Network file server, 110, 111, 112, 114, 115,
    139
Network File Systems, 81, 185
Network information system (NIS), 81
Network Integration Services, Inc., 348–349
Network management, 39, 112, 139
Network needs, 41
Network operating systems
    functionality with, 39
    information about, 29
Network printers, 63–64

Network Redirector, 189
Networks, vulnerability of, 95. *See also*
    Bullet-proof networks
Network security, 92
Network services, 113, 114, 116, 138,
    140–141
    audits of, 188
Network solutions, 4
Network topology, 209
New Age Consulting Service, Inc., 316
newaliases, 83
Newsgroups
    internal, 89
    Linux-supporting, 167, 176–177
Novell-based networks, 38–39
NT boot loader, 149, 150–151
NTCRACKER, 185
NT Integrators, 292
Nugent Telecommunications, 298–299

O
Object/oriented model, 182
Objects, 188
Office productivity, 110, 112, 115, 138
    boosting, 221–222
Office support solutions, 213–214
Online support, 146
onShore, Inc., 288
OpenLinux, 223–224
Open Source Definition, 5
Open source software, 5–7, 46, 144
Open systems, 182
    Microsoft and, 197–199
Open systems authority, 228
Operating systems (OSs), 143. *See also*
    Desktop operating systems; Linux oper-
    ating system (LOS); Network operating
    systems
    adding to the BOOT.INI file, 158–159
    comparison of, 109
    Linux versus Windows NT, 180–181
Operating system vendors, 14, 44–45
Oration, LLC, 262
OS/2 subsystem, 184
Outsourcing, 72

P
Pacific Digital Interaction Corporation,
    115–116
Packet filtering, 94
PA dot NET, 327

Paktronix Systems, LLC, 304–305
Partitions, 149, 160
Passwords, 52
Patent lawsuits, 197
Paul C. Eastham's Linux Consulting, 255
Paul J. Mech Consulting, 317–318
PCMCIA cards, 87
PC operating systems, 29
PCs, Web and, 126
Penguin Technical Services, 336–337
Perl (Practical Extraction and Reporting Language), 60, 85–86, 162
  code for, 21
  scripts for, 11
Perl Archive Network, 61
Phaedo Consulting, Inc., 343–344
ping command, 161
PIR Corporation, 299
Platform stability, 15
Plug-and-play functionality, 29
Point-to-Point Protocol (PPP), 45, 86
POSIX (Portable Operating System Interface for Linux) subsystem, 37, 183
Post Office Protocol (POP3), 66, 80
Practical Network Design, 317
pradmin, 133
Predictive Science Consulting, 262–263
Printer controls, 63–64
Printers, network, 63–64
Printer Working Group (PWG), 118
Printing strategies, 118–122
Print queueing, 120, 121
  single-point, 128
Print servers, 110, 112, 114, 115, 131–132, 138
  duplication in, 124–125
Print system, 116–137
Priority management, 41
Private network addresses, 81–82
Privileges concept, 6
Processes, 34–36
Process ID (PID), 34, 56–57
Process identification number (PID) logfile, 33–34
Process Manager, Windows NT, 182
Process tracing, 35
procmail, 65
Product, strategic use of, 40–48
Production kernel, 31
Programming tools, advanced, 75

Progressive Computer Concepts, Inc., 283–284
Promethan Consulting, 288–289
Protected subsystems, Windows NT, 183–184
Protocols, 86–88
Proxy servers, 99–100
pserver, 135
pserver1, 129
pserver2, 129
Psytronics Consulting, 309

Q
qmail, 64
QuickStart Group–Linux Installation Help and Hotline Support, 263
QWK.Net Communications, 285–286

R
Rahim Azizarab Consulting, 286
RAID systems, 63
RAM, for a bastion host, 97–98
rawrite command, 160
rcs (revision control system), 75
RCT Design, 263–264
Rdist tool, 134
REALM Information Technologies, 244
Real-time operating systems, 222–223
Realtime Software Solutions Corporation, 114–115
Reboot Inc., 302
Red Hat Linux, 167, 234
Red Hat Package Manager, 72
Red Hat Software, 23, 52, 57, 101, 104, 105, 160, 164, 165, 168, 171, 239, 240
  support system of, 166
Remote File Sharing (RFS), 185
Remote Procedure Calls (RPCs), 187
Request for Proposal (RFP), 13
Research and development (R&D), 18
Resources, Internet/Web-based, 231–232
restore, 63
RG Consulting, 264
Rindy Corporation, 349–350
Robert Dale Consulting, 324–325
Roger A. Prata Consulting, 349
Rogers Cable Company, 113
Root diskette, 160
Routing Information Protocol (RIP), 81
rpc.nfsd, 57
rpm, 72–73

RT-Linux, 224
Rueb Group Ltd., 320–321
Run level, 33

S

Samba (SMB), 128–129, 147. *See also* SMB
    servers
    accessing, 176
Scalable server concept, 20, 45
Scripting languages, 74
Script names, 33–34
Scripts, for recurring tasks, 58–61
SCSI capability, 62
Sean Harper Consulting, 348
Secure Sockets Layer (SSL), 66
Security, 75–76, 92–100, 166, 169. *See also*
    Filesystem security; Firewalls
    Linux, 190–191
    mail, 65
    system, 5–6
    Windows NT versus Linux, 187–190
Security audits, 187
Security mission statement, 94
Security Reference Monitor, 183, 189
Security servers, 99–100. *See also* Bastion
    hosts; Firewalls
Sehnert Engineering, 274–275
sendmail, 64, 65, 82–83
Sendmail configuration file, 53
Sendmail seminars, 45
Sequential Query Language (SQL), 162
Serial Line Interface Protocol (SLIP), 86
Seruntine, Cliff, 102–103, 107
Server configuration, 70
Server Message Block (SMB) file-sharing pro-
    tocol, 189
Server rebooting, 45–46
Servers. *See also* Backup server; Linux server
    multiple, 36
    rebooting, 45–46
Service groups (sgroups), 129–131
Sheer Genius Consulting, 330
Shell *csh*, 59
Shell scripts, 58–60
Shell *sh*, 58
Shell *tcsh*, 60
Sifry Consulting, 265–266
Simple distributed database (SDDB),
    132–133, 137
Simple Mail Transfer Protocol (SMTP), 80, 82

Simple Network Management Protocol
    (SNMP), 11, 134, 137
SimsCon Services, 344
Slackware, 160, 165
Small-tool philosophy, 20
SMB servers, 63
Softcraft Impresa, 266
Software. *See also* Red Hat Software
    backup, 63
    desktop, 178
    free, 69–70, 106
    included on the CD/ROM, 233–238
    Linux, 165
    Linux-supporting, 170–173
    logging, 98
    office, 221–222
    open source, 5–7, 225
    professional, 105
Software authors, contact with, 42–43
Software bugs, 6
Software development, 110, 113, 114, 116,
    138, 139, 141
Software development kits (SDKs), 186
Software/operating system interaction, 6
Software selection, corporate, 25–26
Software solutions, characteristics of, 25–26
Software systems compatibility, 187
Software vendors, 40
Solutions
    competitive, 46–47
    customizable, 15–21
    in-house, 108–116
    levels of, 41–48
    Linux-based, 23
    off-the-shelf, 11–12
    technological, 91
Solutions provider, becoming, 47
Sony Worldwide Networks Corporation, 111
Source code, 186
    advantages of reading, 27
Spectrum Office Systems, Inc., 344–345
Staff, internal, 41
Stand-alone mode, 32
Standards compliance, 37, 38–40, 90–91
Star Office, 105, 106, 221–222
Starshine Technical Services, 244–245
Start script, 33–34
Start-up routine, 160
Steve Hedlund Consulting, 305
Steven Jackson Consulting, 326–327

Stock charting, 215
Storage units, 208
Subnetting, 81
Sun Solaris, 203
Support. *See also* Decision support; Linux
consultants
commercial third-party, 43–44
contract, 44
global, 46
operating system vendor, 44–45
philosophy of, 45
third-party, 166–167
Windows NT, 184
Swatch, 98–99
Symmetric multiprocessing (SMP), 22, 31,
167, 182
Sys Admin magazine, 44
System administration tools, 39–40
System bugs, 96
System configuration, 69
System crash, 33
System management tools, 177
System needs resolution, 12–13
System resources, 71–72
availability of, 15
monitoring, 55–58
Systems administrators, 39–40, 41
Linux, 227–229
resources for, 10–11
role of, 49–50
System stability, 104–105
Systems transactions, synchronized, 27

T
tar standard, 63
Tasks, scripts for recurring, 58–61
TCP (Transmission Control Protocol), 80
TCP/IP firewalls, 93–94
TCP/IP network diagnostics, 39
TCP/IP protocol, 79–80, 123
TCP wrappers, 100
Technical specifications, 21–24
Technical support, 146
Tech Support Consulting, 267
Telnet, 80
Tempest Harding Incorporated, 280–281
TerraBytes Computers, 340
TES, Inc., 318
THEBUC.COM, 292–293
Threads, 182

Three Point Consulting, 337
Tiger, 98
Token ring card, kernel modification for, 161
Token ring network, 160
Tom McDonald Consulting, 335–336
Tony Mendoza Consulting, 287–288
Top command, 55–56, 59
Top program, 35
Torvalds, Linus, 42, 168, 171, 195
Total cost of ownership (TCO) assessment,
202–203
TraiCom Services, Inc., 318–319
Training, 38. *See also* Linux training environ-
ment
Training machines, 18
Triangle Software Corporation, 245
Tripwire, 98, 99
Tri-State Networking Technologies, Ltd., 319
Triton EDT Corporation, use of Linux by,
139–140
Troubleshooting, 33
TSCNet, Inc., 346
Tummy.com, ltd., 275–276

U
U.S. Army, use of Linux by, 141
U.S. Navy, use of Linux by, 140–141
UFS, accessing, 175–176
UHW Corporation, 337–338
uncompress command, 161
Unix, 168, 202, 203
growth of, 197
history of, 19–21
philosophy of, 19
Unix philosophy, 19
Unix servers, 123
Unix tools, 51
Un*x Amiga Emulator, 175
Upgrades, 23, 50
Uptime command, 56
Usenet news groups, 167
User accounts, managing, 54–55
User Datagram Protocol (UDP), 80
User identifications (UIDs), 35, 189
User interface, Windows NT, 184
User mode, 181

V
Vendor list security resources, 76
Vendors, operating system, 44–45

Vendor Web sites, 52
Vennerable Consultants, 267–268
VFAT filesystem, 175
vi, 53, 132
Virtual Memory Manager, 183
Viruses, 75–76

W

WarpWare, 338
Waypointe Information Technologies, 299–300
Web interface, 134–135
Web pages
  internal, 89
  reworking, 134–135
Web servers, 84. *See also* Apache Web server
Web sites, 36
  operating systems used by, 203–204
WellThot Inc., 289
Westphila.net, 327–328
WhitePine Consulting, 350–351
Wide area networks (WANs), 39
William Rozmiarek Consulting, 350
Willson Consulting Services, 346–347
Win32 subsystem, 183
/WIN95DOS switch, 158
/WIN95 switch, 158
Window manager, 68
Windows 2000, 202
Windows 95 bootsector file, 152, 153
Windows 95 installation disk, 151
Windows 95 SYS.COM, 153
Windows 98, 143, 144–145
  integrating Linux with, 147–148
Windows-based applications, porting to Linux, 185–187
Windows emulator, 176

Windows Interface Source Environment (WISE), 186–187. *See also* WISE emulators
Windows NT, 145, 146, 147
  filesystem security of, 189–190
  history of, 180–185
  Linux tools for, 185
  versus Linux, 179–191
Windows NT executive services, 184
Windows NT Process Manager, 182
Windows NT Setup diskettes, BOOTABLE, 151
Windows programs, running, 176–177
WINE project, 176, 186
WISE emulators, 186
Working Version Consulting, 297–298
Worldmachine Technologies Corporation, 297
Worldwide Solutions, Inc., 276
Wrappers, 100
WSI.com Consulting, 290

X

xprt Computer Consulting, Inc., 338–339
X servers, 185
X utilities, 161
X-Windows, 67–69, 110, 112, 114, 115, 137, 140, 141

Y

Yggdrasil Computing, Inc., 268–269
ypserv, 57

Z

ZEI Software, 307
Zip drives, 168–169
Zot Consulting, Inc., 324